MICROCOMPUTERS IN EDUCATION:

A Nontechnical Guide to Instructional and School Management Applications

Lee M. Joiner

George J. Vensel

Jay D. Ross

Burton J. Silverstein

Learning Publications, Inc.
Holmes Beach, Florida

Library of Congress Number: 81-84658

Co-Editors:
  Edsel L. Erickson
  Lois A. Carl

Learning Publications, Inc.
P.O. Box 1326
Holmes Beach, Florida 33509

ISBN 0-918452-31-7

Cover Design by Melinda Frink Kabel

Printing: 1 2 3 4 5 6 7 8 Year: 2 3 4 5 6 7

Printed and bound in the United States of America

We dedicate this book, with love to Clifford and Kathleen Joiner of Rochester, New York, John and Margaret Vensel of Butler, Pennsylvania, Jean Silverstein of Forest Hills, New York, and in memory of Leonard and Laura Ross and Morty Silverstein.

PREFACE

Written by and for educators, this book is the first to describe what microcomputers are all about in understandable, non-technical language. It began three years ago when we heard more and more educators talking about microcomputers and wondering how they could get ready to take advantage of this powerful new technology.

Most educators that we were involved with as consultants had absolutely no formal training in the information sciences, computer programming, or instructional design. Educators pioneering in the use of microcomputers in schools were working on their own, learning through trial and error and informal professional contacts. In working with school districts in different parts of the country we saw many exciting applications evolving. Sometimes we felt like a walking newspaper, spreading the news about what educators were doing with microcomputers.

So, we started planning a book that would give educators a look at what's been accomplished with the microcomputers in the schools and the opportunities for continued development. We wanted a very basic book that we could use in workshops with teachers and administrators who have no knowledge whatsoever about computers. We wanted a book that would raise stimulating issues, take a hard look at the problems and limitations of microcomputers in the schools, and would provide the reader with detailed information about vendors, organizations, publications, and the state of the art. These were the goals that guided us in our writing.

Our first chapter introduces the reader to microcomputer concepts, looking at micros from the standpoint of their probable impact on curriculum, instruction, and the teaching profession. Next, we address the question of how to immediately begin building staff skills in microcomputing. Cost saving applications, how to insure the effective adoption of microcomputers, and computer literacy are some of our major themes.

The third chapter explains how a microcomputer center was organized in a rural school and what was learned about staffing, teacher and student involvement, and how micros help build school-community ties. Planning a system, evaluating courseware, and questions concerning what hardware to choose are considered in chapter four.

Chapters five and six are about classroom applications and special education. We have described a number of interesting micro projects throughout the country and have also included a major section on the newest and perhaps most important breakthrough in instructional technology: computer assisted video.

Our chapter on micro assisted administration, number seven, looks at financial accounting and reporting systems that can save schools money. Testing, word processing, scheduling, inventory control, deriving meaning from data, optimal bus routing, and other micro applications that free administrators from time consuming and burdensome chores are discussed. The new management information systems, what they can and can't do for school organizations and administrations are explained in chapter eight. Much of our material was drawn from what business leaders, already well ahead of educators in computer applications, have learned.

Our last chapter, "Computer Confrontation," looks at the struggle that is taking place between vested, organizational, bureaucratic interests in large computer systems and those using locally controlled microcomputing.

ACKNOWLEDGEMENTS

This book could not have been written without the support and assistance of the many teachers and administrators who shared their ideas and insights with us. New and exciting ways of using microcomputers have greeted us in every school system we have visited where microcomputers are being used. We extend our thanks, especially, to Gerald Hansen, Bill Heck, and Richard Quast, pioneering Minnesota educators who gave us their ideas and materials to work with. Curt Johnson, a high school student in Ortonville when this book was started, represents the first wave of a new generation of microcomputer professionals. His enthusiasm, dedication, and hard work resulted in several of the applications we have described.

In our discussion of special education and management information systems we drew heavily from the ideas and development work of Dr. Richard Weatherman, Director of the Upper Midwest Regional Resource Center and Dr. Warren Bock, President of Bock Associates.

Dr. Burton Nypen, Superintendent of the Ortonville, Minnesota, school system, has provided outstanding administrative support for a remarkably effective microcomputer adoption. It has been a pleasure to work with him and his able staff. Larry Goldsmith, Director of the Southern Illinois Educational Service Center, has taken the initiative in building staff skills by providing a solid in-service program for rural teachers. Many of the issues he raised helped us organize chapter two. Dr. Thomas King, editor of the Association for Educational Data System's **Monitor,** permitted us to reprint some of the material we have published in that journal.

Preparing a manuscript is a difficult undertaking. Fortunately for us, we could rely upon the painstaking and competent editing of Ken Burzynski and Dr. Pamela Miller. The manuscript itself was typed by Perfectly Clear Printers of Carbondale, Illinois, under the supervision of Lin Sweazy, expert in word processing. Sherry des Jardins prepared the graphs and figures. It's remarkable how many unforseen problems arise in producing a book. Cynthia Sills Worden was our masterful problem-solver.

And finally, we thank Dr. David Sabatino, our department chairman at Southern Illinois University for providing the encouragement and academic climate so crucial to creative work.

TABLE OF CONTENTS

Chapter I

MICROCOMPUTER CONCEPTS

As an educator, chances are that you've wondered what microcomputers can and cannot do, their costs, and what the "computer revolution" means for curriculum and to your role as a teacher. If so, you're among the growing number of educators whose involvement with computer issues has coincided with the expanded application of electronic computing or "information processing" in our society. Getting and using information is the essence of the learning process. Thus, a technology that is able to radically alter how information is stored, transmitted, and accessed is of tremendous significance to educators.

A NEW CONSUMER PRODUCT

Most Americans are aware of the remarkable growth in the availability of computers since 1975. Throughout the nation, retail computer stores are opening their doors to a public that is just beginning to realize the computer's many uses in the home, school, and business. Shopping malls and airports find rapt patrons crowded around computer games with sophisticated graphic displays. If a customer returns to his drugstore to have a prescription renewed, he may find that a complete record of his medication purchases has suddenly become part of a microcomputer "database" for the pharmacist to review.

Late in 1980, the Wall Street Journal was overflowing with articles and discussions concerning the impact of the recession on numerous sectors of the economy, as well as the woes of businesses suffering from surging interest rates and a decline in sales volume. For small computer retail stores, however, the story was quite different. Compushop units in Texas and Illinois were 50 percent busier than ever and reportedly, for the first time, retail computer sales were experiencing a Christmas market. Computerland, a national retail outlet, planned five new franchises per month for 1981. Both Xerox and IBM entered the microcomputer market place in 1981-82.

Undoubtedly the post-war years have witnessed an avalanche of new consumer products: stereos, color televisions, microwave ovens, CB radios, instant cameras, and fast foods. Is the microcomputer just another consumer product in the "long chrome line" or does it represent the beginning of a major change in how people work, learn, and communicate? To answer this question, we will consider what a microcomputer is and how it relates to education in an information oriented society.

WHAT IS A MICROCOMPUTER?

The microcomputer, also known as the home computer, personal computer, or stand alone system is usually about the size of an electric typewriter. Although reduced in size, it has the capabilities of room size computer units of a decade ago. Size reduction was made possible by the metal oxide semiconductor, a microcircuit embedded in the surface of a silicone or crystal chip. With miniaturization, production costs were reduced.

Some major microcomputer manufacturers who now appear most active in the education market are: Radio Shack, producer of the TRS-80; Apple Computers, Inc., producers of the Apple II; and Commodore, Inc., the manufacturer of the PET system. Generally, a simple microcomputer system contains:

1. a microprocessor similar to the central processing unit in a large scale computer;
2. a typewriter-like keyboard for entering instructions or data or for responding to computer prompts;
3. a cathode ray tube (CRT) of the T.V. type for displays;
4. a cassette tape and tape player, or disk drive unit, for storing and loading programs.

In addition to these components, a variety of secondary or "peripheral" equipment that expands the capabilities of the microprocessor can be added to a basic system as user needs arise.

Peripherals are especially valuable for making input and output arrangements compatible with the user needs. Audio peripherals that permit the computer to synthesize music and speech or access pre-recorded messages can be used by persons with expressive language disorders. Peripherals that allow the machine to respond to voice commands can be used by persons with limited mobility. Learning disabled persons can use light pens to indicate their answer to multiple choice questions displayed on a screen, or to trace figures and line drawings for instant display on the video screen.

Peripherals such as oversized, touch activated keyboards, kneeswitches, and joysticks enable physically handicapped persons to control the microcomputer. Printers provide typed "hard copy" of information displayed on the screen. A special record-like device called a floppy or hard disk and a disk drive can also be added to increase the memory capacity of the machine for more efficient storage and access of information or programs. A device called a modem allows one microcomputer to communicate with another over telephone lines and also allows for the easy transfer of programs. These are a few of the most common peripherals that are available for purchase with microcomputers. New hardware to expand the capabilities of the microcomputer is being developed constantly.

MINIATURIZATION

Microcomputers were first marketed in the mid-1970's after their development in the space program. These miniaturized versions of the large computer use complex integrated circuits that can combine several functions into one postage stamp sized, solid-state chip.

As these chips were reduced in size, they consumed less power. It is through this phenomenon that developments in the computer industry demonstrated the dymaxion concept of Buckminster Fuller...getting more while using less. Prices have declined by a factor of ten every seven years, for equivalent computing capabilities. In fact, prices have declined so markedly that one computer store owner described the computer as "incidental to money making." In his book THE MICRO MILLENIUM, Christopher Evans reported what is now a rather famous quote, originating in the WASHINGTON STAR:

> Had the automobile developed at a pace equivalent to that of the computer during the last 20 years, today a Rolls Royce would cost less than $3, get three million miles to the gallon, deliver enough power to drive the Queen Elizabeth II, and six of them would fit on the head of a pin!

A COMMON DENOMINATOR

The power and flexibility of the computer arises as much, if not more, out of the standardization of information, numbers, words, and images, as out of engineering advances. Early in the development of computers, the insight arose that any kind of information, a picture, a formula, a list of words, a poem, or a melody could be reduced to a "binary code" represented by an "on" or "off" condition of a switch or circuit in a computer. For instance, the image on a television screen is composed of a matrix of dots, some lighted and some unlit. No matter how complex the image, it can be reproduced by a matrix of lit and unlit dots or pixels. The advantage of the binary code is that information in this form is easily communicated and stored through electronic means.

SOFTWARE AND COURSEWARE

Computers function by executing a series of exact instructions called a program. Programs of all types are referred to as software. Software that delivers instruction is called courseware. Herein lies one of the greatest current problems for classroom users of microcomputers.

Because few teachers have been involved in computer programming, most programs now available were written by computer programmers with limited awareness of the principles of learning and curriculum. This situation has resulted in many well composed programs that are poorly suited to classroom use or integration with existing curricula.

There is also a tremendous software incompatibility problem in the computer world. Different computer chips use different operating codes and many higher level languages such as BASIC, FORTRAN, and COBOL are in use. Courseware written in one language will not run on a computer set up to use a different language. And even programs written in the same language, e.g. BASIC, will usually not be inter- changeable on different brands of microcomputers. Potential buyers of educational computer systems could thus end up with a powerful system restricted in usefulness because of the limited availability of compatible courseware.

Solutions to these problems are slowly being realized. One approach to software incompatibility is to design computer programs that can convert courseware for wider use. A software package that converts programs written for the Radio Shack 8080 microprocessor, to run on the Apple microcomputer, is already available (at the time of this writing) at a cost of less than twenty-five dollars from Dan McCreary, Box 16435-WA, San Diego, California, 92116. Although it does not appear likely that the industry will adopt a standard language for educational courseware, a recently developed generic language called PASCAL, written at the University of California at San Diego, can be entered into different brands of microcomputers and will run without modification.

PLATO, the most extensive educational courseware system, has over 6,000 hours of courseware available to users. Owned and operated by Control Data Corporation, PLATO is a timeshare system where terminals are linked to a large central computer. This rich source of educational programs has only recently been made available to microcomputer users and can now be adapted for microcomputer delivery.

Local Courseware

Teachers and students in different communities have unique needs for instructional materials because of the tremendous variation in curricula in our schools. Locally developed courseware, therefore, would seem to be very desirable. For this purpose, special "authoring languages" are available for microcomputers. Using simple commands and standard formats (e.g. multiple choice test format, flash card style format) authoring languages allow teachers to develop microcomputer lessons and drills without having to learn all the skills involved in programming in a language such as BASIC.

To facilitate programming in BASIC, a program called "THE LAST PROGRAM" is now available. This program allows the user to write BASIC programs by responding to queries, but is directed toward business applications.

One of the most prominent courseware authoring languages is TUTOR, specifically designed for the PLATO system and making use of extensive graphic capabilities. For microcomputers, authoring languages include PILOT and ASSIST, a new authoring language for special education applications developed by RMC Research Corporation of Cupertino, California. Teachers have enthusiastically endorsed ASSIST, writing over 1,000 instructional programs in this language.

Some schools have elected to provide trained student programmers as teacher aides in writing local courseware. This approach allows a school to immediately get started with locally relevant courseware, prior to teachers receiving inservice or using authoring or programming languages.

Under the direction of teachers who describe what they need and evaluate end products, students can prepare microcomputer programs originally written for use on other machines.

COMMUNICATION AND MICROCOMPUTERS

The microcomputer and our present telephone communication system are natural partners, allowing almost instantaneous transmittal of programs, data, and messages between microprocessor users via telephone lines. The telephone system becomes the means of transmitting courseware among and between schools and school districts. Encoded text material, graphic displays, and programs can be transmitted at high speed, thereby reducing long distance telephone fees.

DISSEMINATION

Microcomputer user groups and organizations concerned with microcomputer applications (see Appendix I) have multiplied rapidly since 1976. User groups are often informal, and exchange courseware and software developed by members. Formal groups usually require membership fees and either a nominal copying fee for programs or a simple exchange agreement.

Dissemination of software will be greatly enhanced with the expansion of local and national data networks for microcomputer users. Through these networks, such as MICRONET, many different programs can be accessed by group members. A user dials the number of the network, places a telephone in his modem, enters a password, and is then able to access a wide variety of programs stored in central libraries. Software and courseware can also be bought and sold through the network, an area of particular interest to teachers with programming skills seeking additional income while remaining at home.

Microcomputers can also access large data banks, such as Educational Resources Information Center documents. This capability immediately expands the professional libraries of school districts to include the majority of articles, reports, and research pertaining to education, a remarkable resource at low cost. Networks usually charge an initial fee to join and then bill the user according to an hourly fee schedule for "connect time." Hourly fees vary according to time of day and programs or data bases accessed.

THE INFORMATION SOCIETY

Conclusion

Graham Molitor (1981) has reviewed the historical development of human communication and provides a rich context for envisioning the role of computers in future society. He contends that our society is experiencing a major transition from an industrial to an informational base. Examining the distribution of the work force in 1920 and 1976, he noted that in 1920, 53 percent of the work force was engaged in manufacturing, commerce and industry, 28 percent in agriculture and extractive industries and 19 percent in information, knowledge, education and service enterprises. By 1976, only four percent were engaged in agriculture, 29 percent in manufacturing, 50 percent were in information, and 17 percent were engaged in other service occupations. Knowledge is becoming the principle resource in our society.

Changes in how we acquire and use information can be dichotomized according to accessibility and selectivity. Computers, in an information age, become the repositories of vast bodies of knowledge which can be selectively accessed at the time the information is needed. Historically, educators have viewed the individual as the repository of knowledge with the aid of printed materials stored in archives. Major professions such as law and medicine have thrived on their ability to access specialized knowledge. The hallmark of a professional in our society is a storehouse of specialized knowledge.

Many words have been said and written concerning the

knowledge explosion of recent years. Given new insights, concepts, formulae, procedures, and laws that have been produced at a dazzling rate, how can the individual assimilate and understand where we are today in any field? Fortunately, at any given moment the individual is preoccupied with only a few questions. And to these questions a universe of knowledge is hardly relevant. With the selectivity and accessibility that computer assisted procedures allow, the inquirer faces the challenge of interpreting and using only the facts and data relevant to the question at hand.

As we progress into the information age, educators must focus on the changing behaviors of the public in the marketplace, at work, and at home in how they relate to and acquire information. For instance, the largest machine in the world is now the international telecommunications network, consisting of 440 million telephones, 1.2 million telex terminals, data networks, and other specialized communication links. Taking advantage of the power of this system, the British have recently introduced the paperless newspaper, where news is displayed, on demand, on a subscriber's screen. Because of the two-way capability of the network, the viewer may request more detailed information on any news item of special interest.

In the United States, computerized shopping or "tele-shopping" is undergoing experimentation in Coral Gables, Florida where a newspaper is providing a service to owners of personal microcomputers wherein they can see various products displayed on their video screen and type in orders for merchandise which will be billed to their accounts.

In Albany, New York, American Telephone and Telegraph has initiated a trial of the electronic yellow pages, a document in constant need of updating. The cost efficiency of a computer assisted yellow pages system has implications for other advertising methods that require constant up-dating, such as the want-ads appearing in local newspapers. Soon, we may be seeing, on a large scale, rapid transactions between individual buyers and sellers at remote sites linked by the telecommunications network.

EDUCATION'S INTRODUCTION TO THE COMPUTER

Thus far, most educators have had little, if any, directed exposure to computers and lack the preparation to respond to these changes. Teacher education programs have rarely included computer related courses, perhaps because computers were originally expensive and exotic machines; access to which was rationed even for expert users. Computer literacy was also rationed and regulated, remaining a virtual monopoly of engineers, accountants and information scientists. Even the most mundane computer related activities spawned terms and phrases (see Glossary) that heightened the mystification of computing and promoted the rise of a computer elite, now threatened, incidentally, by microcomputing.

It is interesting to note that the most significant event in the microcomputer revolution was an article appearing in 1975 in POPULAR ELECTRONICS, "ALTAIR 8800 - The most powerful minicomputer project ever presented - can be built for under $400." With that article, the computer mystique was shattered.

Schools first became involved with computing through "timesharing" where a remote central computer served their needs. Front line educators, in the pre-microcomputer days, had little control over what got done, how it was done, or when it was done. Computer services to state education agencies and larger school systems (the only ones who have had reasonable access to computer resources in the past) were under the control of experts who were frequently more concerned with computer protocol, doing things the "right" way than meeting the needs of a variety of users. User needs often took second place to "system needs" and considerable dissatisfaction existed among front-line educators, who had little to say about computer systems operation (Foecke, 1979).

According to Sippl (1977), "small decentralized computer systems usually produce better results than large systems because the latter force users to conform too rigidly to 'total' systems...there is always a tendency in computer systems to 'solve the wrong problem'." This can easily happen when the computer system is designed for the computer center personnel and not the appropriate user of the services. With a microcomputer system, the computer becomes a tool rather than a service. At the same time, the democratization of computing creates new responsibilities, opportunities and training needs for local school staffs.

MICROCOMPUTERS VS. TIMESHARING SYSTEMS

One of the most extensive timesharing systems that has been used in education is PLATO. PLATO is a sophisticated computer based education system linked to a central computer that makes courseware available to children and adults in curriculum areas ranging from advanced mathematics to tutorial reading for learning disabled adolescents (Joiner, 1978). Microcomputers, however, appear to possess five distinct advantages over large timesharing systems: initial cost, ease of installation and servicing, limited effect of "down time," accessibility, local control, and no need for a cadre of experts. These advantages are discussed in the following sections.

Five Advantages of Microcomputing

Cost. Economically, microcomputers possess the advantage of requiring a relatively small capital investment. Microcomputers can be purchased "turnkey" or ready to run, for between $300 and $7500. A system for classroom drill and practice and limited simulations, costs about $1000. For school business management, a system would cost between $2600 and $4000. When contrasted to leasing a terminal connected to a large time sharing system at a total cost between $900 and $1300 per month, the microcomputer's economic benefits are obvious.

Installation and Servicing. A microcomputer can be purchased at a local retail outlet and installed in a classroom on the same day. There are no intricate wiring or complex installation procedures required. There is no need to arrange for a telephone link to the central computer or to learn the codes and procedures for "logging on" or entering the system.

Reliability of microcomputer hardware is well established. Most units carry a 90 day parts and labor warranty and a one year parts only guarantee. Extended maintenance contracts can often be purchased at a cost of about 5% of the initial purchase price of the equipment. The Ortonville, Minnesota public schools have acted as a trial site for a number of microcomputers and have recorded the instances and types of equipment failures over a one-year period. Failures were few and generally easily corrected (Joiner and Silverstein, 1979).

It is more efficient to transport the equipment for instructional applications than the user. The timesharing system method of scheduling children and moving them to the stationary terminals directs staff resources away from the instructional process and is time consuming. Microcomputers can easily be transported and temporarily installed in a resource room, a corner of the library, an office, or a classroom with little advance site preparation. In Ortonville, the microcomputer center is staffed by high school students who are responsible for transporting the equipment to various users in the K-12 building. The microcomputers are transported in much the same manner as conventional audio-visual equipment.

Effects of "Downtime". In timesharing situations, when the central computer is being repaired or maintained all terminals are unusable. If the system "crashes" during peak load hours, usually those hours during which educators are most likely to be using the equipment, the educational process that relies upon it is disrupted. Disruptions of direct instruction, especially of special education students, are more critical than those in nearly any other type of computer application (Suppes, 1966). Some exceptional learners would become very upset and difficult to manage if they were brought to a terminal in anticipation of using it, only to find it inoperative. It would be even more stressful to be disrupted in the midst of a computer tutorial lesson, having to begin anew when the system was reactivated.

In contrast, since a microcomputer is self-contained, a

malfunction inconveniences only one person or small group. Most schools can afford to purchase an extra microcomputer just for "back up." If a microcomputer fails, the back up can be immediately substituted. Routine maintenance is unnecessary for the microcomputer.

Accessibility and Response Time. Accessibility and speed of response to commands are related. In timesharing systems, it is very common to encounter busy signals when attempting to access the system. Busy signals indicate that the system is being used to its fullest capacity. When this happens, repeated dial-ups and frustrating delays impede the educational application.

A related problem of time sharing system, when they are being used for instruction, is the speed with which the computer will respond to a student's answer. If there is a large number of people using the computer at the same time, the response or feedback from the computer "degrades" or slows, to perhaps 10-15 seconds rather than the .5 to 1.0 second response latency to which students are accustomed. Users of timesharing systems always voice their annoyance at being required to wait to make their next response. Slow downs or "response degradations" are not a problem for the microcomputers since in most applications there is only one person interacting with each machine.

Local Control. The centralization of authority in education has been a subject widely debated during recent years by educators, parents, and school board members. What is at stake is the amount of control over the schools that will continue to be exercised at the local level.

Regardless of the pros and cons of the argument over how much local control is justified, there is undoubtedly a strong trend toward the centralization of authority in American education.

How has the centralization of authority in American education happened? One major theme is that as America became more urbanized and the population shifted away from rural communities, there emerged an increasing gap between the provisions for education that the small school districts could offer and those available in the larger districts. This maldistribution of population and resources fostered a centralization of school districts in rural areas in order to provide an economic and population base for a broad curriculum taught by qualified professionals.

The centralization of school districts, however, is not necessarily a threat to local autonomy because these associations gradually evolved with grass-roots support. Considerable control over school budgets, personnel policies, and curriculum remained in the hands of locally elected school boards.

In recent years, however, there has been an astonishing growth in the number of state and local laws that govern the conduct of education. And the corollary of these laws and regulations is a complicated record keeping and reporting system that the schools must adhere to. State and federal reporting requirements place severe burdens on local schools. As schools engage in uniform data acquisition and reporting in order to meet the requirements of federal and state laws and regulations, there is a tendency for uniformity to evolve within local school systems. However, a certain degree of autonomy is retained as long as local schools have control over school budgets and can exercise independent judgments in disbursements.

While there is a pervasive sentiment among school boards and professional educators that further centralization of authority is a threat to the concept of local education, the advent of computer support systems has provided a "painless" and almost invisible means of centralizing authority even further. It arises from the fact that educators are seeking to reduce the burden of complex reporting requirements. To relieve these problems, computer assisted management seems ideally suited. Unfortunately, the centralization of information in today's world by computerization is analagous to the centralization of power.

Uniform financial accounting and reporting requirements is a good example. Suppose that a state requires that school districts adopt these procedures. And let us further suppose that the system of uniform accounting and reporting is supported by a centralized computer system and staff. If that were true, state education agencies would be provided with a high power telescope to gaze into the financial activities of every school district, whenever they saw fit to do so. Direct and continuous access to local financial information by state and federal "big brother" agencies would undoubtedly influence the behavior of local school districts in regard to their budgetary decisions. A state's interest in these local financial data could easily be interpreted as a preliminary step toward intervention in, and finally control over local decisions.

But if microcomputers, owned and operated by the local schools, can serve to meet the reporting requirements of uniform systems, control over fiscal matters is more likely to remain in the hands of local schools. And the fact of the matter is that microcomputers can indeed serve this function (see Chapters Seven and Nine).

MICROCOMPUTERS AS TEACHERS

Generally when educators respond to the word computer, they think of computer assisted instruction (CAI). Dr. J.C.R. Licklider of M.I.T., in a recent report (1979) to the National Science Foundation proclaimed however, that as we enter the information age computers are everywhere but in the classroom. Has American education, an institution that made possible the scientific achievements that led to the microcomputer, turned reactionary? Have computers become a threat to the teaching profession? Do teachers lack the literacy and world view to adopt this technology on a large scale?

Actually, classroom involvement with "automated instruction" has had a long history. The roots of computer assisted instruction are in "Pressey Boxes," teaching machines, programmed instruction, talking typewriters, and the vision of the infinitely responsive learner environment of educational technology guru O.K. Moore. Appealing to the post-war educational philosophy of "individualism at any cost," the fundamental rationale for this family of methods is that the student is freed from the tyranny of the group, liberated to pursue learning at a uniquely suited rate of speed.

Nurturing the vision of computer as teacher has been the recent promotion of the technology by commercial vendors, whose sales approach stresses the presumed savings in direct instructional costs that could result in a landscape of electronic classrooms. According to some of these vendors, computer assisted instruction is the answer to the question of how to provide instructional equality for students in rural schools where small enrollments threaten to limit course offerings to the barest minimum. They also claim it is a painless and efficient way to teach basic skills to reluctant learners.

Few educators in today's schools, however, have gained enough computer sophistication through their teacher preparation programs to allow them to challenge such hyperbole. Educators have little awareness of the relative costs, benefits, and limitations of computer assisted instruction. Consequently, some teachers have already assumed a defensive posture, expressing fears of technological displacement.

In his monumental evaluation of the TICCIT computer-assisted instruction system for Educational Testing Service, Alderman (1978) wrote, "The resistance of classroom teachers represents the greatest single impediment to the implementation of instructional technology in our schools." Citing the earlier work of Armsey and Dahl (1973) and Anastasio and Morgan (1972), Alderman attributed teacher resistance to fear of complex technologies, ignorance of the computer's capabilities and limitations, and "the clash of values that arises from the teacher's perception of the computer as a replacement for personal interactions with students." Nonetheless, school boards continue to yearn for the materialization of the tireless, unpaid, uncomplaining teaching robot as a defense against escalating costs of education and "Proposition 13ism."

To bolster the position of the resistant teacher, the argument is posed that the computer is "dehumanizing." In doing so, the same educators reject the notion that the individualizing capabilities of computer assisted instruction may in fact lead to greater curricular flexibility and sensitivity to personal needs.

Robert Travers (1978), however, is an example of an educational leader who is an ardent critic of computer assisted instruction, believing the method too individual. He contends that social learning experiences, group instruction, and cooperative activities are already underemphasized as important ingredients of the curriculum of our schools. Even without computer assisted instruction, we adhere too closely to the doctrine of individualism, to the long term disadvantage of our society. It should be noted, however, that computer assisted instruction can have a group, rather than an individual, orientation (see Chapter Five). To do this requires imagination and a new look at microcomputer capabilities.

Fortunately, as educators gain more first hand experience with computer assisted instruction, their consciousness of its price and promise is elevated above the level of socio-political discourse. Direct experience reveals that the successful employment of the computer as teacher depends on many human variables such as the adequacy of the design of the courseware, the "off-line" follow-up activities conducted by teachers, the consistency of course objectives with student interest, and the way in which the computer assisted instruction experience is integrated with the student's instructional and socialization program (Thelen, 1977). Teacher concerns about technological displacement are further relieved when one realizes that the student's involvement with computer assisted instruction is limited by necessity. One student typically sits before one terminal. And there is a definite limit to how long he or she can sit there.

Thus far, research contains no real answers as to how much time students can profitably spend each day interacting with a computer terminal. Some authorities recommend a maximum of twenty to thirty minutes. A limited exposure is required because the computer forces student attention. And, the students generally tire more quickly than they would in group instruction involving changes of pace, wider perceptual fields, and social experiences.

As far as efficiency is concerned, research suggests that the time required for learning can be shortened. After thoroughly reviewing the literature on the effectiveness of computer assisted instruction, Thomas (1979) concluded "...it is clear from the studies reviewed at all levels, that CAI reduces the time required for a student to complete a unit." While Edwards et al. (1974) concluded, on the basis of some very sparse research available at the time, that long-term retention appeared worse for computer assisted instruction than for conventional instruction, Thomas noted that studies reported since that time "lean more toward equal retention."

As far as saving money is concerned, administrators should note that if the rate of learning were to be accelerated for all learners using computer assisted instruction, there would certainly be no saving. Rather, a need to extend the scope of the curriculum would emerge, resulting in increased instructional and material expenditures. Students would cover, and hopefully retain, more material during their schooling. If school systems were to adopt the provisions of California or Florida for early graduation through proficiency testing, however, there might indeed be a saving of money by adopting computer assisted instruction.

THE COMPUTER AS MANAGER

Long before questions concerning the adequacy and appropriateness of the computer as teacher are answered, the computer will become institutionalized and tamed as "manager." The assimilation of the computer into the American school as manager will emerge from the fact that education, like most other sectors of our society, has become immersed in seemingly uncontrollable record-keeping and documentation functions -- paperwork.

In the education of the handicapped, for example, the

individualized educational program (IEP) with all its record keeping and information gathering features has been widely endorsed as the major ideology in the field. In fact, Public Laws 94-142 and 94-482 mandate individualized instruction. Despite its many commendable features, individualized instruction consumes resources voraciously. Teachers must maintain detailed records of student performance and match students with instructional resources. These record keeping and documentation functions for teachers move instructional resources away from direct service and into clerical work -- an uneconomical practice. Moreover, the resulting snowstorm of paper buries individual items of information that become increasingly difficult to find and interpret as the drifts accumulate.

The task of the IEP is so burdensome and difficult for teachers to perform unassisted that government, by mandating it, has created a vast market for computer manufacturers and a prime job market for computer experts. Control Data Corporation, for example, has responded to this opportunity by attempting to assist the teacher in organizing and accessing information. According to these vendors, the paperless classroom with computer managed instruction (CMI):

> "...guides each student through a curriculum along a learning path which is designed by the student's instructor, maintaining records of student achievement for use in evaluating the effectiveness of the educational resources." (Control Data Corporation, 1977).

While assisting teachers in the management of instruction, computers have already proven their worth in the business management of the school. Administering a modern school involves record keeping and accounting procedures that parallel those of the business community. Purchasing, budgeting, inventories, forms management, personnel, "compliance" management, and the reporting of data required by the government are all part of the educational leadership role. Computers can do all these things rapidly, accurately, and inexpensively.

A FINAL THOUGHT

The reduced costs and expanding capabilities of microcomputers and their peripheral devices are making the
purchase of such equipment more and more attractive to
educational leaders at all levels. At the same time, many
questions concerning the acceptability and cost-benefits of
microcomputers in the classroom remain unanswered.

Because microcomputers are so available, they represent a
technological innovation that cannot be ignored by educators.
Commenting on the response of teachers to computers in the
classroom, Andrew Molnar, manager of science education at
the National Science Foundation, reportedly said, "teachers
have deluded themselves that they would be able to retire
before the computer actually became part of classroom
learning." In view of the widespread and growing distribution
of the technology, it is apparent that teacher preparation
programs and inservice will need to be designed so as to lay
the groundwork for a "technical conversion" within the
profession.

Chapter II

BUILDING
STAFF SKILLS

To most schoolteachers and administrators, the computer expert's image is like that of the early auto driver: engineer, mechanic, daredevil, wizard. This is because most educators have had little involvement with computer people or the evolution of the computer sciences. As ubiquitous as computers have become, access to them, until the advent of microcomputers, has been controlled by computer technicians and information scientists. Differing from the average educator in many ways, these experts sometimes adopted a pose of intellectual superiority because of their arcane knowledge. Their relationships with educators have been marked by great social and professional distance.

However, placing microcomputers in the hands of frontline educators may be the beginning of the end of the old professional barriers. Microcomputer development and implementation will probably not be treated by educators as a separate discipline, distinct from the "old-fashioned" part of education. One important consequence of this will be the growth in the production of educational software by educators; until now the product of a small, select group of educational technologists and programmers.

But a bright sunset often precedes a dismal night. The recent history of education discloses that when innovations such as computer-assisted instruction have been introduced into school systems, only small amounts of money have been spent to improve teacher competencies to use the computers. A staffing study by the former U.S. Office of Education documented that schools spend about as much money on staff development as on substitute pay. And there is the ill-conceived but definite tendency for schools to hire an additional staff of computer people, at added cost, rather than retraining the current staff and assigning them new functions (Hyer & McClure, 1973).

Overcoming traditional professional barriers and poor management of the introduction of new technologies are problems that must be considered when planning a staff development program. A third involves reducing the fears and preconceptions of many teachers and administrators.

Any effort to design a staff development program must be undertaken with an awareness that teachers have already acquired concepts and attitudes concerning what computers are, what it takes to make them work, and how their own abilities stack up to the perceived requirements. It is very easy for teachers to feel "intimidated by technological considerations, especially if they are forced to participate in forums where they do not understand the language or the objectives" (Hadalski, 1979).

Teachers also have very real fears of technological displacement by computers. Most educational writings, up until now, have dismissed the idea that computers could ever replace teachers. This perpetuates the idea that machines cannot serve as human interaction agents. Teachers are told that "such expensive pieces of electronic machinery do no more than save the teacher the trouble of saying to each learner such things as two times two is four, not three or five." (Alvir, 1977).

The implication of Alvir's pronouncement is "don't worry, computers won't change how you do things...just make them easier." Licklider (1979), speaking from the platform of the prestigious National Science Foundation, is less reassuring. Citing the remarkable improvement in cost-effectiveness of computer hardware, he turns in contrast to education, a 50 billion dollar a year enterprise with 41 million students...most money being spent on teacher salaries. Licklider (1979) writes, "The fact that education is highly labor-intensive must be taken into account when thinking about the near-term future and about transition into an improved regimen." In Licklider's view, that improved regimen will entail fewer teachers and more "very sophisticated educational applications" of computers.

Already, Stanford University has introduced fully computerized instruction. A course in logic has been prepared where no meetings occur between students, instructors, or assistants. The authors believe that reductions in public, political, and financial support for education (Guthrie, 1981) may begin to exert irresistible pressure toward full computerization, at least in certain curriculum areas.

Moursund (1979) is skeptical that microcomputers will solve the "computers-in-education problem." As Chairman of the Association for Computing Machinery's Elementary and Secondary Schools Subcommittee, he believes that there are massive barriers preventing the schools from achieving computer literacy for all students, making computer-assisted instruction universally available, and providing students opportunities to acquire advanced computer skills. These include:

• Lack of enough hardware
• Insufficient software and courseware
• Teachers who lack training
• School administrators who lack training
• Lack of awareness and support by school boards, parents, and taxpayers

The unavailability of hardware and the fragmented and insufficient supply of software are economic phenomena that microcomputers certainly can't alter directly. Nor can microcomputers change skills, awarenesses, or community support. However, the growing visibility of microcomputers in homes and businesses, along with the fact that individuals can now realistically expect to purchase their own computer equipment sets the stage for a successful staff development effort. Except for the availability of comprehensive courseware, the problems noted by Moursund are all correctable through carefully planned and implemented staff development programs. The "computers-in education problem" is basically a staff development problem.

COMPUTER LITERACY

Computer literacy is a topic that has been widely discussed during the last few years (see Appendix L for recommended readings). While some consider computer literacy to be a matter of knowing how to operate and program computers, the more widely accepted view is that computer literacy includes not just the nuts and bolts of computer operation, but also:

1. the social and economic implications of computers
2. the past, present, and future capabilities of computers
3. how computers can be used in business, education and at home.

Assessing Computer Literacy

Before embarking upon a program to develop computer literacy, it is advisable to determine where you are now. This is a process known as assessing computer literacy. Supported by a two-year grant from the National Science Foundation, Minnesota has performed one of the more extensive assessments. The Minnesota Computer Literacy and Awareness Assessment[1] consisted of 120 items pertaining to: hardware, programming, computer applications, algorithms, software, data processing, complex applications and the impact of computers on society. Results from students in grades seven through twelve revealed that about one-half of the content had already been mastered. An 18 percent increase in knowledge was recorded after a semester of instruction about computers.

---

[1]Educators wishing to obtain a copy of the Minnesota Computer Literacy and Awareness Assessment should contact the Minnesota Educational Computing Consortium, 2520 Broadway Drive, St. Paul, Minnesota 55113.

Results of a "Computers in Education Survey" developed at the University of Nebraska were reported by Stevens (1980). Findings revealed that teachers, student teachers, and teacher educators strongly advocated computer literacy for students, but felt ill-prepared to teach computer skills. In addition, Stevens notes that:

> "A professional attitude was demonstrated by many participants in expressing a desire to learn the computer skills necessary to respond to the technological needs of students."

For inservice sessions, it is desirable to provide a short computer literacy survey as a starting point. The results can be used for planning subsequent activities and for discussion purposes. A very useful instrument was developed by the Robbinsdale, Minnesota Area Schools called "Micro-computers in Education." Part I of the survey included 12 attitudinal questions that are for detecting how a group of teachers feels about computers in society. To what extent do you agree or disagree with the following statements?

I would like to learn more about computers..............

Computers sometimes scare me.......................

I would very much like to have my own computer........

I enjoy (or think I would enjoy) using computers in my classes...

I feel uneasy when I am with people who are talking about computers....................................

I enjoy (or think I would enjoy) working with computers..

I feel confident about my ability to use computers.......

Computers are gaining too much control over people's lives...

All students should have some minimal understanding of computers..

All students should learn about the role that computers
play in our society.....................................

Computers can be a useful instructional aid in many
subject areas other than mathematics..................

Computers provide more disadvantages than
advantages in education..............................

The information portion of the "Microcomputers in
Education" assessment includes a number of basic questions
designed to reveal staff knowledge of computers. (See
Appendix K for answers.)

(True or False)

1. Computers cannot be used to assist in teaching English
   grammar.

2. People often use computers to store large amounts of
   information that they wish to use over and over again.

3. Computers help people make decisions by providing
   correct answers to any question.

4. Computers help people make decisions by telling them if
   their problem is important.

5. Use of computers in education always results in less
   personal treatment of students.

6. Privacy is an issue whenever there are files containing
   personal information about people.

7. The increased use of computers in our society both
   eliminates and creates jobs.

8. Using computers can free one to do more creative tasks,
   but this may lead to more dependence upon machines.

9. In order to use a computer, a person must know how to
   program.

10. Computers are not good for tasks that require:
    a. speed
    b. accuracy
    c. intuition

d. something to be done over and over again
e. I don't know

11. If your charge account bill has an error, it was probably caused by:

a. breakdown of the computer
b. mistakes made by people
c. poor design of the computer
d. general weaknesses of machines
e. I don't know

12. The main duty of a computer programmer is to:

a. operate a computer
b. prepare instructions for a computer
c. schedule jobs for a computer
d. design computers
e. I don't know

13. Which of the following is a limiting consideration for using computers?

a. cost
b. software availability
c. storage capacity
d. all of the above
e. I don't know

14. In order to program a computer, a person:
a. can use any English language words
b. can use any English or foreign language words
c. must use programming language numbers, not words
d. must use the words from a programming language
e. I don't know

15. A computer program is a:

a. course on computers
b. set of instructions to control the computer
c. computer generated presentation
d. piece of computer hardware
e. I don't know

16. Choose the correct output for the computer program shown below:

```
10  LET C = 6
20  LET D = 8
30  LET E = C+D+2
40  PRINT E
    END
```

Output
a. 6
b. 14
c. 8
d. 16
e. I don't know

17. Computer software is a term describing:

a. computer programs
b. electronic components encased in soft plastic or rubber
c. people who work with computers
d. mechanical and electronic parts of a computer system
e. I don't know

18. When in operation, a computer:

a. follows a set of instructions written by people
b. thinks just like a person
c. recalls answers from memory
d. translates data from digital to analog code
e. I don't know

19. What is the main purpose of the following program:

```
10   INPUT A, B, C, D, E
20   LET S = A+B+C+D+E
30   LET M = S/ 5
40   PRINT S,M
50   END
```

a. store A, B, C, D, and E in the computer
b. print the letters S and M
c. print the sum and average of five numbers
d. calculate large sums
e. I don't know

20. The computer must have two types of information to solve a problem:

a. the problem and the answer
b. the name of the program and user number
c. the data and the instructions
d. the name of the program and your name
e. I don't know

Achieving Computer Literacy

A great deal of material that can be used in developing computer literacy has already been prepared. And like any subject, there is always more to learn regardless of an individual's present state of knowledge. For educators interested in developing computer literacy among students, a number of courses have already been developed and indexed by unit and lesson content (Hanson, Klassen & Anderson, 1979). In short, a teacher doesn't have to begin at ground zero.

Dennis (1978) developed a model for training teachers to teach with computers. Twenty-four knowledges and skills that are fundamental for educators wishing to use computers effectively in their programs were identified and are presented in Table 1.

TABLE 1

Important Knowledge or Skills for Instructional Computing (Dennis, 1978)

1. Familiarity with computerized teaching materials (i.e., instructional programs) in a variety of fields.
2. Ability to integrate computerized teaching materials into a course.
3. General knowledge of the functioning of CMI (computer-managed-instruction) systems.
4. Understanding of effective design of drill and practice materials.
5. Ability to apply computerized drill and practice in a variety of teaching situations.
6. Familiarity with computer simulations and models.
7. Experience in preliminary design and construction of a simulation.
8. Knowledge of the uses of simulations as teaching tools.
9. Ability to evaluate the effectiveness of a course that uses computerized teaching materials.
10. Ability to determine the computer needs of a school.
11. Ability to draft specifications (request for proposals) which set down the needs and desires of the school and invite proposals/ bids from potential suppliers.
12. Ability to be highly critical of suppliers' proposals and their machines.
13. Ability to assemble data about proposed equipment to facilitate decision-making (cost, performance data,

hardware characteristics, software support, etc.).
14. Familiarity with instructional games.
15. Knowledge of how to use instructional games appropriately and effectively in teaching.
16. Physical familiarity with computer equipment, i.e., everyday operation and use of a range of different machines.
17. Knowledge of trouble-shooting procedures and means of access to professional help, i.e., knowing how to determine if a piece of equipment is ailing, and if it is, knowing who to call to fix it.
18. Knowledge of sources for computer materials.
19. Knowledge of how to improve less than adequate instructional computer programs.
20. Ability to evaluate the effectiveness of instructional computer programs.
21. Ability to instruct others in the social role and impact of computers in society.
22. Knowledge of alternative uses of computers in schools, e.g., as class-record-keepers, term-paper-editors, etc.
23. Awareness of the value of involving students in the development of computerized instructional materials.
24. Knowledge of processes of involving students in instructional materials development.

For schools that are interested in getting started in microcomputing, a materials kit has been prepared for use on Apple II microcomputers that should provide staff and students alike with a grasp of the fundamentals. Called "Apple Seed," this kit consists of six parts that can be used for self-instruction:
- computer literacy show and tell kit
- computer discovery
- computers and education
- microcomputer systems and Apple BASIC
- Applesoft tutorial
- educational software directory.

Included in this kit are workbooks, instructor guides, texts, examples of real computer components, and tutorial materials. The cost of this program, in 1981, was approximately $500.

Less expensive is an excellent interrelated series of papers on training teachers in the use of computers, also applicable to microcomputers. These materials were developed by the

University of Illinois under a grant from the EXXON Education Foundation. The materials have been extensively tested in pre-service and inservice programs. Each is available at a cost of 50 cents from ISEAC, Department of Secondary Education, 396 Education Building, Urbana, IL 61801. The program includes:

* A Teacher's Introduction to Educational Computing

* Designing Instruction for Teaching with a Computer

* The Question Episode--Building Block of Teaching With a Computer

* Evaluating Materials for Teaching With a Computer

* Tutorial Instruction on a Computer

* Drill and Practice on a Computer

* Computer Simulation and Its Instructional Uses

* Instructional Games and the Computer Using Teacher

* Computer Managed Instruction and Individualization

* The School Administrator's Introduction to Computing

* Computer Applications in Science Education

* Computer Applications in the Teaching of English

* Practicum Activities for Training Teachers to Use Computers

* Documentation of CTRS--Computerized Test-Result Reporting System

* Documentation of CAISP: A Small Computer CMI System

* Documentation of INFO: A Small Computer Data Base Management System for School Applications

* Documentation--A Small Computer Attendance Keeping System

* Documentation--A Computerized Instructional Resource Management System

* A Look at Computer Assisted Testing Operations

* Getting Started in School Computing: Preparing the Purchase

*A Teacher's Introduction to Administrative Uses of Computers

The International Council for Computers in Education, a non-profit professional organization of educators, has developed three 48-page booklets that are useful for staff development. The following booklets are available from ICCE, Department of Computer and Information Science, University of Oregon, Eugene, OR 97403:

*School Administrator's Introduction to Instructional Use of Computers (D. Moursund)

*Teacher's Guide to Computers in the Elementary School (D. Moursund)

*An Introduction to Computers and Computing (J. Rogers)

Overcoming Fear of Hardware

An effective microcomputer literacy program requires that many opportunities be provided for educators to manipulate the machinery while under direct supervision. The authors have concluded that fear of hardware is a major obstacle to getting teachers enthusiastically involved with microcomputing.

Fear of hardware probably has been partly induced by the limited instruction that preservice teachers receive in how to operate mechanical devices such as film projectors and videotape recorders. A universally shared teacher experience is the failure of audio-visual equipment at critical moments, often before an audience of merciless students. The embarrassment and management problems stemming from these failures can produce strong avoidance reactions by teachers to all kinds of machinery in the classroom.

Although microcomputers are both durable and reliable, an inexperienced user is often convinced that they are fragile, temperamental, and ornery devices. To counteract fear of hardware, some intensive programs have been developed to train teachers how to disassemble and reassemble microcomputers, locating and correcting mechanical problems. The final activity is for the instructor to build a mechanical problem into the equipment, requiring teachers to locate and fix it.

While a training experience of this magnitude may be unrealistic for many school districts, there are a number of items relating to hardware maintenance that teachers should know, for example:

1. Static electricity can "scramble" computer chips making it necessary for users to ground themselves before using the micros. This can be done by wiring a small metal plate to an electrical ground and touching the plate to discharge the static buildup. Some grounding mats for use on the floor at each microcomputer workstation are also available.

2. Power surges through the lines caused by lightning, can heavily damage equipment. Isolators are available which detect the surge and break the connection before equipment is affected. Brownouts or low power situations generally will not damage microcomputer equipment but will disrupt whatever work is underway.

3. High temperatures and high humidity can adversely affect microcomputers, again, without permanent damage. Small fans are available for some micros to help prevent overheating. Most school environments should not present a problem, even if they are not air-conditioned.

4. Radio frequency signals produced by microcomputers can cause T.V. interference and rarely, several micros operating in close proximity may interfere with each other. Recent shielding requirements by the Federal Communications Commission greatly reduce this problem.

5. If the equipment fails to operate:
   - make sure it has power available
   - if that's not the problem, unplug the micro, ground yourself, take off the lid and firmly but carefully press down on all the chips to be sure they are properly seated in their sockets...this happens due to expansion and contraction of the chips as the temperature changes
   - if a peripheral piece of equipment is not functioning properly, unplug the micro, ground yourself, remove the appropriate interface card from the slot where it is

plugged in and gently clean the contact surfaces at the base of the card with an eraser or a cotton swab dipped in alcohol before plugging it back in.

AN INSTRUCTIONAL DESIGNER ROLE FOR TEACHERS

When computers have been introduced into business and production situations, some jobs have been eliminated, some added, and many changed. The microcomputer revolution will certainly offer rich opportunities for educators with the foresight to become computer literate and the flexibility to adjust to changing role requirements. One of the new dimensions of teaching will be the task of instructional design.

Without technology, teaching has been principally a human relations activity wherein a teacher plans experiences, locates relevant materials, and distributes knowledge through direct encounters via the oral tradition. The learner has been the focus of the teacher's thinking and planning.

In order to take advantage of the microcomputer's capabilities for instruction, we will need to look more closely at the organization and presentation of the educational content itself. This does not mean that the learner as a person will be secondary, or unimportant; only that we will also be dealing with the creation of a lasting educational product. These instructional products will become a major determinant of student progress, whether they progress rapidly with a feeling of success or become confused, bored, or frustrated.

An indication of just how far we have to go in developing instructional design skills among teachers is the prevailing tendency of teachers to give vague specifications to programmers who are "authoring" lessons (Jacobson, 1973). Even the most skillful programmer can't transform poor quality and vague specifications into good courseware. If educators are to be uninvolved in the writing of computer courseware, they must at least learn to be quite precise and detailed in describing what is needed. They will need instructional design skills.

Roblyer (1981) has noted some of the methods of instructional design that distinguish it from "authoring" or programming:

* Instructional designers base their work on a model. An example of one model that is sometimes used is BLOOM'S TAXONOMY OF OF EDUCATIONAL OBJECTIVES. This model classifies educational goals according to a hierarchy of cognitive skills:
  - knowledge
  - comprehension
  - application
  - analysis
  - synthesis
  - evaluation
* Written design documents spell out in detail what the final courseware will look like, prior to starting programming. These written documents describe prompting flow, standards for judging successful completion, specifications for dictionaries of terms, graphics, number of repetitions, branching, and the instructional logic (introducing, sequencing, and terminating).
* Instructional design is a team effort. It has been shown that courseware designed by teams is of higher quality, probably because systematic errors are reduced. The design team engages in much cross-checking of each other's work.
* Instructional design involves continuous evaluation of lesson content by subject matter specialists who observe individual students as they progress through courseware in classroom field-tests. In this sense, instructional designers need some of the same skills provided educational evaluators in their training.

Robyler (1981) has also provided a summary of the major stages and activities of the instructional design process as shown in Figure 1.

In designing courseware, a detailed mastery of the subject that is being worked with is required. Gaps in knowledge or incomplete understanding of concepts make it impossible to design quality courseware because these deficiencies become magnified, readily detected by informed reviewers. Teachers who are functioning in an instructional design capacity are aware that their work is going to be the object of professional evaluation. This is quite different from teaching in a closed classroom, a relatively invisible activity, shielded from professional observation. Providing greater public visibility for teaching is a powerful incentive for quality performance,

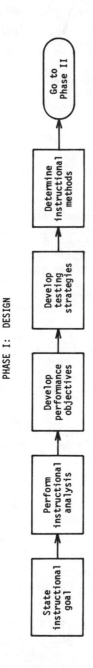

ROBYLER'S INSTRUCTIONAL DESIGN PHASES

PHASE I: DESIGN

State instructional goal → Perform instructional analysis → Develop performance objectives → Develop testing strategies → Determine instructional methods → Go to Phase II

PHASE II: DEVELOPMENT

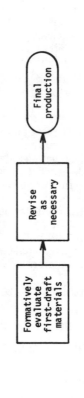

Develop activity flowcharts → Develop frame storyboards → Review and revise flowcharts, storyboards → Develop first-draft materials → Go to Phase III

PHASE III: EVALUATION AND REVISION

Formatively evaluate first-draft materials → Revise as necessary → Final production

Figure 1

but not all teachers are anxious to accept that challenge.

Another benefit arising from having teachers function as instructional designers is the increased sensitivity to the learning process that they can gain. Observing students while they work with instructional software can provide valuable insights into individual differences in learning style, problem solving skills, and task-orientation. With a reduced emphasis on the teacher as a performer, as in acting, careful observation of learners becomes a more fundamental part of the teaching role.

Incentives

Designing, authoring, and reviewing microcomputer courseware are all rewarding and creative activities for skilled teachers. Especially needed today are detailed reviews. Many educators are reluctant to purchase courseware without previewing it, an opportunity that is rarely available. Published professional reviews are an alternative to first-hand knowledge, but preparing them is a long and costly process, hardly a viable commercial enterprise. (See Appendix E for software review sources.)

School MicroWare (see Appendix E) made an interesting offer to subscribers recently. If a courseware review, using their form, is performed and accepted, the reviewer will receive one or more free copies of SCHOOL MICROWARE REVIEWS, thereby saving a cost of $30 per volume. We expect that nationwide software review networks will become one of the principle mechanisms for quality control in educational software.

Teachers who design and author educational software can market it themselves through MICRONET, a national communications network, (see Chapter Four) if they are subscribers. Locally produced software can be leased or purchased by remote parties, a potential source of added income for teachers.

Some teachers may want to apply for grants to develop specialized software in their area of interest. One opportunity to receive support is provided by the Apple Education Foundation. Awards are given to both individuals and institutions to develop new methods of learning with microcomputers. A few of their recently supported projects are:

- Hand-eye Coordination Skills Acquisition System
- Computer-Based Exercises in Fractions and Decimals
- Computer-Assisted Instruction in Reading Skills
- Planning Nutritious Meals

Integrated Curriculum Development

Partly due to the professional barriers that have separated computer people from the mainstream of classroom teachers and also because major computer-assisted instruction development efforts have been undertaken outside the school environment, in companies, universities, and labs, much computer-assisted instruction is poorly integrated with existing instructional procedures and curriculum.

Jacobson (1973) was attuned to this problem and described how integrated curriculum development might proceed in order to insure appropriate and effective use of computers in the classroom. Integrated CAI curriculum development is very similar to developing programs with varied texts, individual projects, supplementary media experiences such as films and video cassettes, field trips, and group projects. Computers, in this model, become one resource that can be used to enhance the overall effectiveness of curriculum. Computer applications should not be developed outside the general context of overall program development.

Here are some of the principal questions that are addressed in the process of integrated curriculum development (Jacobson, 1973):

*What objectives and skills will be addressed?

*What learning conditions must exist?

*What materials and experiences will promote the acquisition of these skills and objectives?

*What is the best way to use these materials and experiences?

For example, Jacobson (1973) suggests that:

> Dienes blocks would be used to teach place-value notation
> because of their appropriate perceptual qualities; computa-
> tional algorithms would be taught largely by group
> discussion and practice sheets because verbal exposition and
> practice produce the optimal learning of such skills; and
> inquiry and problem-solving skill would be taught using
> particular types of interactive computing routines which can
> respond to an individual's needs by generating the right kind
> of problem with appropriate assistance available.

The integrated approach to curriculum development for
microcomputer applications results in varied experiences that
relate to each other and the whole. Concepts, terms, sequence
of presentation, and emphasis can be controlled. The
inevitable redundancy that occurs when multiple, independently produced "packaged" educational programs are
used is surely reduced and hopefully eliminated.

COST SAVING APPLICATIONS

As we noted earlier, cost reduction has been a paramount
goal of the introduction of technologies in education. If one
accepts this view, an important part of staff development is to
help educators recognize applications that have potential for
savings.

Teacherless Courses

How can small, rural schools faced with declining
enrollments, burgeoning federal and state controls, a
competitive job market for graduates, and the economic
realities of the "Age of Less" provide academic equity for
their students? Increasingly, rural schools are abandoning
courses that are not cost-effective. And what this means is that
courses with low enrollments, such as foreign language,
chemistry, and computer programming are casualties, even
though these courses might be considered essential in medium
and large school districts. Isolation, a fact of life for teachers
in many rural schools, limits professional development
opportunities for staff and further hinders prospects for
academic equity for students.

In tackling this problem, the Littlefork-Big Falls Independent School District, located in northern Minnesota along the Canadian border, developed a self-instruction center. The center offered students several forms of self-instruction and assessed the relative costs and feasibility of each.

Carpeted and sound-proofed to provide a quiet atmosphere for individual study, the self-instruction center houses 14 study carrels and table space for small group study. Its equipment includes two film strip cassette players, six audio cassette players, two printing terminals linked to the statewide computer network, three Control Data PLATO terminals, and an Apple II microcomputer. Twenty-seven new courses were added to the secondary school curriculum during the first year using four major types of self-instruction: 1) PLATO computer-assisted instruction; 2) extension courses offered by universities through correspondence; 3) audio-visual courses; and, 4) video-tape courses.

Beyond resources, one of the biggest threats to academic equity through self-instruction is the difficulty of monitoring student progress. Most secondary students lack the skills and experience to work completely on their own and need external support in learning self-monitoring and self-evaluation skills, both of which are necessary to success in self-instruction. To help in this, a microcomputer program was developed for the Apple II that allowed each student to enter daily information concerning goals, progress, and attitude. Each day, a student's progress is graphically displayed, in color, on the T.V. monitor. And a group summary can be obtained on demand by the instructional manager.

Reduced Training Time

Cost savings are to be had whenever computers can be used to reduce the length of time that students are involved in an educational experience if student costs are not fixed. A good example of this is inservice education for teachers.

Schools typically provide, at considerable expense, paid inservice days for teachers. Because computer assisted instruction can reduce instructional time by as much as one-half, schools might be able to reduce the number of paid inservice days, while receiving the same staff development benefit.

The present authors designed microcomputer based training procedures in response to a request for a proposal issued by the Illinois Department of Children and Family Services. The agency is controlled by a complex set of regulations that are constantly being revised. Frequent, expensive, face-to-face staff development sessions are needed in order to keep staff appraised of the new rules. Video-tape instruction, written materials, and other media presentations are very cost-ineffective because of the constant need for revision. Microcomputer courseware, on the other hand, is relatively inexpensive to produce and easy to modify to reflect changing regulations. It could be administered individually and at times of convenience to the employee. Inservice could be scheduled so as to minimize disruption to on-going work.

Paraprofessionals

Cost savings will occur when computers are used to increase the ratio of paraprofessionals to fully certified teachers. In computer assisted instruction, several paraprofessionals under the supervision of a trained teacher can assist students who are working individually or in small groups. Paraprofessionals can assemble and distribute supplementary materials, handle the logistics and scheduling problems, collect and compile written assignments, and deal with various technical and user problems.

Labor Intensivity

Cost savings can be realized when computers are used in highly labor intensive areas such as special education. Reduced class sizes and requirements for higher levels of teacher preparation make special education programs the most expensive that schools provide. Many of the services offered by special education entail tutorial instruction supplemented by drill and practice. Both of these are among the simplest computer assisted instruction applications and therefore show great promise for cost reduction in the schools.

Non-Teaching Functions

Another way that microcomputers can be used to reduce school costs is to free teachers and other highly paid professionals from documentation and paperwork functions. As early as 1972 it was determined that approximately one-quarter of a secondary school teacher's time was spent in non-instructional activities (English and Sharpes, 1972). Paperwork represents an ever increasing activity of teachers. To the extent that this burden can be reduced, instructional resources can be shifted back into direct instruction. At the same time, the need for paraprofessionals can be reduced.

Reducing Management Costs

Schools have generally been very unsuccessful in containing the growth of management costs. While no technology can reduce administrative over-staffing (a political and organizational phenomenon), microcomputers will help reduce the cost of the clerical work. One has to be very careful, however, that the work doesn't expand to fill the time available to do it. More efficient (faster) paperwork, without a reduction in clerical staff, is no saving.

In order to take full advantage of the cost-reduction potential of microcomputers, major policies governing education will need to change. A deterent to the universal application of microcomputers in the classroom as a cost-saving mechanism is that their principal strength is to reduce the amount of time required by a student to complete a given unit of instruction. As long as schools adhere to fixed schedules, days per week, hours per day, days per year and years per certificate of graduation, reductions in the time needed to complete courses will result in greater, not less costs. Curriculum would need to be expanded to allow for the students' accelerated growth and learning. The movement of some states, such as Florida, toward early graduation based on the achievement of competencies, could open the way to major cost reductions through microcomputer assisted instruction.

ADMINISTRATIVE SUPPORT

There are many support services that districts can provide to teachers that will help staff members improve their computer-related skills. Some of the following services might be provided by regularly employed staff; others might be contracted if funds are available.

- Provide on-site visits to teachers who are using micro-computers in their classrooms. Visitations by colleagues or outsiders who have considerable expertise in classroom applications can be very encouraging and a good source of ideas. It is a good idea to have teachers supply a list of questions to the resource person in advance of the visitation in order to gain most benefit.

- Arrange short, group presentations on new developments in microcomputing, hardware, software, and ideas. Round table sessions, after school, concerning special topics such as computer graphics or word processing are effective.

- Arrange training sessions for larger troups of teachers representing a single subject area or grade level. Outside resources may be required for this. Be sure that concrete materials are made available during these sessions and that the program is carefully structured. Detailed outlines of training sessions should be available in advance. If written materials are to be used, participants should have access to them in advance of the training sessions.

- District-wide newsletters are an economical way of keeping teachers interested and informed of new developments in microcomputing. Producing a newsletter is usually an assigned task for one or more school staff, but this service could also be contracted. Newsletters must be brief, highlighting sources of help and information. Noting quality software or courseware can also be an important contribution of a newsletter. Most important, newsletters help emphasize district policies and goals by keeping a particular topic highly visible.

- Courseware exchanges can be established to give teachers an opportunity to share their work with others and to get professional feedback. Courseware exchanges also maximize the volume of local or commercially purchased courseware that is available to teachers. Members of exchanges duplicate programs if they are not protected by copyright.

- A directory of key teachers involved with microcomputers can be prepared. Robbinsdale, Minnesota used this approach effectively. Teachers were identified by school, experience, educational background and area of interest for microcomputing.

INVOLVEMENT WITH NATIONAL ORGANIZATIONS

An important aspect of staff development is communicating and working with other educators who have similar interests. National organizations provide a forum that encourages communication and professional development. The major organization in the United States concerned with microcomputers in education is the Association for Educational Data Systems.

The Association for Educational Data Systems is a private, non-profit educational corporation founded in 1962. AEDS was created by a group of professional educators dedicated to providing a means for the exchange of information about the impact of modern technology upon the educational process. Membership is available to all persons interested in learning more and keeping informed about current developments and direction in educational data systems and computer technology. Included in the membership are educators and technical experts from all over the United States, Canada, and other countries representing public and private schools, higher education, state and provincial departments of education.

The Association publishes three quarterly publications--the AEDS BULLETIN, a newsletter; the AEDS MONITOR with short timely articles; and the AEDS JOURNAL containing technical articles. A special JOURNAL was recently published entitled THE SELECTION AND APPLICATION OF MICROCOMPUTERS.

Additional activities include an annual international convention, special seminars and workshops, a computer programming contest for students in grades 7-12, and up-to-date information on legislative activities impacting educational technology. Eighteen geographic chapters and one functional chapter are affiliated with AEDS; others are currently in the process of organization.

The Association of Educational Data Systems is head-quartered in Washington, D.C. at 1201 Sixteenth Street, N.W. Individual membership fees are $35 per year; student membership is $10.

There are a number of other organizations that professionals interested in microcomputer applications may wish to explore. These organizations, listed in Appendix I, provide professional development experiences in the form of workshops, publications, and special programs.

MATERIALS AND IDEAS

Getting started in microcomputing can be difficult because it is a new and constantly changing field. There are many small vendors and manufacturers active today, and it is impossible to locate a single source of all or even most of the information that you need to get started in the right direction.

Recognizing the possibility that rapid changes in the field could make some of the information obsolete, the authors nonetheless felt it to be desirable to include several lists of sources of materials and aid. The listings found in the appendices are not comprehensive and should be viewed only as a number of good places to begin seeking information. Listings in the appendix include:

- Vendors
    Microcomputers
    Printers and Video Displays
    Miscellaneous Peripherals
    Software
- Software Reviews
    Newsletters
- Magazines and Journals
- Directories and Catalogs
- Organizations
- Recommended Readings on Computer Literacy

SOME QUESTIONS AND ISSUES

Video Display Problems

Educators who intend to begin using microcomputers for

instruction should be aware that there has been some discussion of potential health hazards associated with improper use of video display terminals. The National Institute for Occupational Safety and Health has taken a leadership role in investigating any potential health risks.

One area of investigation has been x-ray emissions of cathode ray tubes associated with their high voltage requirements. Most researchers are convinced that there is no problem for human health and the FCC has established standards, but some say that how x-ray emission relates to established exposure limits for humans hasn't been determined.

An area of greater concern to the National Institute for Occupational Safety and Health is the higher rates of vision problems reported by terminal operators. Some think that the refresh flicker of the cathode ray tube, where images are actually re-created electronically at a rate of 25 or more times per second cause serious eye fatigue. One thing is certain; it is very important to allow terminal users to adjust the contrast and the position of the terminal relative to the user.

Some manufacturers are working to design greater flexibility into computer workstations. Moveable keyboards, adjustable screens, and glare reduction are all priorities. Glare reduction screens, available for separate purchase, have already proven invaluable in preventing eye fatigue, particularly in environments where considerable light is reflected by the screen.

Several suggestions have been made for reducing video terminal user problems (Business Week, July 22, 1980), including:
- Provide frequent breaks
- Use chairs and keyboards that are adjustable
- Add glare reduction equipment to screens
- Don't dismiss complaints as imaginary, follow-up on them
- Control lighting so as to avoid direct reflections into the screen
- Don't place the CRT near a bright light source such as a window

- For children who wear bifocal lenses, consult with parents and physician before having them work with video displays.

Memory Load

Video displays provide students with no "hard copy" of material as it is presented. The displays of information, instructions, illustrations, and graphics are rapid and transitory. Together, these conditions result in what researchers call high memory load. Studies conducted at the Florida State University Computer-Assisted Instruction Center have provided evidence that low ability students have great difficulty in coping with the uninterrupted flow of information without being able to refer to material presented earlier (Brown & O'Neil, 1971). Certainly this problem must be considered when designing courseware for low ability students.

Copyright Provisions

Educators purchasing software from commercial vendors should be aware that it is often illegal to duplicate the software for multiple users. Before duplicating any software it should be determined if it is "public domain." Usually, software is "public domain" if it was developed entirely under a grant from a federal agency, such as the Department of Education. Public domain materials belong to the public and can be reproduced without permission.

If software is copyrighted, be sure that the seller owns the copyright or accepts any liability that arises from its distribution. Schools that purchase copyrighted software, according to the 1976 Copyright Reform Act, are allowed very limited copying privileges under the "fair use exemption." For instance, it might be possible to make one back-up copy to insure against loss or destruction. However, be sure that the meaning of "fair use" is concretely described in the sales agreement. When in doubt, the best thing to do is to contact the person or organization holding the copyright. Infringement of copyright can result in fines, confiscation of illegal copies, and in some cases criminal prosecution.

Ownership of Software

Software and courseware have economic value as recognized by copyright provisions. There is an available market for these materials that is relatively easy to access. When public school employees produce written materials, such as units or lesson plans, there is only a slim chance that these products will be marketable. The publishing industry is relatively closed, in contrast to the software industry which is open.

As more and more teachers become involved in the development of educational software, legal issues concerning ownership and royalties will undoubtedly surface. A state department of mental health, in a recent conflict over ownership of media produced by employees, took the position that employees would have to surrender any copyright interests in what they produced during the period of time that they were employed by the state. This matter was not resolved in court because the employees resigned.

School districts are likely to become more involved in legal issues pertaining to copyright interests in software when they realize that there is a potential for obtaining considerable income from the sales of these materials to the public.

FORMAL TRAINING

As school staffs become more involved with microcomputer applications, it is likely that some teachers may wish to pursue formal training that will permit them to assume leadership roles. Several colleges and universities have established programs at the master's and doctoral level that prepare educators for this new career opportunity. Each of the following institutions offers degree programs in instructional technology with skill building degrees in microcomputers. These are education degrees with a computer applications emphasis, not data processing or computer science degrees.

Columbia University
Teachers College
525 West 120th Street
New York, NY 10027
Attn: Dr. Steven M. Gorelick, Assistant Dean

Lehigh University
School of Education
524 Brodhead Avenue
Bethlehem, PA 18015
Attn: Dr. Leroy J. Tuscher

Lesley College
Graduate School
29 Everett Street
Cambridge, MA 02238
Attn: Dr. Nancy Roberts, Director
        Computers in Education

NOVA University
Office of New Programs
3301 College Avenue
Fort Lauderdale, FL 33314
Attn: Dr. Robert L. Burke

Stanford University
School of Education
Stanford, CA 94305
Attn: Dr. Decke Walker or Dr. Robert Hess

State University of New York at Stony Brook
Nicholls Road
Stony Brook, NY 11794
Attn: Dr. Ludwig Braun

University of Illinois
Department of Education
1310 S. 6th Street
Champaign, IL 61820
Attn: Dr. Richard Dennis

University of Oregon
Department of Computer and Information Science
Eugene, OR 97403
Attn: Dr. David Moursund

Chapter III

A MICROCOMPUTER CENTER*

MR. LYNCH'S PREDICAMENT

On May 14, 1979, an article entitled "A Computer Error: Trying to Use One in Your Own Home" by Mitchell Lynch appeared in THE WALL STREET JOURNAL. In the article, Mr. Lynch recounted the tribulations of a micro-computer owner attempting to use the manual to make the machine work. Lynch wrote, "Experts say people like me have neither the technical training nor technical inclination to make a home computer--in my case a Tandy Corp. Radio Shack TRS-80--strut its stuff." What seems to be happening is that "there is a tremendous gap between what the computer can do and what most people can make it do." One analyst reportedly described the microcomputer, as merchandized for home use, as "a solution looking for a problem."

Despite the lack of skills of the average purchaser, estimates reported in the same article indicated that by the end of 1979, 600,000 microcomputers will have been installed in homes and 500,000 will be in offices, laboratories, and schools. It is now conservatively estimated that "sometime in the 1980's microcomputers will be a consumer product."

---

*This chapter is an edited version of: Joiner, Lee Marvin, Silverstein, Burton J., and Ross, Jay Dee. "Insights from a Microcomputer Center in a Rural School District." EDUCATIONAL TECHNOLOGY. 20(5). May, 1980, 36-40.

ORTONVILLE RESPONDS

A small rural community, such as Ortonville, located on the southern-most tip of Big Stone Lake on the boundary between Minnesota and South Dakota, would seem an unlikely place to search for a response to Mr. Lynch's predicament. To think so would be wrong. In fact, the Ortonville Minnesota public schools have been involved in a major "transfer of microcomputer technology" into rural education for several years. This chapter describes this process and what was learned by the participants.

To find out what microcomputers can do for a rural school and community and how to use microcomputers effectively, Ortonville established a microcomputer center in its grades K-12 school building. An "in-house" project run by students and local school staff, the Microcomputer Center was established to study the feasibility of microcomputers for school management, computer assisted instruction, computer literacy, computer programming and community service.

TESTING THE HARDWARE

One of the center's original goals was to conduct on-going testing of various microcomputers. To that end, several popular microcomputers were purchased and installed:
• Radio Shack TRS-80 Level I 4K
• Radio Shack TRS-80 Level II 16K
• Commodore PET 8K
• Tektronix 4051
• Micro-33
• NCR 7200
• Digital 11V03
• Apple II
Hardware was selected on the basis of availability, performance tests and recommendations by the Minnesota Educational Computing Consortium.

WHY ORTONVILLE CHOSE MICROCOMPUTERS

In addition to the cost, ease of installation, and availability considerations that are causing educators nationwide to begin taking a hard look at microcomputers, the Ortonville staff had four important requirements in mind that they believed could be met by microcomputer systems:

- Transportability--it was desirable to have computers that could be moved from class to class or better yet, building to building.
- Group application-- it was desirable that a computer possess the capacity for graphic display to a group.
- Multiple input--the school wanted computer capacity for handling input from different kinds of devices; e.g., keyboard, card reader; and multi-user capabilities, a machine that would allow at least three different and simultaneous users, performing a variety of computer operations.
- Random access files--as opposed to sequential, because in administration applications there is a need for efficient data file manipulation.

HARDWARE PROBLEMS

Despite the characteristics of low maintenance and durability widely proclaimed for microcomputers, there were problems. The problems Ortonville staff encountered, by type of equipment, for a period of approximately six months is described in the following section. While most of these problems were ultimately resolved, they are presented to remind the readers that systems can be fallible.

PET

Problem or inadequate system feature:

* Data files read incorrectly
* Data files can't be edited
* System "locks" due to incorrect chip installation

*Out 5 weeks for service
* If the answer to an input runs onto next line, PET ignores the part that ran over. Under certain conditions an input statement will allow truncation of data entered
*Tape won't read or save--out 3 weeks

Radio Shack TRS-80 Level I

Problem or inadequate system feature:

*No editor
*Sent in for repair--tape advance with no control
* Only one "if then" can be used per line--nothing can be put after an "if then"
*Wave action on monitors--cured by moving monitors farther apart
*Sent monitor for repair--won't accept keyboard entry

Radio Shack TRS-80 Level II

*Trouble loading
*Trouble saving
* "Keybounce"--entering double characters when a key is depressed once
* An "echo" effect
*Incorrect reel alignment on cassette recorder which contributed to the "loading and saving" problems

Tektronix

*No subscripted string variables
*Tab function nonstandard
*Undesirable system features omitted from the manual

Micro-33

*System failure
*Sent in for repair--used "loaner"
*Didn't work when returned

STATEWIDE HARDWARE STANDARDIZATION

Around mid-year, it was learned that the Minnesota Educational Computing Consortium (MECC) endorsed a standardized, statewide, microcomputer; the "Apple." An advantage of standardization, other than an economy of scale, is that users develop programs. These programs can then be distributed to other users through the statewide time-share system by "uploading" the locally developed programs from the district to the time-share system through the telephone lines. Centrally stored programs can be selected from a control library and downloaded onto local microcomputers. In the event of statewide conversion to new hardware, revised master programs can be prepared at the central site.

STRENGTHS AND WEAKNESSES OF THE APPLE II HARDWARE

Since the Apple II was endorsed for statewide distribution, the Ortonville staff was careful to note the specific strengths and weaknesses of that system. These include:

Strengths

* Color graphics
* Speaker
* Easily uploaded & downloaded
* Hard copy easily attained
* Fast disk drive
* Manuals are well written

Weaknesses
* No print using format
* No lower case alphabet
* Some high resolution colors do not show
* File handling is sometimes cumbersome
* It does not print characters on the high or low resolution screen above the bottom four lines. A character file must be created.
* Every other vertical line drawn in high resolution graphics is invisible if drawn in any color other than white. This becomes important when a program uses moving shapes. For example, if one were displaying a blue car traveling across the monitor, gaps would appear in the shape as it traveled laterally
* Saving programs and reading from cassette tape has not been reliable

When considering standardizing microcomputers for statewide applications it must be noted that no one unit is suited to meeting the computer assisted instruction requirements in all subject matter areas. For instance, the Terak provides character flexibility that would be of great importance in foreign language calligraphy where different alphabets and diacritical markings are involved. Tektronix equipment provides special graphic capabilities relevant to geography, geology, and other subject areas where spatial analysis constitutes an important analytic activity.

The Commodore Pet's ability to use upper and lower case letters may make it more suitable than the Apple II for special education involving any reading activities. Special education students often experience problems with different orthographics and therefore might suffer from the lack of a lower case alphabet.

UNANTICIPATED PROBLEMS IN UPLOADING

Because of the presence of telephone interference, or "line noise," there is a need for editing at the uploaded level to correct any errors caused during transmission of the program over the telephone. One procedure would be for the person entering the program to recall it and scan it manually. A more efficient procedure would be for the time-sharing system to develop a program to compare the uploaded program with the original copy, i.e., verify.

INSTRUCTIONAL APPLICATIONS OF MICROS

Ortonville has developed several instructional microcomputer applications to date. First, the top twenty statewide time-sharing programs, in terms of rate of use, were adapted for micros. For example, a simulation relating to agriculture and farm management was developed. Included were such items as cost analysis of purchasing beef cattle, management of sow herds, depreciating farm equipment, and optimized livestock feeding programs. In addition, numerous drill and practice arithmetic, spelling, reading and grammar programs were presented via computer assisted instruction.

Four high school seniors in Ortonville created several drill and practice programs for use in the elementary school. Drills in phonics, German grammar, beginning chemistry, geography, spelling, arithmetic, graphic geometry, physics and a fish life cycle game have all been programmed by high school students at Ortonville.

Of particular interest to Ortonville students were vector and projection simulations in the physics program, the fish life-cycle simulation, and the geography quiz. Vector and projection concepts are reinforced by requiring the student to key in the correct angle for the simulated trajectory of an artillery shell. A student fires the artillery and watches the trajectory of the shell across the monitor. If the trajectory is correct, the shell destroys an enemy tank. Based on where the shell lands, the student adjusts his angle of firing. In two other programs, LUNAR and MARS1, the student attempts to safely land his craft by firing retro-rockets...speed and distance from the surface are displayed while graphics show the craft "falling." Gravity is computed for the Moon or Mars depending on which program is being used. If the impact is above an acceptable level, the craft crumbles. If the landing is successful the pilot is congratulated. There are many correct combinations of retro-fire that will allow a proper landing.

Simulating the life cycle of six different species of fish, another microcomputer program poses problems of survival. In this game, the student assumes the role of a fish. Attacking, escaping to deep or shallow water, or attempting to prey on a series of different aquatic creatures, are choices available to the student (fish). If choices appropriate to the species of fish involved are selected, the student (fish) will survive.

Geography drill and practice is provided by another engaging program. Graphic outlines of the states, with the capital cities starred, are presented successively. The student is requested to type in the name of the state. If the first response is correct the computer congratulates and then asks the name of the state capital. Again, congratulations are given for the correct answer and a new state outline is drawn. If an incorrect response is given, the computer consoles the student and displays the first letter of the state or capital. Another mistake calls forth more hints until the student responds correctly.

One of the programs adapted for micro from the statewide network is Oregon Trail. Oregon Trail simulates a settler family's journey by covered wagon, from Missouri to Oregon. Budget allotments must be made before the journey. The settlers' survival hinges on the judicious allocation of funds for clothing, medicine, supplies, ammunition, food, and emergency cash. Settlers can periodically choose between hunting for food, stopping at a fort (purchasing expensive supplies), or continuing on their journey. Hunting is simulated with the space bar on the keyboard serving as a rifle which fires bullets at a deer running across the screen. The settler may select the degree of perception and eye-hand coordination required to kill the running deer, or attacking bandits. Hailstorms, breakdowns, illnesses, injuries, bandit attacks, all take their toll on the settlers and their resources. And if their marksmanship or planning is inadequate, the family will not survive.

Oregon Trail has been a great challenge for sixth grade students. It has potential for stimulating individual class projects and for microcomputer-curriculum integration. Possible integration activities include:

- Students can be directed to write a log of events based on the experiences presented by the computer.
- Students can write letters home and recount their trials as intrepid pioneers.
- Each child can make a map and highlight the major events of their journey.
- Students can do research on personal accounts of actual pioneer journeys.
- Drawings or paintings can be made of events, scenes or wildlife.

During the 1977-78 school year, Oregon Trail was run over 63,000 times on the Minnesota time-share system, and Ortonville used it heavily. After adapting it to micros, that version was used exclusively. It was more appealing because of the graphics, lack of busy signals, and transportability to individual classrooms. As more schools use micro-Oregon,

Ortonville expects a considerable savings on line time to the time-share system.

Ortonville staff are convinced that computer assisted instruction must be used for integrated conventional classroom instruction and that giving a game playing function to the computer is educationally unsound. First through sixth grade classes have used student written programs for drill in arithmetic, phonics, and spelling. Both teachers and students are enthusiastic about the learning experience and the performance of the computer programs. In addition, several teachers are taking computer programming courses on microcomputers. These skills will become increasingly valuable as computers become a greater part of everyday life. The broadening uses of micros are described in the following section.

BEYOND INSTRUCTION

The prospects for the use of the computer as an information storage and retrieval, environmental monitoring and control, and management system in the home and small business will require that schools expose students to many computer applications other than as respondents to computer assisted instruction. To be instructed by computer requires little active knowledge of what computers can be made to do and how to get the machines to do it. Emerging applications of microcomputers in the home and in business will cause American schools to begin offering courses in how to use microcomputers in all of the administrative and management capacities now identified with the large networked systems.

Ortonville demonstrated that microcomputers can support an orderly and efficient management process at the school board level and at the school administration level. Prior to the availability of computer support, the week leading up to the school board meeting was hectic. Much clerical, accounting, and data retrieval activity was involved, all performed by hand. After a microcomputer system was developed, a young person who had completed the high school data processing class was able to assume payroll responsibilities. As a bonus over manual methods, this person was able to perform additional duties such as keeping records, preparing federal reports relating to the lunch program and so forth.

Class scheduling also consumes school resources voraciously. Without computer assistance, the process of class scheduling occupies much of the summer; at least two weeks of professional level time is involved and even more clerical time. Microcomputers can organize this information with about one week of secretarial level input.

Here is a list of school management reports and records that Ortonville's microcomputer center produced:
- monthly budget reports
- payroll and accounting reports
- general ledger
- revenue reports
- voucher and bill lists
- summary reports
- census tabulation and record keeping
- staff personnel records and reports
- purchase orders
- student scheduling

BUILDING SCHOOL-COMMUNITY TIES

In the context of the microcomputer as a consumer product, one of the benefits of the Ortonville project is that it builds capabilities within the local school in anticipation of, rather than in reaction to, emerging community needs. Projects that are closely tied to felt community needs enhance the quality of local education by building and maintaining strong community support for the schools.

For example, only since the inception of the Ortonville project has it been feasible to offer night courses in computer programming to community members. The micro is seen as an accessible technology because of the availability of the hardware and continuing decline in costs. Small business operators and others such as Ortonville's county engineer and the business manager of the local hospital are anxious to learn how to use microcomputers to make their work more efficient and to enhance their own productivity.

STAFFING THE MICROCOMPUTER CENTER

Schools that are contemplating adopting microcomputer technology should be advised that someone will need to manage the operation. As awareness of computer instruction capabilities grows, teacher use accelerates along with a need to schedule equipment, provide special assistance in operating, and write instructional programs requested by classroom teachers. In order to integrate microcomputers with the conventional curriculum it is important to: (a) provide physical accessibility of hardware in the classroom, (b) create computer assisted lessons tailored to the felt needs of individual teachers. Ortonville's center was staffed by a full-time teacher and four students aides.

In operating a microcomputer center, staff will need to know BASIC if they are to be involved in programming. Also, they must be able to read the manuals pertaining to the various machines they are working with. No formal provisions were made for staff training as part of the project; skills were acquired on the job or in the case of students, through programming courses. Teachers are still being introduced to classroom applications and a major challenge is to help them overcome any avoidance reactions that may have resulted from cultural conditioning: a mystification of computers and computing.

NEW SKILLS AND HABITS

A number of new staff skills are emerging from the project. Secretarial staff, for example, are learning to provide more detailed and complete reports. And the task analysis that is prerequisite to programming focuses attention on efficiency considerations. At the instructional application level, teachers and paraprofessionals become more sensitive to design quality and lesson structure because unlike conventional instructional materials, courseware modification and improvements can be initiated at the user level (teacher). In preparing courseware, you must first "teach" the computer, an activity that causes the teacher-author to become more sensitive to sequences, pacing, need for variety, and inconsistencies.

Student aides involved in the project were very fortunate because the project provided a means of contributing to the school in a creative and productive sense. Opportunities also become available for exploring career options such as computer sciences and teaching. Their responsibilities encouraged student aides to be sensitive to the needs of others and the difficulties entailed in creating effective instruction.

Future plans include the involvement of elementary level students with programming. It is anticipated that starting with programming at a younger age will greatly increase high school level programming skills. And therefore, programming students at the secondary level will require teachers who are better prepared and able to take their students much farther than they are today.

INCREASED TEACHER ACCEPTANCE AND INVOLVEMENT

Now that Ortonville has microcomputers, they log more hours of computer use in computer assisted instruction in one day at the elementary level than they did in a year using timeshare. Having the microcomputer in the room is attractive for many reasons: (1) the classroom teacher is directly involved in the operation of equipment, (2) it is very inconvenient to send one or two students to a remote site for computer assisted instruction, especially when the involvement of the whole class is desired, (3) busy signals on the phone wrecked many a lesson plan, making any attempt at scheduling an exercise in probability. Teachers are understandibly unwilling to continue planning for computer assisted instruction after such encounters on time-sharing systems.

COMPUTER CAVEATS

It seems that the whole range of possible computer assisted instruction experience has pitfalls that must be avoided. For example, the possibility exists that computer assisted instruction could become nothing more than the step-by-step approach to predetermined goals as in the manner of programmed texts which peaked and fell from favor in the 1960's. In our conversations with teachers, it was clear that the first suggested idea for development of educational software would be that of programmed instruction. We do not mean to imply that programmed, i.e., step-by-step instruction shouldn't be developed, but rather that we must extend our vision. We might do well to consider a network of experiences with many interconnecting branches rather than linear isolated strands. The unique versatility of the computer is lost if we do the same old things with them.

CONCLUSION

What we have seen of educational software produced by computer experts represents material of little long-term worth. This is understandable for two reasons: (1) computer experts are not necessarily educators, and (2) the market has not been alive long enough to produce high quality software. Educators must be careful to insure that what they develop and release is of the highest quality; failing to do so increases the danger of providing a platform for disillusionment and eventual rejection by the users.

We believe that programmers are becoming more available, being trained in the advanced computer programming classes in high schools. Student workers are performing this service very nicely in the Ortonville school system. What we feel is most important is a classroom teacher with the imagination to provide educational opportunities for the computer. The idea of "Oregon" was much more important than the writing of the program.

Chapter IV

PLANNING A SYSTEM

We doubt that any responsible educator would begin the curriculum development process in a bookstore under the guidance of a bookseller. Curriculum is more than books alone. It represents broad traditions and knowledges, a concern for the school as a social organization, long-range development strategies, and procedures for judging the quality of outcomes.

It is also true that an effective microcomputer application in the schools involves looking beyond hardware and software. Nonetheless, we have already begun to see educators purchasing microcomputer systems on impulse, usually under the guidance of commercial vendors and promotional brochures.

This chapter is for the educator who would like to get involved with microcomputing, wants to do it right, but isn't too sure how to go about it. We emphasize careful preparation, beginning with an awareness of the rules for introducing microcomputers. Next we describe hardware options that should be considered. Finally, our discussion turns to developing software and judging its quality.

RULES FOR INTRODUCING MICROCOMPUTERS

From the experience of business and educational organizations that have introduced computers into their operations we have learned some important principles. By following these simple rules, your chances for success will be increased.

1. Many educators are hesitant about the role of computers in the schools so it is a rare situation when the entire staff is enthusiastic. Organize a group of staff members who are interested in getting started in microcomputing. Don't forget to include interested students and parents as they may already have micros at home and have knowledge that could be of great value to your school. Observing successful applications may cause other teachers to want to become involved. Some staff, however, will never use microcomputers for instruction or anything else and there is little that can be done about it.

2. If funds are available, or if the state can provide it, find someone with a reputation for quality inservice on micros in education. Micros are a hot topic and the technology is only five years old, so many are talking but not all make sense. Get recommendations from other schools on inservice.

3. Early microcomputer applications should be in the performance of routine and repetitive tasks. From these applications your staff will reap visible and immediate benefits. Typically, applications such as handling school attendance, cafeteria receipts, and locating substitute teachers are threatening to no one.

4. Introduce microcomputers in situations where staff are already inadequate to perform the needed functions. This procedure minimizes job displacement and demands little, if any, restructuring of occupational tasks.

5. Introduce microcomputers in situations where large numbers of learners are expected to be exposed to the same content or engage in identical activities, using the same computer programs.

6. In classroom applications, begin at the lower levels of computer capability, but keep moving up. Milner (1974) developed the following gradient of computer applications and their demands on computer capability, from most complex, to least:

Greater potential capability of computer	Student-designed automation
	Student-developed simulations of real systems or processes
	"Open-ended" problem-solving (student solution of complex and/ or student-posed problems)
	Student programmed automata
	Student-developed instruction (e.g., tutorials)
	Exploration of simulated systems or environments (computer simulated experiments)
	Interactive information retrieval
	Generative CAI; multi-level branching; artificial intelligence applications
	Instructional management systems
	Calculation (electronic sliderule)
less potential capability of computer	Tutorial (computerized programmed instruction or "multi-choice" CAI)
	Testing and record keeping
	Drill and practice

7. Heed Papert and Solomon's (1972) warning to avoid "using bright new gadgets to teach the same old stuff in thinly disguised versions of the same old way." In essence, be creative.

8. Find applications that can decrease training time or increase student-teacher ratios. Using computer assisted instruction in training paraprofessionals, and teaching children with learning disabilities are good possibilities. (Butman, 1973).

9. Give very careful consideration to the first application attempted. Select an application where there is a high probability of success. Fully tested software should be available for these microcomputer applications, prior to making any substantial commitment to purchasing hardware.

10. Start developing staff skills and knowledges before implementing a microcomputer application. "If you can't understand it you won't use it." (Wells, 1979). Carefully analyze how jobs will be affected. And make sure that intermediate level management is supportive. The authors have observed that support from clerical level staff is often more readily forthcoming than support from their supervisors. In a recent situation, the opposition of a small college registrar caused major obstacles and delays in the computerization of registration procedures, despite strong support from clerical staff and faculty.

11. "Start small. Build slowly. Incremental growth you can manage; instant sophistication is risky. Success, not glamour, is what counts." (Wells, 1979).

12. Avoid placing responsibility for microcomputer applications in the hands of a single "expert." It is far better to build across-the-board involvement and skills among school staff than to rely upon a single individual. This approach lessens the disruptive impact of staff mobility. Also, there is always a tendency for empire building when power and authority over computer applications are placed in the hands of one individual or a small elite group.

13. Orderly curriculum development pertaining to microcomputers is a must. A fragmented approach where teachers go off on their own, in all directions, is poor practice because it leads to duplication of effort and a tendency to produce page-turning, simplistic courseware. Microcomputer curriculum development must at least be a school-wide, if not district-wide, effort.

14. Don't undertake the introduction of microcomputers into your school without sufficient financial support. If new funds are unavailable, there may need to be a re-allocation of existing funds.

15. When you hire consultants or persons to staff workshops, make sure that they are first teachers and second, technologists.

LOOKING AT HARDWARE OPTIONS

Without discussing how they do it, just what can micro-computers do? Besides doing numerical calculations, such as those done with hand-held calculators, microcomputers also:
- Compare data entries
- Store and retrieve large volumes of data
- Conversationally interact with users
- Logically evaluate data
- Graphically display data
- Generate and recognize speech
- Generate music
- Control external devices

All computers - whether micro or otherwise consist of five modules:
1. Input: information and commands are transmitted through these devices to the computer.
2. Memory: a storage device and medium onto which software programs and data are written for later reference.
3. Central Processing Unit (CPU): the part of the computer that performs all the calculations, comparisons, and manipulations of data.
4. Control: the CPU is monitored and controlled by software (programs).
5. Output: information gained through input, control, CPU, and memory interaction is transmitted to display devices such as a printer or video screen.

These modules are discussed in the following section.

Input

Microcomputers typically input data through a typewriter style keyboard, but other devices are now available. A proximity keyboard is flat and responds to a touch on the appropriate key marked on its surface. A special proximity keyboard for the handicapped has one-inch square keys with one inch spacing between keys. Plastic overlays can be placed on the keyboard to assign new symbols to the keys.

Light pens are devices which allow the computer to read a response when the pen is touched to the television screen. Some light pens can be used to draw on the screen.

A digitizer pad converts lines and angles, as in graphs and maps, into digital information for the computer to store when the figure is traced on the surface of the pad with a special stylus. Similarly, images from a video camera can be digitized and transmitted into the computer.

Another device enables the computer to understand and respond to spoken commands, greatly simplifying the operation of computers for most people. A device that reads information from pencil-marked cards is available for microcomputers and can be used to analyze questionnaires or grade tests, when the cards are used as answer sheets. Other input devices include joysticks, buttons, knobs, switches, thermometers and scientific instruments.

Memory

Memory has been an expensive part of microcomputer systems but memory costs are dropping 30 percent per year (Bork, 1978). Memory capacity is often expressed in units of K which equal 1024 bytes (one byte or computer word could stand for one letter or numerical digit). A 48K memory would store 49,152 bytes.

Solid state memory chips provide the fastest access to data but they are the most expensive method of storage. Magnetic tape (including standard cassette tapes) are the least expensive method but are the slowest.

A "floppy" or flexible disk system uses a rapidly rotating disk or magnetic material with a moving recording head. Depending on disk size, they provide rapid access to anywhere from 80 to 1,000K of data. Disks can be changed like records on a turntable so that a system using a disk drive can have a library of programs and data on interchangable disks.

Expanding memory further are the hard disk drives that permit storage of 2 to 50 megabytes (millions of characters) of information. Hard disk memory costs two thousand dollars and up at the time of this writing.

Laser read optical videodisk systems are now being linked to microcomputers to store digital information, visual images, and auditory signals. In addition to the videodisk's extended life due to no mechanical wearing of surfaces, its memory capacity is measured in gigabytes (or billions of bytes). According to Wood and Soulier (1981), "the present videodisk / microcomputer systems of 1981 could store the entire National Union Catalog, produced by the Library of Congress, on one disk (with digitized data storage), with the average access time of 2.5 seconds, at a cost, including hardware, of less than $5,000."

Magnetic bubble memories use moving patterns of magnetic domains in a solid state chip to store data. These devices have no moving parts and are relatively small in comparison to other mass storage systems. Intel, IBM, Texas Instruments, and Rockwell International are producing or developing bubble memories. Bell Laboratories recently announced a major breakthrough in bubble chip design which results in a four fold increase in storage capacity, ten times faster operating speed, and a substantial decrease in cost (Libes, 1979). The durability and small size of bubble memories make them an attractive option if they can be produced at a cost which is competitive with the disk systems.

Many people assume that the microcomputer has limited memory. This is true if you provide no memory device other than the chips internal to the computer itself. A standard Apple microcomputer without a peripheral memory device has memory capacity for 49,152 characters. However, as noted in the following table; this can be expanded 255,000 times by interfacing the microcomputer with an optical disk memory system.

Equipment	Memory	Translates to
48K Apple	48 Kilobytes	20 to 25 book pages
48K Apple and floppy disk	150 Kilobytes	60 to 80 book pages
48K Apple and hard disk	10 Megabytes	About 10 books of 300 pages each

48K Apple and   12.5 Gigabytes   About 12,000 books
videodisk

Central Processing Unit

Most micros marketed in 1981 have 8 bit microprocessor
units which means they use 8 binary digits (e.g. 10011101) in
each byte. A byte then stands for a letter, number or whatever
is assigned that particular code. Using 8 bit bytes, a computer
can use 256 different codes, and have a 64K byte maximum
directly addressable memory size.

Several 16-bit microprocessors are being marketed and
some microcomputers use them: Alpha Microsystems,
Rexon, IBM 5100, and Texas Instrument 99 / 4. These have an 8
million byte directly accessible memory. Increases in
addressable memory allow working with larger data bases
(bigger school populations), higher resolution graphics (more
pixels on the TV screen), and better multi-user capabilities.
Large computers such as the IBM 370 use 32 bit processors and
several chip manufacturers have 32 bit microprocessors
available for equipment manufacturers. Capabilities of these
new CPU chips are quite remarkable but are sure to be
exceeded in performance, and reduced in size, power
requirements and price by future developments.

Control

Instructions for the computer are called programs,
software, or in the case of instructional programs, courseware. Binary code (0's and 1's, e.g. 01100111) is actually used
by the computer and early programmers had to work with
strings of this code, an unenviable task. Higher level
languages were gradually developed which allowed a symbol
or word to stand for one or more bytes of binary code.

Some of the higher languages available for micros include:
COBOL, FORTRAN, PASCAL, and PL-1. These are the same
languages that are used in controlling the large mainframe
computers. Most familiar, however, to microcomputer users
is BASIC. BASIC is actually a family of languages since it has
many versions, a few of which are:

Alpha BASIC	Applesoft II BASIC	StarDOS BASIC
Super BASIC	Microsoft BASIC	Benton Harbor BASIC
Level I BASIC	BASIC 800 I	Tiny BASIC
Level II BASIC	Microworks BASIC V 2.10	Waterloo BASIC

Often, a particular version of BASIC is used with a particular microcomputer.

Many schools have realized the importance of computer literacy and are teaching computer programming to students and staff in the BASIC language. This instruction should be considered an introduction to the concepts of programming because BASIC will certainly be displaced as the most popular microcomputer language. Several recently developed languages that promise easier use and greater flexibility include SMALLTALK, LISP, FORTH and, for education, LOGO. Schools need to be sensitive to the rapidly evolving language situation to keep instruction from becoming obsolete.

Output

Microcomputers are generally set up to display text and graphics on cathode ray tube television sets. Eye strain caused by the flicker of cathode ray tubes is a problem which may be resolved by the development of flat screen displays that don't use electron beams to create images. These flat screens can be as small as one square inch or up to an entire wall. Mass production will bring the cost of flat screen displays down to a level competitive with cathode ray tubes.

Hard copy of text and graphics can be provided through a printer controlled by the microcomputer. Many types of printers are available over a wide price range. Thermal and electrostatic printers use special papers to produce images but the lower price of this type of printer may be offset by higher paper costs. Dot matrix printers strike an ink ribbon with tiny rods selected from a matrix of rods to create the desired character. Standard typewriter quality printers use rotating spheres, wheels, or thimbles to type at speeds up to 50 characters per second. Several brands of electric typewriters can be converted for computer control but are slower, typically about ten characters per second. Ink jet printers use changing electrostatic fields to direct a spray of ink onto the paper. They have fewer mechanical parts but are prone to clogging problems in the spray jets. Improvements may allow ink jet printers to capture the market since they have good color printing capabilities.

Computers have been capable of speech generation for some time, but rapid advances in the technology have dramatically improved speech quality. Originally developed for handicapped users, speech output when coupled with speech recognition will permit verbal dialog with computers. Several manufacturers are developing computerized typewriters that will type whatever is dictated to them. A 93 percent accuracy rate has already been achieved and should increase. What this means as far as the number of people who need to learn typing is fairly obvious. Skilled typists will be needed for rapid editing work but certainly most computer users will not suffer due to a lack of typing skills. Again, the evolving technology requires educators to reconsider what skills students will need in the near future.

Outputs may be directed to other devices for control purposes. Microcomputers can be connected through standard wiring to appliances and lights in the home. Tape recorders, slide projectors and video tape players can also be controlled by the microcomputer.

In short, a typical microcomputer system will consist of:
- Microcomputer with some internal memory in chips (16K to 64K in an 8 bit machine).
- Mass memory storage on magnetic tape, magnetic disk or videodisk in the range of 100K to several billion bytes.
- Input device(s)
- Output device(s)
- Software for desired applications.

BEFORE PURCHASING

Before making any purchases, decide what the microcomputers are to be used for. This can be done through a committee or at an in-service session for all staff. Once applications are determined, a review of available equipment can begin. No single microcomputer is best for all applications. For example:

1. More applications mean more expensive equipment. Micros for use exclusively in elementary instruction can generally be of the least expensive type (Commodore PET, VIC-20, TRS-80 Color Computer, etc.) while micros for multi-subject high school use will have to be more flexible (Apple II, NEC 8000, Atari 800).

2. Administrative applications need expanded memory (two disk drives or recently developed high density disks) and preferably, an 80 column display screen for word processing. Examples include the Commodore CBM 80, Archives, TRS-80 Model II, Apple II with several additional devices or the Apple III. A printer will be needed for report generation.

3. Choose a micro that has software available for your desired applications. Trade magazines, professional journals, other districts and consultants can provide this information. Salespersons are not always your best source.

For instructional applications, determine the subject areas of interest and consider the following:

1. Are color graphics desirable?
2. A graphics tablet is needed for use in art.
3. Advanced music instruction will require additions to the micro.
4. Is speech recognition and synthesis desired?
5. Do you want hardcopy for any classwork?
6. Will the micro be interfaced with video equipment for complex instruction?

The more you want the microcomputer to do, the more it costs. To hold down initial cost, equipment should be expandable to adapt to future instructional applications that are more complex or specialized.

Costs for micro systems in 1981 range from $500 for a low cost machine with cassette tape memory storage to over $5,000 for a unit with multiple capabilities. The more expensive micros can generally be used from the elementary classroom to the main office. Hardware is improving and costs are dropping, so the situation is fluid. The best advice, as always, is caveat emptor so spend some time considering these things and look to other educators for their experience.

One of your best sources of information is educators in other school districts who have already purchased equipment and used it. An important question to explore is the extent and quality of dealer support provided. This, of course, is one of the difficulties you face when trying to take advantage of the lower prices offered by mail-order computer retailers. Some educators advocate not only having local service available but also a provision for obtaining a "loaner" written into the sales contract to cover break-down at critical times.

QUESTIONS FOR THE SALESPERSON

Here is a list of questions you may want to take with you when you start shopping for microcomputers.

1. Is the system expandable? This means, can random access memory be added later so that the system can run larger programs?
2. Does the price quoted include all cables and interfaces so that the system will run as shown. We are assuming, of course, that the purchaser has been given a demonstration of the microcomputer under consideration.
3. Does the quoted price include a printer interface, if a printer is part of the system purchased?
4. Are clearly written programmers aids, operators manuals, and instruction manuals included?
5. Where is service available? How long will it take to have any required service and repairs performed?
6. What are the conditions of the warranty provided by the manufacturer?
7. What mass storage devices, floppy disk, hard disk, or "mag" cartridge are available? Are the operating systems for these devices compatible with the system under consideration?
8. Does the mass storage device allow the user to access the entire disk for the creation of larger data files? Some

disk drives can be "chained" together to act as one large disk.

9. If you are purchasing a printer, is the printer set up for parallel or serial interface? What interface is on the microcomputer? Is there an additional charge for the interface? Is the printer a standard type or is it the vendor's unique product?

10. What peripherals are available, such as music, joysticks, game paddles, or speech synthesizers? Are they added at extra cost or are they included in the system you are purchasing?

11. What programming languages can be used with the system?

12. Can the system be used as a terminal in a timesharing network?

13. Does the vendor provide any staff training and are there any charges for this service?

14. Does the vendor support a toll free "hot line" for problem solving?

15. Does the system have special environmental requirements such as temperature and humidity control?

16. What software is offered by the hardware vendor?

WHERE TO PUT THE COMPUTER

A microcomputer is valuable equipment and it is important to control the location of hardware so that a balance is achieved between security needs and needs for maximum use rates. Allocation of microcomputer resources in a school generally follows one of two models: the computer center and distributed classroom use.

If there are only a few micros and staff interest is low, the computer center approach may be best. (See Chapter Three for an extended discussion of a Microcomputer Center.) All the micros are in one room with a manager, possibly a teacher's aide. Teachers send students to the center for specific work on a pass system.

Alternatively, micros can be placed on carts and moved from class to class on a prearranged schedule coinciding with classroom activities. A combination of center and distributed approaches can also be devised. Some teachers may wish to have a micro in their class at all times even while the school provides a distribution service or center.

CONTAINMENT OF SYSTEM FAILURES

No electronic device is absolutely reliable, although because of the relative simplicity of their design microcomputers are much less prone to failure than their large-scale counterparts. Fortunately, the reliance on microcomputers for instructional or school management support can be made even less vulnerable to breakdown by providing for local system back-up. Implementing system back-up at the local level with microcomputers (system redundancy) is simply a matter of retaining one duplicate set of hardware and software. The low cost of microcomputers makes this provision economically feasible.

The back-up microcomputer does not have to be kept idle, under lock and key. It is probably desirable, however, to exclude back-up hardware from routine distribution to classrooms. If a school is large enough to support an instructional media center, the back-up hardware and software may be kept in that location and used for testing programs that the school system is considering acquiring.

Effective use of microcomputers in the instructional program entails considerable planning, scheduling, and logistics. System failures and interruptions can be a major source of disillusionment with computer assisted instruction and it is the wise administrator who takes time and steps to reduce the impact of hardware failure.

SOFTWARE DEVELOPMENT

While the costs of microcomputer hardware have been declining rapidly, the costs of developing software and courseware to use with them has been increasing due to the fact that it is a labor intensive activity. If hardware costs continue to decline, software development will become a larger and larger determinant of overall computer costs. How can development costs be contained? Should the schools count on purchasing software from commercial sources? Should they enter cooperative arrangements with other schools for joint development work? Should each school system develop its own software?

If schools choose to buy software they will find that there is extensive marketing of these products although the quality varies widely. However, it is unadvisable to buy software sight unseen without the strong recommendation of a reliable source. Administrative software is generally of better quality than courseware since business has provided strong incentives for quality programming for years. Some commercial vendors provide support for their materials after the sale. If so, get it in writing. Once purchased, some commercial programs lend themselves to modification to better fit your needs. When considering this option, have a programmer look at the software to determine its flexibility.

Schools that are starting to use microcomputers usually acquire their software through formal or informal user networks or try to develop their own. The impulse to develop software and courseware locally is strong because teacher salaries are a fixed cost. If teachers can develop courseware, no new costs or extra costs other than hardware purchase are entailed in adopting computer technology.

Software and courseware that is of local vintage, unfortunately, is often inferior to that which is available through networks or purchased from commercial sources. There are two reasons why this is true. First, not everyone can design courseware anymore than everyone can write interesting novels. Courseware writing and instructional design are creative activities involving both technical programming skills and the ability to compose, organize, and display educational content in an effective and interesting manner. The skills and interests that generate effective courseware design are different than those that go along with being an effective classroom teacher. That is why teachers have shown only limited interest in learning computer programming and few computer programmers are astute observers of how children learn.

Second, programs that are developed locally are not subjected to as much field trial, "de-bugging," and revision as are programs developed for statewide networks or commercial distribution. Multiple users increase the chance that inadequacies in programs will be detected and user feedback becomes a valuable resource for subsequent revisions.

If the local development option is relied on, there is the danger that only a few people that are highly interested or motivated, often the science or math teacher, will develop programs and make use of the equipment. This is contrary to the principle that microcomputer adoption should be horizontal, across curricular areas, within the school.

The development of programs at the local level is something that should be encouraged, but it should represent only one level of access to computer software and courseware. An important function of local courseware and software development is to further the professional growth of the teaching staff. Some important benefits pertaining to better understanding of the subject matter and the learner are to be derived from trying to program a microcomputer. Programming is the same thing as teaching the computer the content so that it can in turn teach the student. Through this process the teacher can gain insights into how students learn and how to organize material to meet their needs.

One way to help teachers develop their own courseware is to use one of the special courseware authoring languages described in Chapter One. Bell and Howell offers an authoring system for use on the Apple computer which they are marketing under their own trade name. Several of the large publishing houses are also developing simplified development packages for educators. Authoring languages are improving rapidly and should be the first option for local courseware development without expert programmers on the staff.

Another option, used in the Ortonville, Minnesota school system, is to provide trained student programmers as teacher aides in writing original courseware. This project has been successful and it bypasses the need for training teachers to program (Joiner, Miller and Silverstein, 1980). Students have written original programs for classroom instruction. These same students have also translated programs written for use on one machine so that they will operate on another machines. Here is an opportunity for schools to provide talented student programmers experience in working on real world applications.

Consider purchasing materials from schools such as these or through their state network systems such as the Minnesota Educational Computing Consortium. Generally, these programs are less expensive than commercial materials and if the programs were developed under a federally funded project, they should be available for cost of reproduction only.

Some courseware has entered the public domain, that is, no copyright restrictions apply to its use. Educators have donated many of these programs or they were developed with public tax monies. A joint effort by the San Mateo County Office of Education and the Computer-Using Educators organization in Redwood City California, has produced an educational software library of public domain courseware. Visitors to the Microcomputer Center may copy these programs without charge and disks of the programs are available through mail-order (see Appendices). Computer-Using Educators and others evaluate, edit and organize the contributed programs into the SOFTSWAP library.

Approximately 200 of these programs are available for TRS-80, PET, Atari, Apple II and Compucolor micro-computers. Other educators are encouraged to use and contribute courseware to this laudable project.

If schools have common needs they can organize consortia composed of several neighboring school districts for the purpose of developing microcomputer programs. Organizations of this type provide several advantages:

1. Development costs are spread over a larger number of users resulting in lower unit costs.

2. Duplications of effort are fewer than would occur if schools operated independently.

3. Chances of identifying "bugs" in programs are increased because each program is reviewed by multiple users.

4. A professional atmosphere is provided, involving an

exchange of ideas encouraging program development and giving recognition to the individuals developing programs.

5. The identification of similar or "common" requirements, helps prioritize programming, i.e. common needs are addressed first.

Networks

With the advent of microcomputer technology, states like Minnesota have been converting some of the more popular time-shared computer courseware to microcomputer. In order to access these programs, the microcomputer is used as a terminal, a process resulting in little gain over non-micro provisions, or the centrally stored programs can be "downloaded." Downloading is the transmitting of programs from a central computer to a remote microcomputer. Once a program is downloaded, the microcomputer can then operate independent of the central computer.

The advantage of accessing programs that are stored in the statewide networks is that quality control is usually good. These programs have been used time and again. User statistics accumulated by the statewide networks are an index of the popularity and usefulness of the courseware. Typically, consultants who are principally educators and secondarily computer specialists have reviewed the programs prior to their inclusion in the central libraries. User problems have been noted and modifications made accordingly in the programs.

A disadvantage of programs available through the statewide networks is that the content of the programs is very diverse. It is difficult to find several CAI programs that relate to each other, systematically, in a particular content area such as science and at a particular grade level. It should be said that this problem exists in almost all catalogs of microcomputer courseware. Development has arisen from many sources and has therefore been piecemeal. Alaska is currently developing more complete courseware in a variety of subject areas for statewide use which could begin to solve this problem.

Computer networks that make programs available,

nationally, to microcomputer users are likely to multiply in the commercial sector. A computer network (commercial) generally charges an application fee ($10 to $100) that may be refunded by discounting charges incurred by the user when accessing of the network begins. These services offer the user the opportunity to use, purchase, or sell software that is stored in a central location. The system is accessed by telephone line to service centers usually located in urban areas. If the center is remote, long distance charges often make this type of service unrealistic for schools. Charges are determined by the amount of time that the microcomputer is connected to the network, usually less than $10 per hour, and any software purchases. A printed catalog of programs that are available from the commercial network is usually available to those interested in participating.

Development trends in microcomputers have led to the proliferation of equipment, the programs for which are often incompatible with other equipment. Because of the compatibility problems of hardware, which in turn leads to incompatibility of software, greater uniformity is likely to emerge within the schools. Some states have reviewed microcomputer hardware and recommend certain kinds of equipment for statewide adoption. This facilitates the sharing of programs, but not everyone will be equally satisfied, regardless of hardware selected. One important feature of microcomputers endorsed for statewide purchase is that they must be capable of interfacing with the statewide network systems' central computer, if one exists.

Local school district consortia discussed earlier could set up their own network if they have compatible equipment. Since most states don't have statewide networks and the national nets may not be available through a local call, this might be a good way for most districts to get networking experience and share courseware. Once the network is established it can also be used for electronic mail and conferencing. Messages, questions and answers, reports or data of any sort may be entered into the micro for transmission to the other schools. Some of this may be tagged for specific people (e.g., questions about software to the author and their reply) or made available to all.

DEVELOPMENT MODELS

Whether courseware is developed locally or by central agencies, some process model underlies its production. Figure 2 displays two alternative development models preceded by some of their advantages and disadvantages. The authors favor the adoption of the "Structural Model" as a guide to microcomputer courseware development.

Linear Model

Advantages
Student centered
Consistent with teacher generated programming if and when those skills exist in the profession

Disadvantages
Time consuming
Lacks structure (built in)
Potential redundancies

Structural Model

Advantages
Comprehensive
Coherent-structured
Built-in roadmap for development
Uses existing resources optimally
Cost effective
Broad application
Linked to curriculum and district needs

Disadvantages
Requires considerable preparatory organization work
Requires more centralized planning

MODEL 1. THE LINEAR MODEL

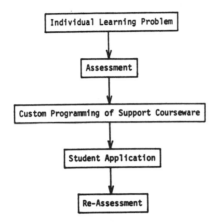

MODEL 2. STRUCTURAL MODEL

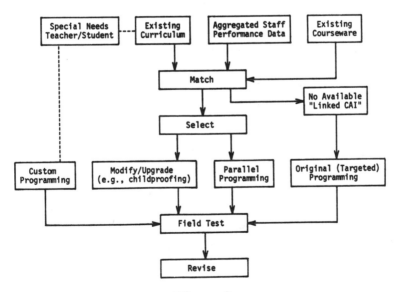

Figure 2

EVALUATING COURSEWARE

Since some of the courseware available is of questionable value, how does one avoid getting stuck with poor quality materials? One way to approach this problem is to read reviews of software prepared by professional organizations, (see Appendix E) or better yet, reviews by educators in field tests. Once acquired, software should be systematically reviewed by local staff to make the final determination of its ability to meet local needs.

Modification of the program or even a return to the vendor may be in order, so the evaluation should occur as soon as possible after receiving the program.

What are some of the standards that should be applied in evaluating the adequacy and appropriateness of courseware for the classroom? Here are some suggested standards for evaluating courseware:

1. Does the courseware take advantage of the computer's unique capabilities or is the material more suited for presentation in another format, e.g. book or workbook?

2. Is clearly written and complete documentation available with the program that tells what it is supposed to do and how to use it?

3. Is the activity educational or recreational? Does it teach or reinforce something previously learned or is it purely entertaining?

4. Is the courseware explicitly tied to classroom curriculum, a taxonomy of objectives or a text series? Are the pages or objectives it relates to spelled out?

5. Are the performance objectives and criteria for success clearly stated?

6. Are the video displays clean, not crowded on the screen with difficulties in finding the key material?

7. Does the program seem to have unnecessary sound or visual effects that contribute little to its educational worth?

8. Does the program accept equivalent answers as correct or must the student answer **exactly** as desired by the program?

9. Does the display "grow" from top to bottom and from left to right? (This is necessary in order to be consistent with eye

movements used in the reading process.)

10. Are the students' instructions simple, clear, and unequivocal?

11. Is there a considerable amount of "flashing" in the displays that might cause the child to feel pressured?

12. Is the volume and spacing of "text" material suited to comfortable reading? Large amounts of text that are used with the program are often better provided as "hard copy" off-line.

13. Is the courseware noisy? If so, using it in a classroom may prove distracting to other students.

14. If color is entailed in the display and is relevant to the selection of answers, is it properly labeled? At present, some distortion in color displays occurs with most microcomputers and CRT's. What is presented and coded as "blue" may not be perceived as "blue."

15. Does the student control movement between frames with the space bar?

16. Are there instances where the program poses a question or problem and then proceeds on without allowing the slower student time to respond?

17. Is the design and format repetitive and boring?

18. Does the student have to make a coded transformation before responding, e.g. blue = 3 on the keyboard? If so, the program is introducing an unnecessary burden on the student that may detract from performance.

19. Are unconventional abbreviations avoided? Materials should reflect good language usage, punctuation, and grammar.

20. Does the student have access to all the information that is necessary to answer any questions posed?

21. Does the program "overreinforce" satisfactory responses with hyperbole such as "great, WOW! You GOT it" time and time again? Age of the student is a key factor here.

22. If the program requires the student to choose from among multiple options, are the options always visible on the screen? If they are not, errors may result from poor recall of instructions rather than lack of conceptual understanding.

23. If the program is designed for young children, can they understand what they are to do, the decisions that they are to make, the options that they are to select from?

24. Is the content accurate?

25. Are student responses correctly evaluated?

26. Are there lengthy delays where the student must wait for the computer to search a file or perform multiple algorithms? Higher levels of computer chess playing programs are examples of extreme delays between input and output.

27. Is the program "kidproof," i.e., if the student hits the "wrong" key at any given time, does the program ignore it and go on or does it shut down, blank the screen and lose all that the student has done up to that point? This is a common fault in much courseware but one that can be avoided by good programming.

Many of the above questions apply to the evaluation of software for administrative and student management applications. In addition to the above, administrative software has some other parameters to consider:

1. Is the program easy for your staff to learn to use? Some programs have complex control codes and structures that take some time to adjust to.

2. Extensive, well written documentation is essential. Look for a large index and perhaps a trouble shooting section to help deal with inevitable problems.

3. Does the vendor / supplier offer any continuing support of the software? Often a phone number is available for user questions or other local users of the same materials should be identified for conferencing on problems. This is another use for the local network.

4. Does the program equal or exceed previous capabilities with a reduction in staff time? Savings and advantages should be measurable.

Have the school library subscribe to one or more of the periodicals that include educational software reviews and / or join a professional organization that is active in software evaluation. In-service your staff in this area and provide them with review sheets of some type to be filled out as they first use the programs. A sample evaluation form follows:

EVALUATION FORM

Program:

Staff Member:

Building/ Room:

1. Is the documentation adequate? Yes —— No ——
Comments:

2. Did the user(s) have trouble running the program? Yes —— No ——
Comments:

3. What grade level used the program? —— NA ——

4. How many students used the program? —— NA ——

5. For approximately how long? —— NA ——

6. What grade level(s) would be appropriate for the program?
   K   1   2   3   4   5   6   7   8   9   10   11   12

7. Suggest any changes that would improve the program.

A FINAL WORD

Careful planning will prevent many future problems so spend some time at it. Some major points are:

1. Form a planning committee that includes interested teachers, office staff, administrators, parents, and if possible, students.

2. Get advice from educators with microcomputer experience by reading the literature, writing to active projects or using reputable consultants. Salespersons are honest for the most part, but their primary task is to sell, not advise.

3. Assess present and near future needs / applications before making any purchases; what you buy depends on this, there is no one best microcomputer system for all applications.

4. Collect feedback from the staff as soon as possible regarding hardware / software for decision making on appropriateness and adequacy.

Chapter V

MICROS IN CLASSROOMS

A few years ago one of the authors was contacted about a serious discipline problem in a class for blind children. It seemed that the blind students were very disruptive, making poor progress in school, and were driving the teacher to the brink. Upon visiting the "problem class," it was apparent that chaos and confusion abounded.

Ample instructional materials of all kinds were evident in the classroom. But there was no system for storing these materials. Each time the teacher changed activities, a different instructional material was required. And the blind children were expected to find what they needed. As a result, most of the students' time was spent seeking things and shouting information back and forth. Establishing a system for controlling the location of these many instructional materials reduced tensions greatly.

What this anecdote reveals is "the trouble with instructional materials." Almost all instructional materials used in classrooms today are single purpose tools. In order to support a comprehensive curriculum you need a lot of them. You need lots of money to buy them, lots of space to store them, and a mental or physical index to link these materials to lessons. For classroom teachers, therefore, the magic of microcomputers may be their multi-purpose nature. Much of the variety that now exists in educational games, kits, workbooks, models, programmed texts, and single purpose devices like hand calculators is captured in a single instrument with intrinsic organizing capabilities: the microcomputer.

COMPUTER MANAGED INSTRUCTION

In the typical classroom, much time is devoted to record keeping relating to assignments and student performance. Computer managed instruction involves using the computer to administer tests, assign study activities, and maintain records of individual progress, both for the teacher and parents. Computer managed instruction also includes the indexing of traditional instructional materials so that they can be located when needed.

Hopkins, Minnesota developed a fine example of a district-wide application of computer managed instruction called Comprehensive Achievement Monitoring. Instructional objectives and parallel test items, developed by 100 participating teachers, were the building blocks of the system.

The computer, acting upon a large data base of test items, generates tests for classroom use. Students are tested on the instructional objectives for the entire year, repeatedly, so that scores start low and increase as students acquire skills. Answer sheets are computer scored and reports are provided to the student and the teacher. These timely reports help students decide what to study and help teachers avoid teaching students what they already know.

Originally written for a large time sharing computer system, Comprehensive Achievement Monitoring has now been adapted to the Apple II microcomputer with limitations on the numbers of objectives and test items imposed by the memory size of the micro system. These restrictions are lifting with the advent of larger capacity storage devices such as Memorex-101 8″ hard disk drives (10 megabytes). Over 25,000 objectives and test items are entailed in this project.

For smaller scale applications, commercial programs are available that allow teachers to prepare tests using the microcomputer. Some programs control printing of tests for classroom distribution; others require the student to take the test at the microcomputer for rapid scoring. Printed tests can be computer scored if the answer sheets are designed for mark sense readers which connect to the micro such as Chatsworth's MR-500 (1981 price = $750). If the tests are computer scored, the results can be recorded directly by an electronic gradebook program that computes averages, percentages, and other summaries. Teachers have rapid access to individual or group data and automatic printing of report cards. Access to records can be controlled with a password system.

Another approach to monitoring student performance is the computerization of student contracts, storing goals, objectives and projected timelines. Student progress is entered into the computer by each student on a weekly basis and the teacher can see how each student is doing on the computer screen or in a printed report as needed. Here's how one district used this microcomputer application to help make a learning center run smoothly and to provide academic equity for rural schools.

The Rural School Crisis

A major challenge for the small rural school district is providing academic equity in an "age of less." Although attention was focused during the 1970's on equality of educational opportunity for the disadvantaged in urban school systems, rural students are now facing increasing disadvantages, especially in the scope of curriculum offerings available to them. In the 1980's, rural high school graduates confront a very competitive job market.

Faced with declining enrollments and increasing state and federal requirements that strain local resources, rural schools have been abandoning courses that are "cost ineffective" as judged by low enrollment. Yet some of these "cost ineffective" courses, such as foreign languages, chemistry, consumer economics, and computer programming would be considered essential features of secondary curricula in urban and suburban school districts.

Beyond economics, it is difficult for small, rural, faculties, working in remote areas, to provide needed support for esoteric courses that students often desire as electives. Professional development for rural staff is difficult because of the reduced opportunity for interaction with a range of professional colleagues and the physical inaccessibility of continuing education programs.

Academic Equity Through Self-Instruction

An approach to providing academic equity that has been undertaken in the Littlefork-Big Falls Independent School District is self-instruction. This tiny, rural Minnesota district organized a learning center for self-instruction. Under the direction of an instructional manager, the center explored the use of four major types of educational technology:
1) computer-assisted instruction via PLATO
2) extension courses offered by universities through correspondence
3) audio-visual courses
4) video-tape courses.

Through these means, fifty new courses were added to the secondary curriculum for 104 students in grades ten to twelve.

Problems In Implementing Self-Instruction

A problem that immediately arose when implementing a technology driven self-instruction center was the difficulty of locating good quality self-instructional programs. Originally, it had been incorrectly assumed that there would be an abundant supply of self-instructional programs and that the chief problem would be one of selection. That idea was quickly proven wrong. The staff had all they could handle to locate enough programs to fill out the curriculum areas that had been targeted for expansion.

Once programs were located and students began their independent studies, however, an even more critical problem surfaced: the need to monitor progress, provide continuing feedback, and personalize instruction, (Miller, Waver, and Semb, 1974) particularly in non-computer courses. Computer assisted instruction courseware, such as is available in chemistry and foreign languages through PLATO, generally has built-in provisions for continuous feedback to students. For correspondence and audio-visual courses, however, these provisions are rather limited, at best. And while correspondence courses are economical, averaging $2.11 per pupil hour in 1980, feedback is slow and reinforcement intermittent.

Because of the slow feedback and intermittent reinforcement associated with correspondence courses, the maintenance of student interest and consistent progress proved difficult. The diversity entailed in fifty different courses taken by over one hundred students also produced management problems. To do an effective job, the instructional manager had to not only function as a content resource, but also constantly monitor the progress of each student. Record keeping was difficult. Furthermore, it was observed that secondary students often lack self-monitoring and self-evaluation skills that must accompany successful self-instruction.

Microcomputer Management of Self-Instruction

A recent evaluation of the TICCIT Computer-Assisted Instruction System revealed that even at the community college level failure to complete courses was a serious threat to the adequacy of "individually-paced" courses (Alderman, 1978). Several other studies indicate that external management of some kind is crucial to the completion of self-instruction courses (Atkins & Lockhart, 1976; Coldeway & Scheller, 1974; Miller, Waver, and Semb, 1974).

Therefore, to add a personal element to self-instruction and to provide an external means of continuously monitoring progress, a microcomputer program was developed for the Apple II. The program allowed each student to enter information concerning goals, progress, and human resources on a daily basis. On the video display, progress is charted, in color, against an anticipated progress curve derived from an interpolation of the student's original goal-setting behavior. And a group summary of progress can be obtained, in hard copy form, by the instructional manager as needed for reporting or student counseling[1]. Also, the program records

[1]Marge Kosel of the Minnesota Educational Computing Consortium served as a consultant in the design of the application. Curt Johnson of the Ortonville Schools did the programming while he was a high school student.

information as to the identity of the "volunteer advisor" who
has agreed to serve as subject matter resource to the student.

To use the micro-manager program, data is entered daily,
at a terminal, by the student or an operator who keys in the
information. Screen activity is as follows (a question mark
signals request for operator input):

```
)RUN

    LITTLEFORK PROGRAM 1.1.1

    REGISTRATION
WHAT IS YOUR NAME?      JANE DOE

    PLEASE STAND BY !!!

YOUR STUDENT NUMBER IS    2
    PRESS SPACE BAR TO CONTINUE

WHAT IS YOUR AGE?     13
SEX (M,F)?
WHAT IS YOUR GRADE POINT AVERAGE?      3.0

    COURSE
WHAT IS THE # OF THE COURSE
YOU ARE ENROLLED IN?     12
COURSE ADVISOR?     MR SMITH
ADVISOR'S TELEPHONE NUMBER?      778-5008

1- VIDEO TAPE
2- PLATO
3- CORRESPONDENCE COURSE
4- AUDIO VISUAL
5- OTHER
WHAT MEDIA IS USED TO TEACH THIS COURSE?     3

UND- U OF NORTH DAKOTA
UWM- U OF WISONSIN- MADISON
ULN- U OF NEBRASKA- LINCOLN
UMM- U OF MINNESOTA- MINNEAPOLIS
UOC- U OF OREGON- CORVALLIS
UIU- U OF ILLINOIS- URBANA
ERA- EDUCATIONAL RESEARCH ASSOCIATION
OTH- OTHER
WHAT IS THE CODE FOR THE DISTRIBUTOR OF THIS
COURSE?     UND

WHAT IS THE UNIT OF STUDY (EX. LESSON, CHAPTER,
UNIT)?     UNIT 1
# OF UNITS IN YOUR COURSE?     3
```

```
DATE TO START COURSE
MONTH?    9
DAY?    15
YEAR?    80
ANTICIPATED DATE TO FINISH COURSE
MONTH?    12
DAY?    15
YEAR?    80
WHEN DO YOU ANTICIPATE FINISHING UNIT 1
WEEK?    1
DAY?    5
WHEN DO YOU ANTICIPATE FINISHING UNIT 2
WEEK?    6
DAY?    5
WHEN DO YOU ANTICIPATE FINISHING UNIT 3
WEEK?    12
DAY?    5
HOW MANY TESTS WILL YOU TAKE?    3

PLEASE STAND BY!

YOU ARE JANE DOE
YOUR STUDENT # IS 2
YOU 13 YEARS OLD
YOU ARE A FEMALE WITH A 3.0 GRADE POINT
AVERAGE. YOU ARE TAKING COURSE # 12. THE
ADVISOR IS MR. SMITH. THE MEDIA IS
CORRESPONDENCE. THE SOURCE IS UNIVERSITY OF
NORTH DAKOTA

   GOOD LUCK!
   AND HOPE YOU FINISH BY 12/ 15/ 80
```

Based on the information that is entered daily, a longitudinal progress report is displayed on the CRT that graphs progress against the goals entered above. Figure 3 shows the daily progress report.

CRT DISPLAY OF STUDENT PROGRESS

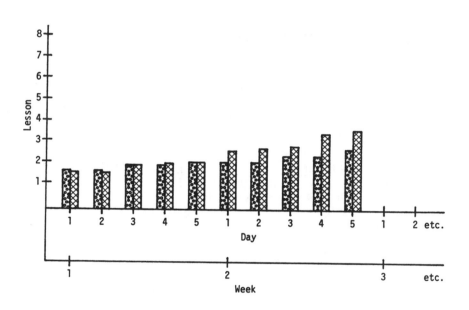

Figure 3

Hard-copy reports of the following type are also produced by the microcomputer program:

LITTLEFORK PROGRAM   PROGRESS REPORT FOR WEEK 1 DAY 1

NAME	ID#	GOAL	LESSON	CONTRACT STATUS	SESSIONS	TIME IN WEEKS
JANE DOE	2	1	1	2	3	2.75

CONTRACT STATUS: 1-AHEAD OF SCHEDULE 2-ON SCHEDULE
                 3-BEHIND

For the instructional manager, a report of the type shown in Table 2 can be produced.

The authors foresee microcomputers as having an important place in improving academic equity in rural schools. While some view microcomputers as a solution in search of a problem, we believe that as educators continue down the road toward technical conversion, they will begin to recognize the needs that can be better met through this technology. In this monitoring of self-instruction, what was at issue was not simply cost but a broader pedagogical issue; the capability of a single staff person to provide individualized instruction to 104 students in 50 subjects.

Any programs developed for computer managed instruction should be evaluated / reviewed prior to purchase. They must be user friendly, i.e. easy to understand, resistant to stopping if improper keys are depressed and have good documentation. If these programs don't save time and effort for the teacher they should not be used.

Table 2. Screen Activity and Sample of Manager's Report

```
MANAGER'S REPORT
ONE MOMENT PLEASE.

1. PRINT MANAGER'S REPORT
2. EDIT MANAGER'S REPORT
3. END
ENTER YOUR SELECTION?  1

PRINT ON:
1. PRINTER
2. SCREEN
ENTER YOUR SELECTION?  1

1. GROUP INFORMATION
2. INDIVIDUAL INFORMATION
ENTER YOUR SELECTION?  1
```

MANAGER'S REPORT

NAME	ST. #	GRADE	AGE	SEX	GPA	COURSE#	MEDIUM	SOURCE	ADVISOR	COST	START	END
CHAD	1	7	13	M	3.5	630	5	UND	BILL THOMPSON	$56.50	1/6/80	5/2/80
DAVID	2	8	14	M	2.67	263	5	UWM	JOE JONES	$57.20	1/6/80	5/2/80
JOEL	3	12	17	M	2.97	369	5	UND	PETE SWENSON	$45.70	1/6/80	5/2/80
LARSON	4	12	18	M	3.45	176	5	ERA	GAYLE ANDERSON	$34.50	1/6/80	5/2/80

COMPUTER ASSISTED INSTRUCTION

Microcomputers can deliver instruction in a variety of ways and are adaptable to individual teaching styles. That's what makes them so vastly superior to the crude teaching machines of the 60's with their uninspired programmed instruction. The electronic classroom envisioned by O. K. Moore and others can now be a reality due to the flexibility and reliability of microcomputers. First, what kind of instruction can be accomplished via microcomputer?

Drill and Practice

Drill and practice is the simplest type of program to develop and use in the classroom. Previously taught concepts are reinforced using a variety of courseware that drills the learner for whatever reasonable length of time the teacher feels is needed. Good courseware will monitor the learners progress and store that data for review. Short drill and practice programs are easy to integrate into an ongoing curriculum and are a good way for teachers to begin using micros. Review may be provided for individual students or groups, depending on the program and teacher inclination. The only advantages microcomputer drill and practice has over worksheets are management capability and reduced reproduction costs. Graphics, sound and gaming parameters can also be included for motivational effect.

Tutorials

Including tutorials along with drill and practice, uses more of the micro's potential. Here, the micro teaches a new concept before reinforcing it. Courseware of this type can either be remedial or provide enrichment for learners. Again, color graphics and sound can increase motivation.

A plus for the micro in tutorial applications is its extensive branching capability, allowing the design of more intricate courseware. When branching is activated, learners are transferred to different locations in the content depending upon the quality of their responses. If the learner is having trouble, similar material may be reviewed, or better yet, a simplified explanation will be sequenced. Learners who are able to move rapidly can follow a fast branch of the program. Several learning styles and a variety of ability levels can thus be covered by one quality piece of courseware, something unavailable in textbooks. Tutoring programs can be brief supplements to instruction or lengthy in-depth courses. Few materials of the latter type are currently available but work is proceeding in the direction of more comprehensive courseware.

Simulations

Simulations are especially suitable for computer delivery. In this mode, the learner is presented with situations requiring decision making and the subsequent chain of events depends on the learner's decisions. Usually, the simulation imitates a real problem, such as a computer simulation of an operating nuclear reactor in which the learner is an operator faced with cooling problems leading to a possible meltdown.

Government and corporations have used computer simulations for many years, most recently in selecting options to pursue in the air traffic controller's attempt to shut-down the air ways. Now the low cost micros make this technique available to schools for teaching students decision making and rational judgments.

Up until now, schools have devoted little time to decision training. Despite the pronouncements of educational theorists, regarding how to be good, school teachers in Bedford-Stuyvesant just haven't had any means at their disposal for teaching decision-making and judgmental skills other than abstract verbal arguments and stories. But microcomputer simulations are powerful instructional devices, entailing complex presentations with color graphics and audio. They are crude mirrors of reality, but light years ahead of textbooks, field-trips, or classroom theatrics.

Whatever type of courseware is acquired, it should meet high standards as described in the chapter on planning. Look for good use of graphic representation to enhance the motivational aspect. Management capabilities to keep track of learner progress are desirable. Poor quality courseware is worse than no courseware at all because the disappointment turns people off and could prevent them from benefiting from this innovation.

Few teachers have had any formal training or experience in how to use microcomputer courseware in the classroom. Don't expect much help from colleges of education in this respect. Despite the remarkable development in computing during the last decade, fewer than a dozen colleges of education have programs that recognize the implications of the information age for education and train teachers to use microcomputing (see Chapter Two). The imagination of colleges of education remains absorbed in antique licensing and certification requirements. Therefore, local schools must take the lead in teacher preparation.

MICROS IN ELEMENTARY SCHOOL

To take a hard look at both the promise and the problems microcomputers offer, three elementary school projects were initiated through a consortium of school districts in Minnesota. Districts housing the projects varied widely in size: the Morgan elementary school had 114 elementary students; Mankato had 3,309 and Robbinsdale 8,322. As will be shown, size affects style and substance in microcomputer applications and the variation among these districts provided for interesting comparisons of how microcomputers can be introduced and used.

Each elementary school project tried to answer basic questions concerning the new technology as it relates to the classroom teacher. For example:

- What are the strengths and limitations of the hardware?
- What constitutes good courseware?
- Can local staff develop cost-effective software and courseware to meet local needs?
- What kinds of staff training are required?

- How long can students effectively interact with computers?
- How can student performance be evaluated?

The projects used the three most widely distributed microcomputers: PET, Apple, and the TRS-80. However, microcomputers manufactured by companies, such as Atari, Texas Instruments, and Ohio Scientific can be used in elementary schools.

As the projects gained experience with computer hardware, it became clear that no single unit was best for all settings. Each microcomputer had its advantages and limitations, the proper choice depending on what the educators wanted to do and how much money they had to do it with.

Robbinsdale staff liked the pricing of PET micros, allowing them to deliver programs to their elementary students at low cost per unit. Mankato chose Apple because they wanted color in their displays and for a student management routine to record and display student progress in math. The Apple disk system provided good capability for the management program. Morgan, while using all three brands of micros, liked the low purchase price of PET and TRS-80, finding the PET to be a cost-effective delivery system for their programs at the elementary grade level.

For some schools, an important consideration is the availability of printed copy. In Mankato, teachers expressed a desire for a printer to create student management reports that could be taken home to parents. Since a printer is unnecessary for most elementary classroom programs, one printer per school can be shared, allowing scheduled access to this resource.

Courseware was developed in all three school districts participating in the consortium and then shared among them. These schools found that the big question, "What does good courseware look like?", had many answers. Relevant to how the question is answered is the educational philosophy of the staff and the goals of their program. These considerations impact the structure and substance of courseware.

Courseware Development Issues

Robbinsdale staff discussed courseware characteristics at some length. First, they contended that "kid-proofing" courseware for elementary students is a must. A program is "kid-proof" when nothing that the student enters on the keyboard is able to break the flow of the program. Insuring this requires special steps in the computer program. According to Robbinsdale staff, the PET lends itself more readily than other micros to total "kid proofing" partly due to the physical attributes of the hardware. It is a single, completely enclosed unit, with no dangling wires.

Another courseware issue is determining the optimal quantity of graphics and animation in a program for elementary students. Robbinsdale staff recommended some graphics as a motivational device, but remained unsure as to the degree of game involvement that is desirable. Mankato project staff warned that the overuse of graphics and games in courseware distracts from the educational objectives of the program. Morgan staff were more disposed toward graphics and gaming because they seem to enhance instruction.

Another courseware issue at the elementary level is personalization; special programming that prompts the student to enter personal data such as his / her name which is then routinely displayed within later segments of the program. Robbinsdale found that some students insert x-rated language into the personalization routines available from commercial sources and therefore deleted these routines. Morgan and Mankato had no problems of this kind and still like the personalization concept.

Should programs be developed primarily as short supplemental units or as a sequential series covering a specific area in depth? Robbinsdale and Morgan wrote supplementary units over a wide range of topics. Mankato, on the other hand, developed a math sequence that entails addition, subtraction, multiplication and division at the fourth grade level. Students work their way through the math sequence at varying rates of speed, each student receiving about ten minutes of exposure to the computer each day. A student management subroutine records the student's name, the unit worked on, number of problems attempted, number of correct solutions, and the elapsed time. Later, the teacher may examine the data as needed or it can be printed out for use in parent conferences. Student performance data is accumulated for the entire year.

Because of differences in approach and in the type of equipment used, programs developed at one site are not necessarily exportable to other sites without some modification. Sometimes, only part of a program may be suitable for another site. Mankato, for example, was enthusiastic about a feature of a program developed by Morgan; the cursor was programmed to indicate each step in the solution of math problems, leading the student along to completion. The cursor remains at the current step until the correct response has been provided by the student. Mankato extracted this subroutine and used it to advantage in some of their programs. Synthesizing and combining ideas like this results in better courseware and is a central feature of development.

Getting Programming Done

Robbinsdale staff worked with the teachers to design new programs and modify existing materials. Three high school student programmers were employed to code and enter the programs into the computer. After the initial programming was completed, the new material was disseminated to three "key teachers" for field testing. A form accompanied each program and was used to record data on student use. Teacher recommendations for improving courseware were also solicited. The programs were then returned to the microcomputer center for modification and final debugging. When the final revisions were complete, the new program was added to the catalog along with a documentation sheet explaining the essential features of the program. Media generalists at each satellite school assembled equipment and programs.

At Mankato, three fourth grade teachers and the project director met with college student programmers once a week to provide direction for courseware development and to suggest modifications in existing materials. District-wide competency tests helped guide the development process and insure that programs fit the normal scope and sequence of math curriculum. Teachers checked for specific weaknesses of students to provide a suitable range of difficulty in each program. Expressing enthusiasm for this approach to development, the three project teachers also praised the effectiveness and motivational qualities of the courseware.

In the classroom, students rotated turns at the micros throughout the normal course of the day. Observations revealed that the students managed the process with little or no aid from teachers, who continued with their routine classroom activities.

Morgan used high school programmers working with project staff to produce and modify programs. This small rural school kept all the computers in one room, elementary students coming to the center under a pass system controlled by their teachers. Each pass specified the exact program or subject area, level of difficulty, and the length of time the student was to work at the center. Closer teacher guidance and full use of a limited amount of hardware resulted from using the pass system.

Morgan's microcomputer center maintained cumulative records detailing the extent of each student's involvement. Working directly with the elementary students in the microcomputer center, an aide maintained the user logs. Teachers furnished ideas for programs at inservice sessions; the aide made suggestions based on interactions with the students; the project director and the student programmers prepared the materials. Interviews with teachers disclosed that an advantage of Morgan's approach was the degree to which courseware was integrated with classroom work.

Estimated Courseware Development Costs

In replicating any of these projects, cost analyses must take into account the time invested by the project director, programmers, and teachers. Because these three projects had different levels of staff involvement, their development costs varied. For example, the use of high school students from programming classes, as was practiced in Morgan, reduced labor costs. Cost analyses must also consider the issue of how to pro-rate hardware. Is the hardware that is used for development work scheduled for subsequent use in classrooms? With these considerations in mind, we estimated that the costs of developing ten minutes of original courseware using student programmers (at $3.00 per hour) were: Morgan, $175; Robbinsdale, $320; and Mankato, $400.

After a program has been developed, costs can be assessed on the basis of the number of hours students use the program. For example, 80 Mankato fourth grade students used a program in 1980-1981, resulting in a cost of $5.00 per student. However, the same program can be used for the next several years and any Minnesota educator who likes that program may have a copy for the cost of reproduction, less than $1.00. As the number of students served increases, costs per pupil hour decline.

Modifying programs is less costly than original development. On the average, less than ten hours of programmer time is required. Another point to consider is that as these projects gain experience, the cost of developing programs declines. For instance, Robbinsdale prepared a series of subroutines that were common to many instructional programs and can be inserted into new courseware under development. This procedure reduced programming time and improved standardization, simplifying subsequent modifications.

Educational innovations have generally been introduced into schools after being prepared and touted by "experts" from somewhere else. If microcomputer courseware can be developed at reasonable cost and / or modified locally as was done in Robbinsdale, Morgan, and Mankato, elementary educators may become enthusiastic supporters of this technology.

BETTER HEALTH PRACTICES

A St. Paul, Minnesota, project, Achieving Student Health Behavior Change Through Personalized Health Appraisal was designed to improve the health practices and lifestyles of junior high school students through: (1) creating an awareness of individual health habits and physical status; (2) establishing personal health goals; (3) developing and expanding health curriculum, and; (4) increasing the involvement of community resource agencies in health education. Using a microcomputer health appraisal to generate a longevity projection and a series of recommendations for changing the student's lifestyle is the key feature of this project. Based on responses to a number of items presented on the Apple video display, students received an individualized, confidential health appraisal.

In order to respond to some items provided by the computer, students complete a Health Information page which includes height and weight, blood pressure, hemoglobin level and a brief family history. A lesson plan was developed by the project teacher so that students could measure their own hemoglobin level and blood pressure in the classroom.

Logistics

Early in the trimester the project teacher installed the microcomputers at each of three junior high schools. For approximately one week, students were scheduled for computer time to complete the health appraisal. Information obtained from the appraisal is confidential and the print-out becomes the personal property of the student. Each student requires approximately 20 minutes to complete the program and the counseling session.

Follow-up counseling was done by the project teacher and a health department consultant. During the counseling sessions, students were encouraged to set short-term achievable goals that would improve their general health. A support person, usually a friend or parent, was chosen to be the student's advisor in achieving the goals set. Goal booklets were used to record these responses and progress toward goal achievement.

MORE CLASSROOM APPLICATIONS

As more microcomputer systems are installed in schools, the software industry produces improved courseware in more subjects in response to a widening market. Programmers specializing in microcomputer applications are already beginning to graduate from schools and their experience should mean even better materials in the future. Here is a sampling of the kinds of applications that produce courseware of interest to many schools.

Alaska's Scattered Villages

Two or three teachers might be working with students in grades kindergarten through twelve in the numerous scattered villages in Alaska. To help these isolated teachers do a better job, microcomputers are being introduced through the Educational Telecommunications Project for Alaska. In preparation, teachers are given a three day training course covering hardware, minor repairs, courseware and the role of the teacher in the instructional process. Subjects that are being taught by microcomputer include Alaskan History, English, General Math, Developmental Reading, General Science and U.S. History.

Word Processing In California

A word processing tutorial has been developed at San Carlos High School in California. Students review computer history and other computer literacy topics while learning to use a microcomputer word processing system in the business department.

Music In Tennessee

Freshman music students at the University of Tennessee use microcomputers in Melodic Intervals Ear Training classes. Computer drill and testing produced higher student scores over traditional drill using audio tapes, probably due to the immediate feedback from the computer.

Preschoolers Learn Directionality

Preschoolers are using microcomputers to learn directionality (above-below-left-right) at the Bing Nursery School in Palo Alto, California. Color graphics enhance the instruction of this important skill which is a prerequisite for both math and reading.

Physical Chemistry in Santa Cruz

Tutorial mirocomputer courseware for Physical Chemistry has been developed at the University of California at Santa Cruz. Simulated experiments are included in the materials.

Economics in Indianapolis

Economics is taught using colorful simulations at The Childrens Museum in Indianapolis, Indiana. Typically, the children spend 20-30 minutes using one of several economics simulations which cover basic concepts.

Bible Study

Microcomputer programs to teach the Bible, the Hebrew language, and Jewish customs have been developed by the Institute for Computers in Jewish Life for use in over 30 Jewish schools across the country.

Computer Literacy For The Gifted

A computer literacy mini-unit has been prepared by Montgomery County Schools, Maryland, for enrichment of their gifted student program.

GROUP INSTRUCTION

As an educational technology, computers have been used primarily for individual or small group instruction. While their effectiveness as a powerful educational media has been documented, their integration into classroom instruction, with larger groups of students, remains relatively unexplored. Underdevelopment of procedures for bringing the computer into the mainstream of conventional classroom teaching may account for what sometimes is interpreted as resistance to computer technology by teachers.

A wider adoption of computer technology by classroom teachers might evolve if we turned our attention to achieving two related goals: (1) developing innovative teaching strategies built around microcomputer capabilities that both solve intractable teaching problems and have strong acceptance by students; (2) improving the cost-effectiveness of computer-assisted instruction, as measured by hours of student use and the acquisition of new skills.

How might this work? Since computers display most of their information visually, several TV monitors strategically located within a classroom, or a large screen projection TV would be needed. Flat screen display devices currently under development would also lend themselves to this purpose. A disk drive with several megabytes of memory, or better yet, a videodisk system, would store large amounts of information needed for lessons.

Creative writing ability is uncommon among students today and is difficult to teach. Asking students to write and rewrite themes is the usual pedagogy, but many students seem to flounder trying to get their ideas onto paper when working alone.

Let's bring a microcomputer with a large screen projection TV into the classroom and load a powerful word processing program into its memory. The teacher might provide a story for the class to rewrite collectively, or students could participate in originating their own story. Any rewriting necessary to produce a quality draft can now be rapidly accomplished using the word processor; all the students can see what's going on. Words, sentences or paragraphs can be changed, deleted or moved to improve the working text. An entire class could be actively involved in the editing process. Examples of different types of texts could be stored on a disk for the teacher to access at the appropriate time.

This electronic blackboard approach would be more efficient than trying to write out examples on the chalk board or cutting and pasting for overhead projection. Data will soon be available on this application, as it is presently under development in Ortonville, Minnesota.

Most teachers are trained for large group instruction so any application using microcomputers in this way should be fairly adaptable to regular classroom activities. A microcomputer simulation called "Lemonade Stand" is used with small groups in the Robbinsdale, Minnesota, schools. Students elect leadership, make decisions and learn to articulate and revise group strategies based on previous outcomes. Courseware of this type makes cooperation and group activities explicit goals. They add to the challenge and excitement of computer education because they capitalize on our social nature.

The cost-effectiveness and adoption of microcomputer courseware will be determined by the breadth and content validity of the available courseware in a given subject area. An index of a project's success is the extent to which it adds significantly to the pool of available courseware resources. The existence of a diverse pool of courseware sets the stage for the increased sophistication and quality upgrading that will follow. If only a small selection of courseware is available within a subject area, even if it is of the highest quality, the likelihood is that the microcomputer will begin to serve the same role as films, a peripheral add-on.

COMPUTER LANGUAGES AS LEARNING TOOLS

Many schools are teaching computer programming on microcomputers, usually in the BASIC language. As long as educators use this process to teach the concepts of programming, this is fine. There is a danger, however, if this is considered an adequate preparation for programming as a vocation. New, more powerful computer languages are being released and this process will continue. In order not to fixate on one stage of language development, these new languages should be introduced to the students as early as possible.

One of the new languages available for microcomputers is LOGO, developed by Seymour Papert and his associates at the Massachusetts Institute of Technology. This interactive language is flexible enough to be used with preschoolers through adults. It is usually introduced to young children through "Turtle" geometry. A marker (turtle) on the display screen can be commanded to move in various directions to draw desired shapes on the screen. Children quickly learn to tie a series of these commands into a program. Once shapes are created, they can be stored under whatever name the student wants as new commands in the language. Shapes can be moved in any direction at various speeds using more commands in simple animation techniques. Allowing the creation of new objects / commands in the language lets it develop with the student and gives it a personal touch.

In his book, MINDSTORMS, Papert says that students using LOGO learn problem solving skills in much less time than in traditional classrooms. Even more exciting is the claim that LOGO helps children go from the concrete to formal operations stage, as defined by Piaget, much sooner than expected. LOGO lets the child "teach" the computer to do something the child wants instead of the computer "teaching" the child.

Languages such as LOGO are adding another dimension to the educational use of microcomputers. In addition to using this innovation to deliver what might be called traditional subjects, the micro can be used by the learner as a flexible problem solving tool. Improvements in computer languages, software and hardware will make the microcomputer an even more powerful teaching aid and learning tool.

COMPUTER ASSISTED VIDEO INSTRUCTION

Video tape is an electromagnetic medium that can store pictures and sound, but it also can store computer programs and text material. Interfaces have been developed that allow the microcomputer to start, stop, search, replay, slow motion or freeze frame the video tape recorder. Until the present time, microcomputer courseware had included text, computer graphics, and occasionally, with difficulty, sound. By wedding the micro to the video tape recorder, video tape sequences can be added to the courseware stored on the magnetic tape. As students progress through the lessons, they might read some text, answer some questions, see a video tape sequence, answer more questions and then be returned for review or advanced according to their responses. This is an interactive media, one that requires student input and branching along several optional pathways according to student performance. Full color video tape sequences add greatly to the effective presentation and motivational aspects of present microcomputer courseware.

Many industrial training applications have this technology and research projects are ongoing in education. What is required and what does it cost?

A microcomputer is needed and at this time the Apple II microcomputer is most often called for by the manufacturers of the microcomputer-video tape recorder interface. However, by Fall 1981, one company has promised to bring out an interface compatible with any micro having a standard RS-232 interface port. All micros used in education can be equipped with this port.

The interface consists of a board with integrated circuits on it that plugs into the micro and has cables leading to the video tape recorder. Several manufacturers are now in business but this technology is just gearing up.

At present, a commercial grade video tape recorder with editing capabilities is needed because these recorders produce a signal (for editing purposes) that the microcomputer can "read" to locate data on the tape. By reading these signals, the micro can search and find any given frame on the tape for branching purposes.

A quality video monitor is also needed for display, the size of which depends on whether the unit is for individual or group use. If one wishes to produce their own computer-assisted video lessons, a color camera must be purchased and a second video tape recorder will be needed for editing. A list of equipment and approximate costs follows:

For instruction:
- Microcomputer - approximately $1,000 to $1,500
- Interface - $500 to $600
- Video tape recorder - $1,000 to $1,500
- Monitor (19") - $400 to $500
- Prepared Tapes - undetermined as yet but estimates range from $50 to $250 each with leasing as a possibility. Mass production would lower costs.
  TOTAL COST - $2,700 to $4,100 plus courseware

For courseware production:
- All of the above except prepared tapes, plus:
- Authoring program from interface manufacturer - $400 to $600
- Second video tape recorder - $1,000 to $1,500
- Color Camera - $800 to $1,500
- Blank Tapes - $12 to $20 each
  TOTAL COST - $5,100 to $7,700 plus blank tapes

As can be seen, prices are fairly high but are dropping as the market expands and competition grows. Another option that reduces cost is to have good video tape courseware converted to the videodisk format. Videodisks are cheap to mass produce ($3-$5 each) and the videodisk player costs $700 to $800. Laser operated videodisks are the near future of this technology but masters will still be made using video tape. Capabilities of these systems vary with the price tags. One manufacturer of computer assisted video interfaces claims that regular video tape recorders, such as those for home use and purchased by many schools, can be converted to produce the signal needed by the microcomputer, but this would void any existing warranty.

Several research and development projects are underway, including several education applications at Utah State University and an economics course being developed by the Minnesota Educational Computing Consortium. To appreciate the power of this technology, imagine a resource program for gifted children in science. Students are at different levels and have different interests. A library of computer assisted video courseware on science topics is available to the students through several work stations. One student is working on an astronomy tape which displays full color photos of celestial objects, provides text materials, quizzes the student and moves from place to place on the tape in response to the student's performance and interest. Headphones can be worn by the student to listen to narrative or music on the tape sequences. Video sequences might show lunar landings, Martian flybys, solar flares or animated graphics of such concepts as black holes. A student management routine in the program logs the daily and cumulative progress of the student for teacher review. Other students are using courseware that they are interested in.

What does the teacher do? Since the individual instruction is being delivered by computer assisted video, the teacher assumes the role of resource person; helping students with questions unanswered in the courseware, directing them to other sources of information and organizing small and large group activities to develop cooperation and social skills. Relieved of the burden of being the content authority (which is impossible anyway when dealing with diverse topics) the teacher can spend much more time observing student behaviors in order to improve their learning and social skills.

Although clearly the gifted can benefit from activities such as these, so can all students. Education is starting to recognize the challenge of handling life long learners and that traditional classrooms just won't work for them. Instruction needs to be tailored for individual consumption at many entry and exit levels. The business world has quickly recognized computer assisted video instruction's cost effective and flexible nature. As the information changes, the courseware can be altered / updated while the equipment remains usable.

Most teachers use the methods with which they were taught. We can follow this trail back into history and although tradition has value, changes are needed. In colleges of education we espouse new teaching strategies but teach them by lecture. Teachers are told to be creative but the schools are predominately lockstep systems where anything out of the ordinary is frowned upon. Like Mark Twain said, schooling isn't education. Students have long complained that schools are not really relevant to the world except for instilling work habits and providing role models (i.e., be on time and be like me). Introducing computer assisted video instruction could be revolutionary; the teacher doesn't have to be an expert in any given subject. They can be prepared as generalists. More time can be spent on analyzing and improving the study / work process skills of learners. More time can be devoted to individual and group dynamics so teachers can relate to and help their students develop emotionally. It's going to be tough on the egos of those educators who are attached to being "experts" and "smarter" than their students in every area.

Chapter VI

COMPUTERS AND SPECIAL EDUCATION

For Bryan R. the words...HI MOM, HI MOM, HI MOM, were a miracle. A twenty-three year old victim of cerebral palsy, Bryan had been helpless all his life. His only way of communicating with others had been to blink his eyes for "no" and to make a sound for "yes." That was until Curt Johnson, staff member at a school computer center, developed microcomputer procedures to let him talk.

In November, 1980, Bryan commenced, belatedly, special education in Ortonville, Minnesota public schools. His aide, Dick Oliva, was convinced that despite the official diagnosis of low mental ability, Bryan had good comprehension of the events surrounding him. Dick Oliva's optimism was based on Bryan's responses to questions about stories that were read aloud, his reaction to jokes, and even his ability to achieve a respectable score in bowling. Still, the absence of expressive language made Bryan a mysterious prisoner in a body that he couldn't control.

When school district employees in the microcomputer center learned of Bryan's near total lack of communication, they decided to link a microcomputer to a SUPERTALKER that could serve as Bryan's voice. The procedure involved displaying a grid of 32 words simultaneously on the micro's cathode ray tube. A telegraph key attached to Bryan's foot permitted him to select words which SUPERTALKER spoke. Another key held in his lap allowed him to signal the end of sentences. A broad vocabulary can be made available by providing several 32 word grids.

You can imagine the drama that unfolded the day that Bryan "spoke" his first words to his mother and teachers.

Bryan's story illustrates how microcomputers are fast becoming one of the most powerful prosthetic devices, joining eye-glasses, hearing aides, and artificial limbs as significant aids to the social, physical, and intellectual adaptation of the handicapped.

TECHNOLOGY TRANSFER IN SPECIAL EDUCATION

Considering the microcomputer's capabilities, it would seem a technology well suited to special education application. But there's more to it than that. We have discussed the statement that the microcomputer is a solution in search of a problem (Lynch, 1979). This statement applies to the use of microcomputers in the home. A question relating to the microcomputer's application in special education is: are we prepared to use microcomputers wisely? Will this new technology be used for the fundamental improvement of the quality of curriculum and instruction or will the microcomputer join the ranks of other panaceas? Worse yet, will the microcomputer accelerate a descent into trivia because of its lack of conscience concerning what or how much information it processes?

These questions are suggested by Callahan's (1970) penetrating criticism of educational leadership in the 20th century.

Callahan's historical study disclosed a pattern of educational leadership preparation that excludes training in technologies, their advantages and limitations, and for that reason he concludes that technical innovations can serve little more than decorative purposes in schools.

This projection may be less apocalyptic for special educators than for their colleagues in general education. The reason for this is that the one pedagogical element that distinguishes "special education" from "other" educations is its record of openness to technical innovations and its assimilation of them into real and continuing practices for the benefit of children with special needs. Talking calculators, variable speed tape recorders, the Optacon, and paperless braille machines are just a few of the technologies that special educators use today.

EARLIER COMPUTER-RELATED TECHNOLOGIES

The microcomputer captures the essence of a series of technical developments wherein educational media designers attempted to meet the special learning needs of the handicapped. Unfortunately, most of these older technologies were unwieldy, expensive, overspecialized, and were mechanically fragile or unreliable. It is interesting to note, however, that special educators have had a clear awareness for a long time of the many ways that instruction can be enhanced and adjusted to special needs through computer-related technologies that can now be supplanted by the microcomputer.

Cleary, Mayes and Packham (1976) listed and described some of the earlier special education technologies that can now be replicated by microcomputers at reduced cost and increased reliability. The theories and rationales for each of these inventions, however, remains intact. These include:

* The Hively Visual Discrimination Apparatus (Hively, 1964) allowed multiple slides to be presented for teaching visual discrimination. A panel was pressed and a bell sounded when a response was correct.

* The Edison Responsive Environment (Moore, 1966) was termed the "talking typewriter." A self-contained, isolated, learning environment, the "talking typewriter" provides audio commands and responses to a child who manipulates a typewriter keyboard. The rationale for the technology was that it was "autotelic" or automatically and infinitely responsive to the learner.

* Touch-Tutor (Cleary and Packham, 1968) contains a visual slide, touch panel, and auditory, pre-recorded, word-tapes. It was designed to teach reading and related visual

discrimination skills to young, pre-school children. Many teachers of the mentally retarded use this device extensively.

* The Language Master was designed by the Experimental Development Unit NCAVAE (1970). Cards with written words or pictures were manually inserted into an apparatus. A magnetic tape strip activated a play-back of the word, aloud.

* The Talking Page, designed by Salisbury (1971) consists of records and books. It is basically a battery operated record player contained within a book format. A pointer is used to select lines that are played back. It can be programmed like a branching teaching machine with visual multiple choice questions for the student to answer.

The fact that the microcomputer is a highly adaptable, general purpose machine that can be programmed with peripherals that easily replicate the functions of most single-purpose instructional technologies, distinguishes it from these earlier computer-related devices.

HOW COMPUTERS HAVE BEEN USED IN SPECIAL EDUCATION

Cartwright and Hall (1974) reviewed the ways that computers had been used in special education up to about 1973. Computers had already been used for direct instruction and testing with hearing impaired, visually impaired, emotionally disturbed, mentally retarded, and disadvantaged students. Program management and teacher training simulations were also prominent special education applications of computers in the early years.

Computers, as teaching aids, have long been attractive to special educators because they are compatible with and reflect some of the important principles by which special education instruction is characterized:
- graduated tasks keyed to individual needs
- a considerable degree of "structure" for the learning task and environment
- and a reduction of learning "stress" wherever possible.

According to Berthold and Sachs (1974), "...(computers) provide clearly defined stimuli and expectations, active responses, immediate reinforcement, and gradual increase in the complexity of the material. Machines have infinite patience, minimize social stress, and often reduce factors like teacher motivation and negative preconceptions about a child's ability."

COMPUTER ASSISTED INSTRUCTION

Hicks and Hyde (1973) described computer assisted instruction as:

> a teaching process directly involving a computer in the presentation of instructional materials in an interactive mode to provide and control the individualized learning environment for each individual student.

For special education, computer assisted instruction has three special features for enhancing learning (Overheu, 1977). These include:

> *the ability to make small or large changes in the level of difficulty when developing skills such as hand-eye coordination, so that the task set for an individual is challenging and neither trivial nor too difficult; and

> *the ability to present routine skill training in an attractive format which minimizes extraneous distractions; and

> *the ability to develop new educational strategies based on a combination of modes of information.

Computer assisted instruction has been hailed by Magidson (1978) as an "educational promise to individualize and personalize the instructional process and to simulate experiences not readily available." He noted that:

> CAI lessons can serve as text, test and tutor while compelling students to be active participants in their own learning. Students work at their own pace while the CAI lesson monitors their progress and commonly prevents them from continuing to more advanced instruction unless mastery is demonstrated. Students are also kept informed of their progress through immediate feedback and achievement summaries.

Three large-scale CAI systems that have been used extensively and successfully by many American school districts are the Interactive Training System (ITS), Programmed Logic for Automatic Teaching Operation (PLATO), and the Stanford Project.

Briefly, the ITS, developed by International Business Machines Corporation, allows the teacher to prepare a computer assisted course without detailed programming knowledge. PLATO, developed by the University of Illinois, integrates knowledge, fact, and information and educates through audio and visual means. The Stanford Project, Stanford University, uses programs and materials with structured curriculum.

Four Types Of Computer Assisted Instruction

Computer assisted instruction can be classified into four categories (Barrette, 1980). These classifications consist of drill and practice, simulation / modeling, games, tutorial and a combination of the first four. Barrette described each of the four categories of microcomputer based instructional application. These include:

Drill and Practice. Programs of this nature are highly desirable to develop mastery skills associated with specific learning objectives. Essentially, items such as math, spelling, syntax, etc. are displayed for the student to practice a specific skill. The built-in random number generator function of a micro is a great help in mixing items. The student is expected to practice mastery. Students however can quickly become tired or even frustrated with this type of program unless it is carefully designed.

Simulation/ Modeling. Programs of this type are generally more complex to write. However, they are also highly desirable and are used by teachers to simulate or model real world events without having students physically encounter the actual forces that shaped the events. Decision making skills are developed. Extensive group discussion occurs. Often data is collected from real world environments and entered into the program. This type of program is often very economical and quite suited to be used with an individual or a group of students.

Games. These programs are fun. Students, as well as adults spend hours with them. They serve a very important educational motivational purpose for many students. In addition, if the programs are well designed, they assist students in developing process thinking strategies.

Tutorials. These application programs are without doubt the most complicated to write. Their purpose is for students to acquire specific knowledge through well designed linear and branching frame sequences. Usually these programs are designed for individual student use. (p. 34)

MICROCOMPUTER CAPABILITIES FOR CAI

Barrette offers a word of caution to educators who might think that microcomputers can do everything as well as larger computers. Microcomputers have capabilities and limitations for different kinds of instructional applications. He has prepared the following chart to compare the capabilities of different size computers. One should pay careful attention to the footnote which implies that technological changes are likely to remove existing limitations.

INSTRUCTIONAL COMPUTER RECOMMENDATIONS

Instructional Application	Micro Computer	Mini and Mainframe Computer
1. Drill and Practice	Yes	Yes
2. Tutorial	Limited*	Yes
3. Problem Solving	Yes	Yes
4. Instructional Games	Yes	Yes
5. Simulation	Limited*	Yes
6. Forecasting	Limited*	Yes
7. Programming	Yes	Yes

8. Testing	Yes	Yes
9. Computer Literacy	Yes	Yes
10. Data Analysis	Limited*	Yes
11. Word Processing	Limited*	Yes
12. Instructional Management	Limited*	Yes
13. Speech/ Sound Recognition	Limited*	Yes
14. Speech/ Sound Synthesis	Limited*	Yes
15. Real Time Analysis	Limited*	Yes
16. Information Retrieval	Yes	Yes

*Current limitations depend heavily upon microprocessor, RAM size program efficiency, disk or virtual memory capacity and analog/ digital pattern circuits. These limitations are likely to be temporary. (Pierre Barrette, August, 1981)

SPECIAL NEEDS LEARNERS LIKE CAI

Undoubtedly it is computer assisted instruction's ease of providing for individualized instruction, required by federal law for the handicapped, that accounts for its appeal to special educators. But in addition, special needs learners seem to respond well to computer assisted instruction.

For instance, the computer has been shown to help students who are poorly motivated become more enthusiastic about learning (Cartwright and Derevensky, 1976). Disadvantaged Mexican-American students who displayed poor attitudes toward learning and who were turned-off by classroom activities showed positive changes when they worked with computers (Crandall and Mantano, 1977). The author's personal experiences and observations are that these positive effects continue over long periods of exposure to CAI and are not simply the result of putting a new gadget into the classroom.

A feature of computer assisted instruction that appeals to reluctant learners is the sense of control that they get during the learning experience. In conventional instruction, the teacher controls what is presented and the rate that it appears. But with computer assisted instruction, the learner is in charge. Tolor (1969) found that measurements of students' "internal locus of control" increased after only eight weeks of computer tutorial experience. McClelland (1969) saw educational technology, particularly computers, as having a crucial role in the development of achievement motivation among students. The key may be that for slow learners, handicapped students, and the disadvantaged, computer assisted instruction provides private, nonthreatening, and reinforcing interactions between learner and "teacher" all the time.

Favorable outcomes using computers for instructional purposes have been documented in correctional facilities and rehabilitation centers. Bagley (1977) described how the staff of the Minnesota correctional facilities successfully used computer assisted instruction to motivate the unmotivated, improve problem solving skills, and provide interesting drill and practice for low ability students.

At the Woodrow Wilson Rehabilitation Center at Fishersville, Virginia, a three-year project jointly supported by the Commonwealth of Virginia and International Business Machines Corporation demonstrated that computer programming was a viable occupation for some physically disabled persons. Disabled students were taught to record their programs and notes on a typewriter-like device at their own rate, to edit and correct this work, and to enter it into the computer via telephone lines. A one hundred percent employment rate was achieved by these physically disabled computer students.

AT THE SECONDARY LEVEL

The most recent comprehensive review of the effectiveness of computer assisted instruction in the secondary schools was done by Thomas (1979). Although special education applications were few in number, there was evidence of some movement in the direction of using this technology. Among the uses noted were: urban disadvantaged learners with remedial needs, accessing occupational information, computer assisted instruction for the deaf and hearing-impaired, and the teaching of reading.

A major effort in reading courseware development for secondary students with learning disabilities was recently completed by Control Data Corporation and the Minnesota State Department of Education with support from Title VI-G funds. This computer-based reading and language arts program is the most sophisticated instructional system now available for the handicapped and is designed around the PLATO timesharing system (Joiner, 1979).

Control Data Corporation is now beginning to make "smart" terminals, which are actually microcomputers designed to interact with a time-share system, available to some users of the PLATO timeshare system. Doing so will reduce telecommunication costs which are high when terminals are continuously linked, over long distance telephone lines, to a central computer. With smart terminals, large sectors of the courseware can be downloaded rapidly for later use, on-site.

COMPUTERS AND THE MENTALLY RETARDED

In teaching mentally retarded students, it is generally accepted practice to reduce instructional content to small, precise units while providing extensive drill and practice. Concepts, skills, and facts once learned are often forgotten and therefore curriculum must allow for review and relearning on a regular, periodic, schedule.

The teacher of the mentally retarded who uses this approach faces the challenge of doing considerably more assessment of skill acquisition and retention than the regular class teacher. Also, with the need for repetition and re-learning it is quite difficult for the teacher to provide sufficient variety and novelty in lessons to avoid student boredom and resistence to learning.

When we examine the fundamental principles of programmed instruction, the same principles that are basic to computer assisted instruction, we see that we're reading a prescription for teaching the mentally retarded:

* educational goals and objectives should be translated into behavioral statements.

* material should be ordered logically and in small steps directly tied to objectives.

* immediate and continuous feedback should be provided and reinforcement should be consistent with the student's personality and preferences.

* students should progress at their own rate through instructional content.

PROJECT TIME: TOTAL INFORMATION MANAGEMENT AND EVALUATION SYSTEM

Minneapolis educators were aware that the degree of detail, assessment, and individualization suggested by good teaching practices for the mentally retarded could only be achieved through computer assisted procedures. Supported by Title IV-C funds, Suburban Hennepin County, District 287, embarked upon a monumental curriculum development program for the trainable mentally retarded. Simultaneously, they initiated a complete computerization of student record keeping and reporting.

Just how difficult it is to manage a behavioral approach to teaching the mentally retarded is revealed in the scope of the areas and tasks identified within the curriculum. Fifty areas formed the basic structure for the curriculum in 1977. More areas were subsequently added.

Examples of curriculum areas would be: toileting, sports, common objects, pre-vocational. Each area was broken down into skills and each skill into tasks. Tasks represented the behavioral statements that translated program goals into behavioral terms, in keeping with the earlier mentioned recommended practices.

Simply listing the areas, skills, and tasks is a major undertaking if it were to be done manually. Fortunately, computer procedures allowed a task directory to be printed in hard copy for ready reference. The following is a sample page from the computer generated "Task Directory":

SUBURBAN HENNEPIN COUNTY JISD- 287

TASK DIRECTORY

AREA: 09 - FAMILY DINING

   SKILL: 01 - TAKING FOODS

      TASK: 01 - SERVE WITH FINGERS

      TASK: 02 - SERVE WITH SPOON

      TASK: 03 - USE SALAD UTENSILS

      TASK: 04 - GRAVY LADLE

      TASK: 05 - USE SERVING FORK

      TASK: 06 - POUR PITCHER/ CARTON

      TASK: 07 - POSITION FOOD

   SKILL: 02 - PASSING FOODS

      TASK: 01 - PASSING PITCHER

      TASK: 02 - PASSING BOWLS

      TASK: 03 - PASS PLATTERS

      TASK: 04 - PASSING SECONDS

      TASK: 05 - ASK FOR SECONDS

   SKILL: 03 - RECEIVING FOODS

      TASK: 01 - RECEIVE PITCHER

      TASK: 02 - RECEIVE BOWLS

      TASK: 03 - RECEIVE PLATTERS

SKILL: 04 - TABLE MANNERS

TASK: 01 - REFUSE FOOD POLITELY

TASK: 02 - FOLLOW HOST EXAMPLE

TASK: 03 - COMPLIMENT HOST

TASK: 04 - TAKE PROPER PORTION

You will note that each task can be referred to by a unique number. For instance, the number 090102 represents family dining (area 09); taking food (skill 01); serve with spoon (task 02). To be able to serve with a spoon is the behavioral objective of instruction. The numbering system allows the computer to locate or store each item contained in the task directory. Printing all the tasks, some of them, or just one, is a simple matter for the computer.

In order to plan and implement instruction, however, the teacher must know, for each child, just exactly which skills have been acquired and which skills remain unlearned. It would be possible to record and access this information manually; each student could have a complete hard copy task directory in a file. Acquired skills might be noted with a colored check mark. A ponderous system, but possible. It would be much more difficult, however, to manually list all the students who hadn't yet learned to "serve with a spoon" in order to put together a small group of instruction.

The Minneapolis special educators concluded that in order for this behavioral objective approach to really work, a number of reports would have to be available to them in order to gauge student progress and plan instruction. The more important reports are:

1. Mastery reports. These reports consist of a computer print-out of all of the skills which a student mastered.

2. Non-mastery reports. These reports provide the teacher with information regarding the skills which the student has not yet mastered but which have been assessed.

3. Year-end profile. This print-out consists of the

information contained in mastery and non-mastery reports as well as a summary statement of that information.

4. Grouping reports. These reports identify all of the students at any location who are identified as receiving instruction in the same skill.

The system just described would be termed a "computer-managed instructional system." It serves the needs of the special education teacher by keeping track of student progress, disclosing groups of students with similar instructional needs, compiling reports automatically, and highlighting inconsistencies in performance. It is the only cost-effective way to implement behavioral-objective approaches to teaching the mentally retarded.

Fortunately, with today's disk storage capabilities for microcomputers, it is quite possible to install a version of this system in any classroom. A system of this type is simple to use and a good place for teachers to start becoming more familiar with microcomputer capabilities. Teachers can develop their own original task directories or borrow from the work that has already been done by others.

COMPUTER AIDS FOR THE HEARING, SPEECH, MOTOR AND VISUALLY IMPAIRED

In 1976, the National Technical Institute for the Deaf surveyed schools for the deaf to identify the type and extent of computer assisted instruction being used (von Feldt, 1978-79). Eleven of 50 states were surveyed, disclosing that 34 elementary and secondary schools for the deaf were using computer assisted instruction systems.

Small computers, generally minicomputers, were the principle form of hardware used. Systems were generally dedicated exclusively to instruction. This is advantageous because competition between instructional and administrative demands is avoided.

Most instructional systems were turn-key, emphasizing drill and practice in academic subjects, especially basic skills. A turn-key system is one that is purchased ready to run. There is no need for on-site, custom programming. Turn-key systems are like textbooks; everyone gets a standardized product. Nearly all deaf educators who responded to the survey were convinced that remarkable growth in the use of computers in teaching the deaf would occur during the next five years (1979-1984).

PLATO And The TELETACTOR

Another example of the computer serving as prosthesis is the use of a PLATO program to teach comprehension to the deaf. Through the computer, words are presented as kinesthetic sensations on the abdomen. To do this, the PLATO auditory disk "speaks words and phrases" that are converted to sensations through a new sensory aid, the TELETACTOR. Sounds of words are perceived as dynamic, flowing, patterns on the skin of the abdomen. And these patterns are learned in the same manner as a conventional language.

The TELETACTOR is one way of reaching children who are unable to benefit from the use of hearing aids. Instead of air vibrations, as perceived on the eardrum, stimulators in the teletactor belt respond to specific frequencies, with output representing the energy available within a given bandwidth. Frequency bands are arranged in the belt from high to low. So a siren would produce a sensation that "moves" across the belt.

Voice sounds, diphthongs, unvoiced stop consonants, and voiced stops all produce unique frequencies that are perceived as a burst of energy at a single place on the belt. Educationally, programming progresses from sound recognition to comprehending words and phrases. Although this program has been developed on the PLATO system, it should be converted for microcomputer delivery as this would be much more cost effective.

Communications For The Deaf

Teletypewriters currently used by the deaf for telephone communications use the "Baudot" coding system to translate typed words into electronic signals for phone transmission. Microcomputers are much more versatile than the old teletypewriters but use the "ASC II" coding system. If a deaf person elects to use a microcomputer for phone communications and other tasks, the system would be incompatible with the large existing network of teletypewriters. However, several packages are now available for micros which can communicate using ASCII or Baudot as needed which make the microcomputer the logical option for telephone communications.

Voice Synthesis / Recognition

Computer recognition of speech is rapidly improving and has many uses in aiding the physically handicapped. Computer programs that control appliances, lights, and telephone communications can be activated and directed by voice recognition giving more environmental control to even severely handicapped persons. The development of typewriters that print out whatever is spoken to them has already been accomplished in several research labs. Typing ability will no longer be a barrier for the handicapped and this technology can also be used for computer control and programming.

Speech synthesis applications like the one presented at the beginning of the chapter, are now common. Older synthesis programs stored a fixed vocabulary of words but newer versions are phoneme based and can pronounce whatever is typed in or chosen from a menu according to a set of rules. Phoneme systems have much greater flexibility and use less memory storage. Voices produced by the computer are also improving dramatically, to the point of having male and female voices to choose from. Conversational interaction with microcomputers will be a reality in the 80's with obvious benefits for many handicapped persons. Talking typewriters and microcomputers are already available for the blind.

Microcomputer Word Boards

For those unable to communicate verbally and with physical limitations that preclude normal typing, word boards provide a method of expression. Older word boards made mechanical selections of desired words or phrases as needed but computers speed the process and allow many possible choices. Special keyboards and a wide variety of switches (buttons, levers, sip and puff switch) designed to meet the specific handicapping condition can be used to make choices from large arrays of words and phrases. Output can be on the display screen, routed to a printer or spoken by the computer. Light pens which detect illumination on the television screen can also be used to make choices.

RECORD KEEPING

Computer applications in special education have involved large computers and have usually been addressed to direct instruction and learner needs. Transferring microcomputer technology into special education may, however, reduce some of the management burdens and increase productivity. Although P.L. 94-142 has been credited with having "codified what has long been recognized as superior teaching practice" (National Advisory Committee on the Handicapped, 1977, pg. 6) its record keeping and documentation requirements are cost factors that may threaten the declining productivity of classroom teachers (Sabatino, 1981). As America enters the "Age of Less," a growing concern for productivity in both the public and private sectors is manifest.

In response to this problem Weatherman (1979) developed some simple microcomputer multidistrict applications for special education "compliance" management. His data collection document was computer generated and available for data collection at the Education Planning Conference. Weatherman's system supplied special education administrators with immediate access to information that would answer the following questions:

1. Have we functioned within the 30-day calendar compliance from the date of referral to the date of placement?
2. How many students are served within our educational unit by disability, by group membership, etc.?
3. By student, how many annual goals were defined? How many of these goals were met? How many specific objectives were met?
4. How much time annually, by individual student, or categorical groups of students, or total number of students is spent within special education services, and what amount of time is spent in mainstreaming activities?

The following are sample hardcopy output from Weatherman's system and represent only a few of the possible reports that can be generated by microcomputers. Weatherman emphasized the importance of the accessibility of a longitudinal-historical data base in special education service delivery, the labor saving aspects of automatic report generating, and the user "friendliness" of the microcomputer system.

Weatherman's experiences working with special education districts in microcomputer applications confirmed Wells' (1979) principle: "Keep it Simple." Wells reminds us that during the sixties a number of monumental computerized planning systems were designed that are now extinct. According to Wells, our experience with computer systems teaches us: "Start small. Build slowly. Incremental growth you can manage; instant sophistication is risky. Success, not glamour, is what counts!"

DEMONSTRATIONAL EDUCATION UNIT *000
GENERAL SUMMARY REPORT

APRIL 20, 1981

DIST	BLDG	STUDENT	ID#	SEX	D.O.B	GR. LEVEL EQUIV.	PRIMARY PLACMT.	%	SECONDARY PLACMT.	%
632	04	Adams, O	2004	M	05/02/72	2	SP	10	LD	5
632	04	Smith, A	3005	M	06/01/73	1	LD	10	HI	5
947	01	Carlson, J	1001	M	04/20/73	1	EMR	50	SP	10
947	02	Jones, J	1002	F	03/15/70	5	LD	25	SP	10
952	01	Dawson, A	7001	F	05/16/70	5	TMR	80	SP	10

DEMONSTRATIONAL EDUCATIONAL UNIT *000
GENERAL SUMMARY REPORT FOR DISTRICT # 947

APRIL 20, 1981

BLDG	STUDENT	ID#	SEX	D.O.B	GR. LEVEL EQUIV.	PRIMARY PLACMT.	%	SECONDARY PLACMT.	%
01	Carlson, J	1001	M	04/20/73	1	EMR	50	SP	10
01	Mark, A	1021	F	06/10/69	6	SP	5	SP	10
01	Sands, S	1030	M	01/16/70	5	TMR	85	OT	15
02	Jones, J	1002	F	03/15/70	5	LD	25	OT	15
02	West, M	1031	M	06/11/72	2	EMR	50	PT	10

DEMONSTRATIONAL EDUCATION UNIT *000
ANNUAL GOALS & OBJECTIVES REPORT FOR DISTRICT # 632

APRIL 20, 1981

AGE	STUDENT	ID#	PRIMARY PLACMT.	# OF ANNUAL GOALS	# OF ANNUAL GOALS MET	TOTAL # OF OBJ.	TOTAL # OF OBJ. MET
4	Ward, J	2501	TMR	5	3	25	20
4	Rick, N	2502	TMR	8	6	15	10
6	Smith, A	3005	LD	5	4	25	22
7	Adams, O	2004	SP	3	3	30	30

IMPROVING CHILD FIND AND ASSESSMENT

The Office of Special Education has been faced with the problem of not being able to find the number of handicapped students, nationwide that equals the 12 percent estimate used for soliciting Congressional appropriations. This is an embarrassment to the agency because critics of special education such as O'Gara (1979), contend that the original estimates were exaggerated and unscientific.

A possible reason for the child-find short-fall is that detection devices are primitive and administered inconsistently. In a study of New York State's screening programs, one of the authors found that most of the assessment devices were local products, subject to little if any quality control. Next to the assessment of language skills, eye-hand condination tasks were the most heavily represented in the screening instruments (Joiner, 1978).

Most eye-hand coordination screening items involve paper and pencil activities, for example the most popular DRAW-A-MAN TEST (Goodenough and Harris, 1963). A paper and pencil assessment of eye-hand coordination is contaminated by a number of uncontrolled circumstances such as environmental conditions under which the test is given, examiner skills and rapport, and ambiguities in scoring.

Converting eye-hand coordination screening tests to microcomputer administration would be simple, economical, and result in more reliable and valid assessments. A series of graphic displays on a screen could be created by the child using a joystick to manipulate a potentiometer. These graphic figures could be automatically scored against standard figures, as in the Frostig Developmental Test of Visual Perception. This "cineopsychometric" program could be branched so that format, detail, and speediness could be adjusted for performance and development level. Scoring would be performed by the program using norm tables stored internal to the program.

NORMALIZATION

Normalization has recently become a guiding principle of special education, an approach to treatment and habilitation that places the handicapped person within the "normal" community-social network. It has been recognized that physically placing a handicapped person in the community rather than in an institution is not normalizing unless the sense of isolation felt by the handicapped is removed. The only way to relieve the sense of isolation is to establish more person-to-person communication between the handicapped and the non-handicapped in the community.

The New Jersey Institute of Technology established a communication link, that can now be replicated by microcomputer, between alert but shut-in women in a nursing home and children at a cerebral palsy center. This novel communication channel proved a valuable source of emotional support for the handicapped children and gave the shut-in women a meaningful activity. This is an interesting microcomputer application that contradicts the stereotype of the computer as "dehumanizing" by bringing about closer contact between isolated people.

DISTANCE EDUCATION FOR THE HOMEBOUND

Students who are unable to be physically present in their classrooms because of physical or mental disorders have been aided by telephone hook-ups with their classrooms and home or hospital sites by teachers who supply tutoring. These homebound and hospital programs of distance education are expensive. And even though the child is able to listen to what is going on in the class and engage in verbal dialog with the teacher, there is still no way to check assignments and practice activities.

Microcomputers can provide better distance education by supplementing visits from tutors and audio hook-ups. Two microcomputers, one in the classroom and one at a distant location, can be connected by telephone, or by radio transmitter / receivers, to provide an instant means of communication, checking written work or taking tests.

THE EFFECT OF INTERVENTIONS

Special education has adopted a quasi-scientific approach to improving educational practices. Modeled after medicine and psychology, clinical methods involving diagnosis, mechanistic and "structured" interventions, and "behavioral objectives" are accepted as the professional norm.

Unfortunately, teachers often lack the resources, time, and energy to engage in the research that is implied by the model and that could adequately document the manner and extent of child growth. By structuring the observation and assessment context and providing automatic analysis of performance data, however, the microcomputer can help bring real practices into better correspondence with professional ideals.

Handicapped students, for example, often display serious language deficits. And the remediation of language deficits is a top-ranked goal for special education programs. Yet it is exceedingly difficult to obtain reliable and valid measures of language deficit. Ideally, the teacher should obtain informal language samples, taken in natural situations, at various times during the school year. Through careful analysis of these language samples the teacher could determine whether vocabularies and the length and detail of utterances had increased. In this case, storage, compilation, and analysis of complex data are all problems.

To address these problems, Montague (1976) began applying a computerized system of verbal content analysis using language samples of pre-school, disadvantaged, black children. He became convinced, on the basis of his experience, that:

> educators can use computer content analysis to objectively study remedial intervention strategies and their effect on the verbal and written language of students.

LOCATING RESOURCES

An important aid in planning instruction for learning disabled students is Computer Based Resource Units. This computerized retrieval system is founded on the idea that "many more ideas, materials, instructional activities, and procedures are actually available somewhere in the nation than most classroom teachers are able to tap." (Gearheart, 1973).

Along similar lines, the three Specialized Offices for the Blind, Deaf, and Other Handicapping Conditions made a significant contribution to the selection of educational media. Qualified personnel from those offices spend hours selecting instructional resources that can be used effectively in special education programs. Information about these items is entered into a computer in the National Instructional Materials Information System headquartered at Ohio State University. The same information is also made available through the National Information Center for Special Education Materials at the University of Southern California and the Lockheed Computer Facility. Altogether, nearly 45,000 entries are contained in these data banks. Information systems of this type are now accessible to microcomputer users who have made the necessary arrangement and have proper equipment.

CAREER COUNSELING BY COMPUTER

Guidance counselors are in short supply in most school systems, a situation that is likely to become worse due to budget cuts and a lessening of public enthusiasm for what some term educational frills. But career counseling is an important part of providing quality education for the special needs learner. The success of special programs is ultimately judged by the post-school performance of students. Can computers help pick up the slack in career counseling?

Sampson and Stripling (1979) reported on the System of Interactive Guidance and Information (SIGI), a direct inquiry system for helping students in the process of choosing a career. Educational Testing Service developed this system.

SIGI's format enables students to progress through six subsystems: 1) values clarification; 2) locating appropriate occupational alternatives: 3) obtaining information on occupations; 4) predicting success in academic course work; 5) planning academic programs; and 6) making career decisions. This computer-based system improves student competence in making rational and informed career decisions, predicting career success based on students' abilities and interests. Because of constant updating of the large data base, the program also is able to respond on the basis of the current job market.

Just recently (1981), the SIGI program has been converted to run on the Radio Shack TRS-80 Model II microcomputer. Institutions purchasing SIGI program user licenses for the first time reportedly may receive a 15 percent discount on hardware purchased from Radio Shack. The microcomputer conversion should make SIGI a realistic and attractive option for smaller schools.

TEACHER EDUCATION

Computers are also used extensively in training teachers to work effectively with exceptional children. Reith and Semmel (1978) outlined the purposes of the Center for Innovation in Teaching the Handicapped whose major objective has been "in using large computers and video technology to mediate instruction on basic teaching competencies." Currently the emphasis of the Center for Innovation in Teaching the Handicapped is on computer-managed instruction for service activities that includes individual education program development, monitoring pupil progress, placement decision making and computer assisted instruction for preservice and in-service teacher training. Center staff would like to use microcomputers for training teachers to comply with the many complex stipulations of Public Law 94-142 and the individual needs of handicapped learners.

Another method of training teachers to comply with the laws that govern education of handicapped children through technology has been the Clinical Teacher Model. This model (Schwartz & Oseroff, 1975) developed at Florida State University and supported by the Bureau of Education for the Handicapped is a "non-categorical teacher education program; designed, field tested and documented as an alternative approach to the manpower preparation patterns in special education." This model uses instructional technology and evaluation research strategies for accomplishing its goal. It is intended to "individualize and personalize per-formance-based instructional curricula for both the clinical teacher competencies and the desired academic and social behaviors for mildly handicapped exceptional children."

THE OFFICE OF SPECIAL EDUCATION MOVES FORWARD

In 1981, the Office of Special Education of the U.S. Department of Education requested proposals from researchers and organizations to conduct a study called "Assisting LEA's to Adopt New Technologies." This planned project will help set the stage for increased adoption of educational technologies in special education over the next five years. It is hoped that through this study, local education agencies will be more able to determine what kinds of equipment to purchase and the types and extent of technical support or assistance that will be needed to use technologies effectively. It is likely that microcomputers will be a major focus of this nation-wide study.

Chapter VII

MICRO-ASSISTED ADMINISTRATION

In a recent trade magazine advertisement two businessmen are shown side by side, walking toward an airplane. They both appear to be carrying briefcases. One briefcase, we are told, contains a complete microcomputer system...the other, a file folder, a magazine, and a sandwich. Judging by their pronouncements concerning the limited capabilities of micro-computers, some current leaders in educational data processing are probably carrying sandwiches in their briefcases.

At the 1981 national conference of the Association for Educational Data systems, John Haugo, former director of the Minnesota Educational Computing Consortium, recited a list of reasons why microcomputers can't "cut the mustard" in school administration. Included among the deficits attributed to microcomputers were the inability to handle the large amounts of data entailed in applications such as scheduling and the difficulty of creating complex microcomputer programs.

Thumbing through recent trade magazines reveals a host of administrative software for businesses available from commercial vendors. These programs work. For example, the business operations of the publisher of the book you are now reading are controlled by Radio Shack microcomputers. In Ortonville, Minnesota, local school staff developed adminis-trative software, including scheduling of classes, that will be described in this chapter. Ortonville's finance programs meet the convoluted reporting requirements of the state, in addition to local payroll and budget management requirements.

Analogous to the current situation in microcomputing is the early history of the auto industry in America. Companies that produced the early cars were managed by experts in buggy-making. And early automobiles bore a resemblance to horse drawn vehicles. As horses, and what they pulled, became less compelling mental images for designers, craftsmen, and engineers, and as younger people entered the industry, the automobile began to assume its own natural shape.

What is happening today is that experienced users of large computers frequently prejudge the microcomputer's capabilities rather than seek ways to extend them. School administrators in large school districts who have used large computer resources for several years have systems that work and no incentive whatsoever to experiment with micro-assisted administration. Nor do the people who make a living by running the big systems. Why tinker with a machine that's running? Therefore, most of the ambitious and creative applications of microcomputer technology in education are being developed in smaller schools and businesses that heretofore lacked computer resources.

MANIPULATING INFORMATION

Usually, in writing, you move from the simple to the complex. We have chosen to violate this principle because we believe that the "information problem" of administrators today is an inability to manipulate and derive sense from information rather than an inability to store it. Like a waterbed, inflated information is easy to store but hard to move. Yet, in our experience, a major part of the administrator's job is absorbed in moving information: rearranging words in written communications, numbers in reports, students and teachers among classes; dates and events on calendars; buses between homes and schools, where books and materials came from and went. And although manipulating information is probably not the first microcomputer application that an administrator will undertake, it's where the real payoff lies.

WORD PROCESSING

Typing consumes more secretarial time than any other clerical activity. Letters, forms, and documents of various types, compose an endless stream of typing chores. Many of the letters that administrators write are routine correspondence requiring only changes in name and address and perhaps a few key words. Yet in many school offices, these letters are typed from scratch every time they're used. Documents or reports are also typed and then revised for total retyping. A large part of this typing time may be saved using a word processing system.

Revisions of documents and second drafts are a major problem for the administrator who cares about the accuracy and appearance of written work. There is always a tendency for new errors to be built into successive typings of documents. That means a careful re-reading of each successive version is required. Moreover, with the low pay scales for clerical staff in many educational institutions, it is impossible to hire highly competent workers. One administrator told us that his secretary was so inept at working with documents that he could ask that a page be copied on the Xerox machine and it would be returned with an error. A joy of word processing is that it insures that errors, once corrected, stay that way and that new errors don't appear in work already proofed.

Word processing software for a microcomputer displays the text, as it is being typed, on a video screen and stores it on a magnetic tape or disk. After the job is completed, the text is sent to the printer to provide hardcopy for review, proofing, and editing. If corrections or revisions are required, the typist loads the original text into the computer from the copy stored on the magnetic tape or disk.

Once in the computer's memory, the text can be edited by using keyboard commands provided in the software documentation. Words can be inserted or deleted, spelling corrected and lines or paragraphs can be moved as blocks to any desired location in the text. These modifications and others, depending on which software package is being used, can be made very rapidly after some practice with a system. It usually takes about a week of practice for a typist to start feeling comfortable using a word processor.

A "global search" feature, often included in the software, allows one to locate a word or phrase wherever it occurs in the text and change it to some other chosen word or phrase. The change will be made simultaneously at each location. For example, you could change the abbreviated CAI to the phrase, computer assisted instruction, each time it appeared in the manuscript, in just one operation. Secretarial time can be saved by abbreviating or using acronyms for long, frequently used, expressions in the original draft and then translating them to English, later, in a simple stroke.

Complete control of the printer means the same text can be printed out in a variety of formats with automatic pagination. Margins can be changed and spacing between lines altered. Left and right justification are generally available to give the document the look of a printed book. Many printers also have different type fonts to choose from. Letter quality printers, while expensive, can replicate the look of "selectric" type on bond paper chosen by the users.

Spelling Control

Few people find spelling an art form worthy of serious study. Although the virtues of being a good speller are extolled, and we still have national spelling bees, executive misspellings abound. For many, attention to the minutiae of spelling interferes with the flow of ideas and words so vital to fluency in writing. Poor writing skills are probably the result of children paying too much attention to a system of education that works backwards, drilling students on unmeaningful details rather than more global expressive skills. Many people remain bogged down in spelling and grammar all their lives, writing little or nothing.

Spelling control software, used in conjunction with word

processing is a painless way to sort out the "i's" and "e's." Fast acting software such as SPELLGUARD detects spelling and typographical errors in documents prepared with CP / M or CDOS word processors. Checking approximately 20 pages per minute, SPELLGUARD uses a 20,000 word expandable dictionary, marking questionable spellings in the text for review by the writer. Special technical words can be entered into the dictionary by the user to expand the software's usefulness.

What is central to word processing is that once entered into the computer, text will not have to be retyped from scratch. Minor or major alterations can be quickly accomplished and all versions of the text saved on magnetic media for future recall. It's an electronic cut and paste process with great flexibility. Most people who have used word processors are loath to return to standard typewriters. Writing is rewriting and these systems make the rewrite easy and fast. This book was written in part using an Apple microcomputer and word processing software.

SCHEDULING AND CONFLICT RESOLUTION

Another time consuming activity that preoccupies school administrators is the development of various schedules and the resolution of scheduling conflicts. Large computers have been successfully used to prepare class schedules but high costs have prevented most school districts from using them. Several microcomputer scheduling packages are now available from schools and from commercial sources. Ortonville has written a program for the Apple II microcomputer equipped with two disk drives that will handle two semesters of eight classes per day (16 different time slots) for a total of 450 students signing up for 88 different courses.

Two alternative methods for determining the schedule are possible using the program. In a static type of scheduling, a schedule of classes is set up and the computer slots students into that schedule with the least number of possible conflicts. In a more dynamic mode, all student choices are entered and the computer offers several choices of a final schedule for administrative decision making. Limitations on the number of students and / or classes can be expanded by using recently available large capacity hard disk drives.

In addition to scheduling students into classes, micro-computers can be used to schedule rooms for classes, obtaining maximum use of school facilities. Computer graphics, as will be explained later, can be used to create displays that will immediately pinpoint overused and underused classrooms.

Balancing teaching assignments against available staff, curriculum requirements, and student enrollments is another administrative application for microcomputers. Manipulating this information into an optimum configuration helps insure that teaching assignments are equitable, consistent with the teachers' interests and experience, and that student needs are met.

Electronic School Calendar

A labor saving use of the microcomputer for the principal or school superintendent is the creation of an electronic school calendar. Field trips, plays, guest speakers, athletic events, exams, reporting periods, and social events can be entered and updated using a microcomputer. These activities are always subject to change and rescheduling so it is a real convenience to be able to immediately access this information and make the necessary changes in a master file.

Probably administrators will find that there is sufficient benefit to be gained from this single application to warrant purchasing a microcomputer for the principal's or superintendent's office. If a printer is available, updated calendars can be produced and distributed to staff and students with ease. The availability of a system of this type encourages flexibility in school programming. Often what appears as administrative rigidity is only a reaction to the clerical difficulties entailed in making adjustments after scheduling has been completed. Electronic scheduling, we should add, can help "smooth" the distribution of events and activities over the semester or school year, avoiding "yo-yo scheduling" where people in an organization are bounced back and forth between boredom and hysteria.

TESTING

Microcomputers have been used to generate teacher-made tests which can be printed out or administered by the computer, one student at a time. For students taking tests directly on the computer, scores are calculated and stored for later reporting. Printed tests can use mark sense cards for answer sheets. This allows a card-reader to enter item responses into the microcomputer for scoring and reporting. Most standardized tests would be amenable to this process if the test makers so desired. Security of the tests and grade files could be a problem but no more than exists with manual testing systems.

The National Institute of Education has recently taken the position that the improvement of classroom testing is fundamental to the achievement of better quality education. Toward this end, the National Institute of Education asked research and development professionals to propose methods of creating improved classroom tests using the Apple microcomputer.

TEACHER SALARY SIMULATIONS

What would be the effect of a ten percent across the board increase in teachers' salaries and a 35 cent per hour raise in paraprofessional pay on the local tax rate? Before microcomputers became available, considerable thought and energy had to be devoted to answering that kind of question. Schools are complex financial organizations and any change in expenditures for major items such as salaries have implications for all other budget line items.

Salary negotiations represent an attempt to find a compensation package that is equitable to both teachers and the school district. To find an optimum solution, it is wise to explore the full financial implications of a large number of possible solutions. The more alternatives that are explored, the more likely it is that an acceptable solution will be found without serious labor conflict or strikes.

With access to a microcomputer and some programming support, a school district can generate simulations or projections of the effects of various compensation plans on district finances. Teacher organizations can engage in similar analyses. The advantage of this approach is that it provides data to talk about; data being an affectively neutral object of discourse.

LOCATING AIDES AND SUBSTITUTES

Finding a substitute teacher, often at the last minute, can be very difficult if you are concerned with selecting the best possible teacher for a particular assignment. The subject to be taught, the teacher's credentials, and the location of the substitute's residence relative to the vacancy must be considered. Finding substitute teachers is an activity that occurs every day and the information that is manipulated undergoes constant revision.

Loomis and Sucher (1972) reported that for the City of Detroit, introducing computer procedures for locating substitutes saved $2,000 per month. That was ten years ago and they were using large, expensive hardware.

Implementing a computer-based substitute teacher system is simple. A master list is compiled that includes the teacher's identification, address, subjects of specialization, certificates, and teacher-specified restrictions such as school locations, grade level, or assignment duration. Requests for substitutes are matched by computer with this file and names and telephone numbers are outputted. If one wants to be sure that time and money isn't wasted on telephone calls, substitutes may be required to call in each evening to activate their status for the coming day. That insures that all substitutes in the master file will be available.

Teacher aides and volunteers can be located in the same manner...through the creation of a microcomputer directory. Robbinsdale, Minnesota, has developed an "Aides Directory" for the PET and is quite pleased with this tool.

OPTIMAL BUS ROUTES

In these days of escalating fuel costs, buses cost school districts more than anything except teacher salaries. In order to hold fuel costs and the number of buses required to an absolute minimum, computer assisted schoolbus routing is desirable. Microcomputers have been used for this purpose. Measured distances between all possible pairs of bus stops and the number of students transported to and from each stop are entered into a program. The microcomputer constructs several alternative routes based on efficiency, time constraints, and the number of buses required. Administrators make the final selection from among these optimal routes.

Alspaugh (1981) described an approach to creating optimal bus routes using the Apple II (48 K) and one disk drive. Larger districts could use multiple drives. Alspaugh's approach was as follows:

The actual computations performed in the route construction process are numerous and complex. The general procedure is as follows:
1. As a starting point, assume that each stop represents a separate route.
2. Search all of the available inter-stop connectors to find which two stops may be joined to form a route with two stops that will save the most distance traveled.
3. Keep a running total on the number of stops, the number of students, and the length of the route.
4. If the route is too long then go to step 7, or else, if the bus is loaded then go to step 8.
5. Find the stop that may be added to either end of the route and save the maximum traveled distance. Add it to the route.
6. Go to step 3.
7. Add stops to the route that are between school and the first stop on the route, and between the last stop on the route and school until the bus is full.
8. Record the route and go to step 2. Continue until all stops have been assigned. (Alspaugh, 1981)

DERIVING MEANING FROM INFORMATION

School administrators often lack sufficient training in the interpretation of quantitative information, especially masses of it presented in statistical tables. It has been noted that an overabundance of data, in undigested form, can paralyze the planning process. And in many larger schools districts, the large high-speed computers have produced data at a dizzying rate exceeding the administrators ability to understand and use it. Sometimes, administrators just ignore data and go ahead with seat-of-the-pants decisions.

Displays in the form of graphs, charts, and maps can enhance the administrator's ability to interpret data, however. In a sense, a picture is worth a thousand pages. Joiner (1979) described computer mapping procedures and an application in southern Illinois where computer maps were used to portray levels of service in five counties to severely handicapped children. Carter (1979) and Ungar (1979) have described thematic mapping and polygon graphics using low-resolution color video terminals. The consensus is that computer graphics help administrators understand data. Alterman (1979) reports that, "businesses currently using computer graphics anticipate increased use of the tool, both in analysis and summation. And they forsee a snowballing trend toward further development in this area."

VisiCalc

Personal Software, Sunnyvale, California, has marketed software which is to numbers what word processing is to words. People who have an aversion to numbers may begin to undergo a change in attitude once they begin experimenting with these programs. Three programs, VisiCalc, VisiTrend, and VisiPlot, put tremendous analytic and graphic capabilities in the hands of any school administrator with access to a microcomputer.

The software performs: 1) quantitative analyses, budget projections, cash flow projections, and simulated outcomes in response to "what if" questions; 2) statistical analyses of trend, forecasting, and linear regression; 3) graphs and charts of statistical summaries, both on the video display and on a printer. About 254 rows and 63 columns of data can be analyzed using VisiCalc.

REPORTING

Reporting involves the periodic bringing together of information that is transmitted from the school to the home or community. Administrators are responsible for the preparation of reports and the accuracy of the data contained in them, spending many hours preparing them. Attendance, grades, school lunch, and overall financial conditions are the major kinds of reports that now can be streamlined by microcomputer.

Attendance

Attendance is important to schools not only because it is desirable to have children attend school as required by law and common sense but also, state funding levels are affected by attendance rates. The key to improved attendance is follow-up by an attendance officer as early as possible in the day. Unfortunately, reducing the attendance officer's hours is sometimes used as a cost-cutting device and this produces pressure on the position.

Despite these pressures, attendance can be improved and reporting streamlined by taking advantage of the capabilities of microcomputers. In a computer based system, teachers' daily absence reports are collected, entered into the microcomputer by clerical staff when received, and a menu of reports is available to the attendance officer or other user. Reports required by the state can also be generated automatically.

The following are sample output from Ortonville's microcomputer attendance program:

Prompting

Ortonville Elementary
Attendance

1. Create attendance file.
2. Alphabetical listings.
3. Attendance recording.
4. Corrections.
5. Add new names.
6. Tallies.
7. Data on individual students.

Enter your selection? 2
.One moment please.

Ortonville Elementary
Attendance

1. Alphabetical list of all students.

2. Alphabetic list of students by grade.

3. Alphabetical list of specific grades(s).

4. Alphabetical list of students by homeroom.

5. Alphabetical list of specific homeroom(s).

6. Return to menu.

Enter your selection? 5

List how many homerooms? 2
Enter the homeroom numbers
1? 26P

2? 24

Sample Listing of Homerooms

STUDENT	HMRM	ABSENCE	TARDY	CONSECUTIVE	SEX
A******* D****	26P	0	0	0	M
A******* R****	26P	0	0	0	M
B****** C*****	26P	0	0	0	F
B**** J*******	26P	0	0	0	F
B****** K*******	26P	0	0	0	F
C****** J*******	26P	0	0	0	F
C********** T****	26P	0	0	0	F
H*** C***	26P	26	0	1	M

Menu

Ortonville Elementary

Attendance

1. Create attendance file.
2. Alphabetical listings.
3. Attendance recording.
4. Corrections.
5. Add new names.
6. Tallies.
7. Data on individual students.

Prompting

Enter your selection? 3
    .One moment please.
Date? (DD/ MM/ YY) 11/ 01/ 1980
Announcements? (yes or no)? yes
Reminder: no more than 80 typing characters per line.

(2 lines on the screen = 80 characters)
When finished press CR.

Entry

?1. There will be play practice tomorrow at 8 o'clock in Room 310.
?
?2. Triple trio will practice at noon today.
?
?3. There will be no band lessons today.
?
?4. Boys Phy-ed will meet in Room 208 today.
?

After each ? type data for each absentee or an announcement
Example: Hogan Orky, 4

(Numeral after student name represents consecutive days absent)

When finished type DONE,1

Output

11/ 01/ 1980

Announcements

1. There will be play practice tomorrow at 8 o'clock in Room 310.

2. Triple Trio will practice at noon today.

3. There will be no band lessons today.

4. Boys Phy-ed will meet in Room 310 today.

Attendance

6	5	4
	Plomma Bunchan	Wachter Laurel
	Roder Laverne	

3	2	1
Beachem Beth	Backstrand Craig	Peteler Gregory
Hills Tracy	Biel Charles	Raaf Melinda
Klages James	Anderson Dale	Lobbins Deanna
	Miller Jody	
	Schaffer Greg	

0

Appledorn Ralph
Block Jennifer
Dahle June
Hage Chad
Keipel Heather

Grade Tally of Specific Homeroom

Grade 1 tally as of 11/ 01/ 80

Females 22
Males   21
Total enrollment is: 43
Total absence is: 81
Total tardiness is: 0
Average absence/ student is: 1.88
Average tardies/ student is: 0

Other Available Tallies

1. Tally of entire school.

2. Tally of all grades.

3. Tally of specific grades.

4. Tally of all homerooms.

5. Tally of specific homerooms.

Attendance Record for Individual Student

Enter name? Prior Deanna

Name: Prior Deanna

HMRM: 180

Absence: 0

Tardy: 0

Sex: F

Grade: 3

Enter name ? done

Full Student Status and Attendance Report for Homeroom

TALLY FOR HOMEROOM 26P

Enrollment:	
Students enrolled	29
Boys enrolled	9
Girls enrolled	20
Transportation:	
Students transported	20
Students nontransported	9
Residence:	
Resident students	29
Nonresident students	0
Status:	
Original entries	28
Re-entries	0
Withdrawals	1

Attendance:
Tardies		1.0
Avg./ student		0.0
Days present		812.0
Avg./ student		97.0
Days absent		66.0
Avg./ student		2.3
Days absent quarter		22.5
Avg./ student		0.8
Days withdrawn		28.0
Avg./ student		1.0
Days membership		878.0
Avg./ student		99.2

Report Cards

Report cards can be printed out under computer control once the grades have been entered into the microcomputer. Programs are available that calculate grades from raw scores and save the data for later report card printing. These electronic gradebooks reduce preparation time and have various methods of maintaining security on the files, such as requiring a correct password to gain access to the records.

School Lunch Reports

To meet federal requirements, all schools must conform to lunchroom reporting standards. At Ortonville, students go through the lunch line with cards having their identification in the bar code used in supermarkets. The cashier uses a wand connected to a microcomputer to read the student identification and then enters the cost of the lunch through the keyboard. Data stored on the floppy disks is later read by the computer to generate the printout of all needed reports.

Financial Reports

Schools engage in multiple financial transactions, and as a consequence must create many different types of financial reports. Microcomputer software to support financial management and reporting is available both commercially and from schools such as Ortonville where microcomputer development is being undertaken. Ortonville's microcomputer programs produce the following types of reports:
• General Ledger
• Accounts Receivable / Payable
• Purchase Orders
• Payroll, Check Printing and W-2's
• Monthly Budget Reports
• Voucher and Bill lists
• Voucher Jackets

Figure 4 portrays the administrative data processing cycle that governs the production of financial reports. Reports that are submitted monthly to the school board, by the superintendent, can be prepared in less than 30 minutes.

As far as savings are concerned, two full-time clerical staff were reduced to a single 4½ day per week position. At an average pay rate of $5 / hr., this amounts to a savings of $220 / week or about $8,000 for a 36 week academic school year. In this case, reduction in the work week for the two staff members involved was voluntary, but worker layoffs due to automation will be a definite problem in many schools. Ortonville found other work, principally teaching support, for the office staff to handle as the load was reduced in any given area.

ADMINISTRATIVE DATA PROCESSING CYCLE

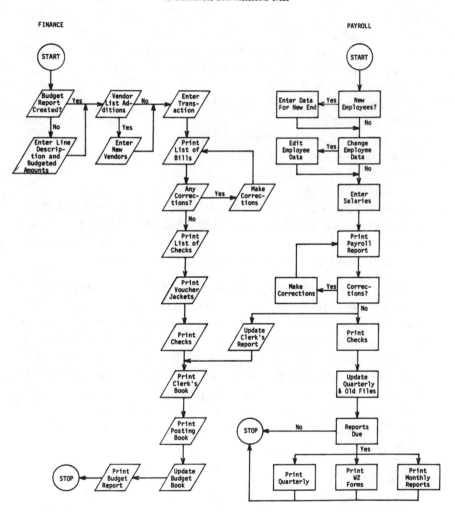

Figure 4

Examples Of Microcomputer Financial Reports

The following are portions of the various financial reports created by microcomputer.

INDEPENDENT SCHOOL DISTRICT #00
SAMPLEVILLE COLORADO
EXPENDITURE GUIDELINE REPORT AS OF 01/31/82

PAGE 1

LINE #	ACCOUNT CODE	DESCRIPTION	ADOPTED BUDGET	REVISED BUDGET	EXPENDITURES TO DATE	BALANCE
GENERAL FUND						
000 DISTRICT AND SCHOOL ADMINISTRATION						
003	01 005 000 000 000 316	DP SER MECC/MIS	2000.00	2000.00	0.00	2000.00
001	01 005 000 000 000 821	REG MBRSHP DU	400.00	400.00	0.00	400.00
002	01 005 000 000 000 822	REGIONAL FEES	6300.00	6300.00	0.00	6300.00
008	01 005 010 000 000 310	SCH BD PER DIEM	2400.00	2400.00	2375.00	25.00
007	01 005 010 000 000 311	CON LEG SER	4000.00	4000.00	7.50	3992.50
005	01 005 010 000 000 366	SCH BRD TRAV	1000.00	1000.00	175.61	824.39
004	01 005 010 000 000 381	CON PR - PUB	2000.00	2000.00	747.85	1252.15
006	01 005 010 000 000 899	OTH SCH B EX	1500.00	1500.00	4567.52	-3067.52
010	01 005 020 000 000 110	SAL SUPT	31200.00	31200.00	7834.67	23365.33
011	01 005 020 000 000 366	TRAV-SUPT	2000.00	2000.00	290.92	1709.08
009	01 005 020 000 000 899	MIS EX SUPT OF	1000.00	1000.00	2579.47	-1579.47
016	01 100 050 000 000 110	EL PRIN SAL	25300.00	25300.00	4683.32	20616.68
015	01 100 050 000 401 110	EL PRIN SAL T1	2800.00	2800.00	0.00	2800.00
014	01 300 050 000 000 110	SEC PRIN SAL	52000.00	52000.00	8600.41	43399.59
013	01 100 050 000 000 366	TRAV-EL ADM	200.00	200.00	49.83	150.17
012	01 300 050 000 000 366	TRAV/SEC ADM	400.00	400.00	22.65	377.35
*** TOTAL DISTRICT AND SCHOOL ADMINISTRATION			134500.00	134500.00	31934.75	102565.25
100 DISTRICT SUPPORT SERVICES						
019	01 005 110 000 000 170	NEX SAL BUS OFF	17400.00	17400.00	7584.07	9815.93
018	01 005 110 000 401 170	NEX SAL T1	3000.00	3000.00	235.74	2764.26
020	01 005 110 000 000 401	BUS OF SUPPL	7000.00	7000.00	5254.82	1745.18
021	01 005 140 000 000 316	CON SER D P	2000.00	2000.00	0.00	2000.00
022	01 005 140 000 330 899	CQE	43000.00	43000.00	28357.78	14642.22
023	01 005 199 000 000 899	SCH ELEC EXP	250.00	250.00	38.80	211.20
*** TOTAL DISTRICT SUPPORT SERVICES			72650.00	72650.00	41471.21	31178.79
200 REGULAR INSTRUCTION						
025	01 100 201 132 000 140	SUB KG TCHR SAL	100.00	100.00	0.00	100.00
024	01 005 201 000 000 140	KGT TCHR SAL	16000.00	16000.00	2564.66	13435.34
032	01 005 203 000 000 140	SUB EL TCHR SAL	4000.00	4000.00	1066.20	2933.80
028	01 100 203 000 000 140	EL TCHR SAL	290000.00	290000.00	45323.16	244676.84
031	01 100 203 000 000 141	TCHR AID SAL EL	3000.00	3000.00	108.75	2891.25
027	01 200 203 000 000 311	CON PRO-TEC SER	1000.00	1000.00	0.00	1000.00
029	01 100 203 000 401 430	INST SUP T1	2000.00	2000.00	0.00	2000.00
026	01 200 203 000 000 430	INST SUP	12000.00	12000.00	9407.96	2592.04
030	01 100 203 000 000 460	EL TXT - WKBK	10000.00	10000.00	12200.94	-2200.94
036	01 300 211 000 000 140	SEC TCHR SAL	400000.00	400000.00	65327.84	334672.16
033	01 005 211 000 000 140	SUB SEC TCR SAL	6000.00	6000.00	50.00	5950.00
035	01 300 211 000 000 141	TCH AID SAL SEC	6700.00	6700.00	1943.09	4756.91
066	01 300 211 000 000 460	SEC TXT/WKBK	8000.00	8000.00	3107.92	4892.08
034	01 300 211 000 382 899	CETA	20000.00	20000.00	5087.66	14912.34

INDEPENDENT SCHOOL DISTRICT #00
SAMPLEVILLE COLORADO
REVENUE GUIDELINE REPORT AS OF 01/31/82

LINE #	ACCOUNT CODE	DESCRIPTION	ADOPTED REVENUE BUDGET	REVISED REVENUE BUDGET	REVENUE TO DATE MONTH	REVENUE TO DATE YEAR	REVENUE BUDGET RECEIVABLE

GENERAL FUND

DISTRICT AND SCHOOL ADMINISTRATION

LINE #	ACCOUNT CODE	DESCRIPTION	ADOPTED REVENUE BUDGET	REVISED REVENUE BUDGET	MONTH	YEAR	RECEIVABLE
001	01 005 000 000 000 001	LOCAL LEVIES	350000.00	350000.00	0.00	0.00	350000.00
002	01 005 000 000 000 005	UNEMP LVY	0.00	0.00	0.00	0.00	0.00
003	01 005 000 000 000 010	CNTY APPORT	15000.00	15000.00	0.00	0.00	15000.00
004	01 005 000 000 000 012	TX FFT SALES	0.00	0.00	0.00	0.00	0.00
005	01 005 000 000 000 019	MIS LOCAL TX	0.00	0.00	0.00	0.00	0.00
016	01 005 000 000 000 035	O/S NON-SCH REV	0.00	0.00	0.00	0.00	0.00
017	01 005 000 000 000 040	TUIT FM PAT	0.00	0.00	0.00	0.00	0.00
018	01 005 000 000 000 050	FEES FM PAT	0.00	0.00	0.00	0.00	0.00
024	01 005 000 000 000 092	INTST INC	40000.00	40000.00	12061.58	14697.57	25302.43
025	01 005 000 000 000 093	RNT FM SCH FAC	200.00	200.00	10.00	10.00	190.00
026	01 005 000 000 000 094	RNT FM OTH PROP	0.00	0.00	0.00	381.00	-381.00
027	01 005 000 000 000 096	GFTS & BEQ	0.00	0.00	0.00	50.00	-50.00
028	01 005 000 000 000 098	UNCLTBL TAX	0.00	0.00	0.00	0.00	0.00
029	01 005 000 000 000 099	MS REV FM LOC S	0.00	0.00	850.29	2427.38	-2427.38
031	01 005 000 000 000 201	ENDOWMENT	20000.00	20000.00	0.00	0.00	20000.00
032	01 005 000 000 000 211	FNDTN AID	800000.00	800000.00	0.00	165803.90	634196.10
033	01 005 000 000 000 220	ST SCH AG CRDT	50000.00	50000.00	0.00	11998.44	38001.56
034	01 005 000 000 000 241	EMGY AID	0.00	0.00	0.00	0.00	0.00
035	01 005 000 000 000 249	OTH GEN AID-STA	5000.00	5000.00	0.00	858.31	4141.69
036	01 005 000 000 000 251	ATTCH MACHNY	0.00	0.00	0.00	0.00	0.00
037	01 005 000 000 000 253	HMST CRDT-R.P.	60000.00	60000.00	0.00	0.00	60000.00
038	01 005 000 000 330 300	CQE	43000.00	43000.00	1749.35	14624.57	28375.43
043	01 005 000 000 465 382	CETA TRNG AGTS	0.00	0.00	0.00	1298.49	-1298.49
042	01 005 000 000 464 382	CETA YETP	0.00	0.00	1500.00	2052.73	-2052.73
041	01 005 000 000 382 382	CETA	2470.00	2470.00	3000.00	6121.00	-3651.00
051	01 005 000 000 817 400	TRD & INDSTRL	4000.00	4000.00	0.00	0.00	4000.00
050	01 005 000 000 814 400	BUS OFF	5000.00	5000.00	0.00	0.00	5000.00
049	01 005 000 000 809 400	CON HMKNG	5000.00	5000.00	0.00	0.00	5000.00
048	01 005 000 000 804 400	DIST ED	8000.00	8000.00	0.00	0.00	8000.00
047	01 005 000 000 801 400	VOC AG	9000.00	9000.00	0.00	0.00	9000.00
046	01 005 000 000 410 400	ESEA PL 89-21	2500.00	2500.00	0.00	0.00	2500.00
045	01 005 000 000 401 400	ESEA PL 89-10	50000.00	50000.00	0.00	6091.00	43909.00
044	01 005 000 000 000 400	OT FED AID WTLD	0.00	0.00	0.00	0.00	0.00
052	01 005 000 000 570 500	GFTD & TAL	800.00	800.00	0.00	0.00	800.00
053	01 005 000 000 000 621	SALE OF MAT	4000.00	4000.00	158.28	539.28	3460.72
054	01 005 000 000 000 622	N-TXBL SALES	200.00	200.00	0.00	228.14	-28.14
055	01 005 000 000 000 623	SALE-REAL PROP	1700.00	1700.00	0.00	0.00	1700.00
056	01 005 000 000 000 624	SALE-EQUIP	1000.00	1000.00	0.00	0.00	1000.00
057	01 005 000 000 000 649	TRANS-OTH FND	0.00	0.00	0.00	0.00	0.00

TOTAL DISTRICT AND SCHOOL ADMINISTRATION   1476870.00   1476870.00   19329.50   227181.81   1249688.19

REGULAR INSTRUCTION

LINE #	ACCOUNT CODE	DESCRIPTION	ADOPTED REVENUE BUDGET	REVISED REVENUE BUDGET	MONTH	YEAR	RECEIVABLE
11	01 005 211 000 000 031	SEC TUIT O/S	120000.00	120000.00	0.00	36964.18	83035.82
19	01 300 249 000 000 050	DR ED FEE	0.00	0.00	0.00	45.00	-45.00

#	NAME	SALARY	OTH SAL	FED TAX	ST TAX	SOC SEC	TRA/PERA	HLTH IN	TSA#1	TSA#2	DUES	OTH DD	TOT DD	NET
1	MCMAHON MARY	3403.95	0.00	684.08	237.65	226.36	153.18	0.00	126.77	0.00	0.00	0.00	1428.04	1975.91
		28778.85	0.00	5469.72	1980.93	1913.76	1295.04	0.00	1140.93	0.00	0.00	0.00	11800.38	16978.47
2	OLSON TOM	2341.74	0.00	322.71	124.58	155.73	105.38	0.00	480.00	0.00	0.00	0.00	1188.40	1153.34
		21075.10	1229.20	3749.17	1434.15	1483.24	1003.66	0.00	1760.00	0.00	0.00	0.00	9430.22	12874.08
3	JACKSON DEBBIE	2171.50	0.00	387.63	150.01	0.00	184.58	0.00	0.00	0.00	0.00	0.00	722.22	1449.28
		19543.50	0.00	3488.67	1350.09	0.00	1661.22	0.00	0.00	0.00	0.00	0.00	6499.98	13043.52
4	OLESEN BETTY	2671.62	0.00	355.82	145.47	0.00	227.09	0.00	160.00	365.00	0.00	300.00	1553.38	1118.24
		24044.30	127.50	3009.63	1252.79	0.00	2054.58	0.00	1440.00	4005.00	0.00	1500.00	13262.00	10909.80
5	OLSEN DICK	610.29	0.00	63.35	25.26	40.58	27.46	0.00	0.00	0.00	0.00	0.00	156.65	453.64
		4930.97	0.00	471.44	190.70	327.94	221.87	0.00	0.00	0.00	77.70	0.00	1289.65	3641.32
6	OLSON ANN	838.75	0.00	104.47	41.92	55.78	37.74	0.00	0.00	0.00	0.00	0.00	239.91	598.84
		6776.75	34.00	803.65	321.50	452.92	306.46	0.00	0.00	0.00	100.10	0.00	1984.63	4826.12
7	BRENER DICK	1677.50	0.00	280.46	107.36	111.55	75.49	0.00	50.00	0.00	0.00	0.00	624.86	1052.64
		13853.50	51.00	2220.33	861.87	924.64	625.70	0.00	450.00	0.00	100.10	0.00	5182.64	8721.86
8	SEVERENSON SCOTT	1679.67	0.00	352.66	99.63	111.70	75.59	0.00	0.00	0.00	0.00	0.00	639.58	1040.09
		13411.03	42.30	2612.78	768.13	874.67	605.42	0.00	0.00	0.00	131.60	95.68	5108.30	8345.23
9	BUSHMACK HARRY	1735.42	0.00	304.25	97.18	115.41	78.09	0.00	15.00	16.46	0.00	0.00	626.39	1109.03
		14021.42	0.00	1822.57	796.06	932.45	630.97	110.40	135.00	148.14	100.10	0.00	4675.69	9345.73
10	PEDERSON MARK	1030.17	0.00	142.60	56.61	68.51	46.36	0.00	0.00	0.00	0.00	0.00	314.08	716.09
		8323.53	603.79	1329.72	459.41	593.70	401.69	0.00	0.00	0.00	131.60	0.00	2916.12	6011.20
11	JOHNSON BETTY	1365.25	0.00	216.42	84.52	90.79	61.44	0.00	0.00	0.00	0.00	0.00	453.17	912.08
		11030.61	0.00	1656.20	653.81	733.52	496.40	0.00	0.00	0.00	131.60	23.92	3695.45	7335.16
12	JACKSON DICK	1189.33	0.00	158.52	66.02	79.09	53.52	0.00	0.00	0.00	0.00	0.00	357.15	832.18
		5067.34	760.00	453.39	222.25	387.55	262.20	0.00	0.00	0.00	77.70	0.00	1403.09	4424.25
13	JOHNSON ANN	1393.50	0.00	192.00	75.65	92.67	62.71	0.00	130.00	0.00	0.00	9.61	562.64	830.86
		11078.86	0.00	1417.58	561.94	736.78	498.54	0.00	1170.00	0.00	131.60	86.49	4602.93	6475.93
14	POINTER JIM	1393.50	0.00	223.20	87.00	92.67	62.71	0.00	0.00	0.00	0.00	0.00	465.58	927.92
		11258.86	17.00	1706.17	673.87	749.88	507.40	0.00	0.00	0.00	131.60	0.00	3768.92	7506.94
15	BRENER JOHN	1219.08	0.00	147.27	64.84	81.07	54.86	0.00	0.00	0.00	0.00	0.00	348.04	871.04
		9849.76	42.50	1092.80	494.85	657.82	445.17	0.00	0.00	0.00	131.60	0.00	2822.24	7070.02
16	OLSON SCOTT	1677.50	0.00	231.36	89.97	111.55	75.49	0.00	250.00	0.00	0.00	0.00	758.37	919.13
		13553.50	0.00	1715.36	676.53	901.31	609.89	116.26	2250.00	0.00	100.10	0.00	6369.45	7184.05
17	BUSHMACK MATT	1393.50	0.00	216.00	84.37	92.67	62.71	0.00	30.00	0.00	0.00	0.00	485.75	907.75
		11222.86	0.00	1639.82	647.44	746.35	505.02	116.26	270.00	0.00	131.60	0.00	4056.49	7166.37
18	SEXXE BETTY	1365.25	0.00	216.42	84.52	90.79	61.44	0.00	0.00	0.00	0.00	0.00	453.17	912.08
		11030.61	136.00	1665.71	663.32	742.57	502.52	116.26	0.00	0.00	131.60	0.00	3821.98	7344.63

```
                              INDEPENDENT SCHOOL DISTRICT #00
                                   SAMPLEVILLE COLORADO
                                  CASH RECEIPTS JOURNAL                                        CR01
-------------------------------------------------------------------------------------------------------------
D                      ORDER        ACCOUNT      TOTAL                              FUNDS
A                   ------------------------------ ALL ----------------------------------------------------
T   1982 JAN         NUM    CODE  CLASSIFICATION  FUNDS  1 GEN  2 FOOD  3 PUPIL 4 COMM 5 CAP  6 BLDG  7 DEBT
E                                                               SERV    TRANS   SERV   OUT    CONS    SERV
-------------------------------------------------------------------------------------------------------------
RECEIVED FROM                       BR FWD>>>>  722612.42        13319.47        1928.43         0.00   705.4
                                                         625155.72        54185.89      12158.88      15158.62
-------------------------------------------------------------------------------------------------------------
01 BEN   KI ELMO       856                      193.80
      02 005 770 000 701 601   SALE OF FOOD .                   179.96
      02 005 770 000 000 606   FD SLS ADULT .                    13.84
02 BEN   KI ELMO       857                      107.20
      02 005 770 000 701 601   SALE OF FOOD .                    96.58
      02 005 770 000 000 606   FD SLS ADULT .                    10.62
03 BEN   KI ELMO       858                      332.66
      02 005 770 000 701 601   SALE OF FOOD .                   261.16
      02 005 770 000 000 606   FD SLS ADULT .                    71.50
03 ZAH                 859                       64.85
      02 005 770 000 701 601   SALE OF FOOD .                    48.60
      02 005 770 000 000 606   FD SLS ADULT .                    16.25
03 BEN   KI ELMO       860                      176.60
      02 005 770 000 701 601   SALE OF FOOD .                   162.85
      02 005 770 000 000 606   FD SLS ADULT .                    13.75
06 BEN   KI ELMO       861                      668.75
      02 005 770 000 701 601   SALE OF FOOD .                   603.74
      02 005 770 000 000 606   FD SLS ADULT .                    65.01
06 ZAH                 862                        9.60
      02 005 770 000 701 601   SALE OF FOOD .                     9.60
07 PUB                 863                       48.75
      01 300 296 000 000 060   GRLS ATH AD SEC GRLS VB    48.75
07 PUB                 864                      733.00
      04 500 505 000 000 040   COM ED TUIT COMPUTER                             81.00
      04 500 505 000 000 040   COM ED TUIT FOODS                                42.00
      04 500 505 000 000 040   COM ED TUIT CALLIG                               64.00
      04 500 505 000 000 040   COM ED TUIT MACRAME                              82.00
      04 500 505 000 000 040   COM ED TUIT MICROWAVE                            36.00
      04 500 505 000 000 040   COM ED TUIT ROSEMALING                           18.00
      04 500 505 000 000 040   COM ED TUIT FIREARMS                              2.00
      04 500 505 000 000 040   COM ED TUIT AEROBICS                            408.00
07 STU                 865                       21.50
      03 005 760 000 000 050   ABTMT & OTH REV APPLETON FB          21.50
07 ZAH                 866                       95.20
      02 005 770 000 701 601   SALE OF FOOD .                    95.20
07 BEN   KI ELMO       867                      230.60
      02 005 770 000 701 601   SALE OF FOOD .                   221.73
      02 005 770 000 000 606   FD SLS ADULT .                     8.87
08 BEN   KI ELMO       868                       73.95
      02 005 770 000 701 601   SALE OF FOOD .                    45.45
      02 005 770 000 000 606   FD SLS ADULT .                    28.50
09 BEN   KI ELMO       869                      100.00
      02 005 770 000 701 601   SALE OF FOOD .                    90.53
      02 005 770 000 000 606   FD SLS ADULT .                     9.47
10 BEN   KI ELMO       870                      125.45
      02 005 770 000 701 601   SALE OF FOOD .                    93.10
      02 005 770 000 000 606   FD SLS ADULT .                    32.35
10 ZAH                 871                       66.65
      02 005 770 000 701 601   SALE OF FOOD .                    65.40
      02 005 770 000 000 606   FD SLS ADULT .                     1.25
```

```
                                    INDEPENDENT SCHOOL DISTRICT #00
                                         SAMPLEVILLE COLORADO
                                       CASH DISBURSEMENT JOURNAL                                          CD01
-----------------------------------------------------------------------------------------------------------------
DATE            ORDER         ACCOUNT      TOTAL                                    FUNDS
                                        -------- ALL -------------------------------------------------------------
1982    JAN 15   NUM     CODE  CLASSIFICATION  FUNDS  1 GEN    2 FOOD  3 PUPIL  4 COMM  5 CAP   6 BLDG  7 DEBT   9
                                                                SERV   TRANS    SERV    OUT     CONS    SERV
-----------------------------------------------------------------------------------------------------------------
PAYABLE TO                      BR FWD>>>>  532811.06          12252.30        11430.31         23.55  625.59
                                                      398856.70         46119.22        38545.89        24957.50
-----------------------------------------------------------------------------------------------------------------
ADM   XP FN           15529                 3539.99
      04 500 505 000 000 899   OTH CIV AC EX                                             73.75
      01 300 294 000 000 140   BOYS ATH SAL                    5.00
      01 300 296 219 000 899   GIRLS TRK                       5.00
      01 005 810 000 000 410   CUSTODIAL SUP                 258.62
      01 005 292 000 000 899   GEN ATHL                      447.17
      01 005 140 000 330 899   CQE                          1532.16
      01 300 294 212 000 899   BOYS CC                        42.00
      01 300 296 226 000 899   GIRLS CC                       42.00
      01 300 294 211 000 899   BOYS FTBLL                    502.00
      01 005 810 000 000 401   OTH SUP/PLNT OP                40.00
      01 300 296 230 000 899   GIRLS VBALL                   262.00
      C1 300 258 000 000 430   VOC MUS SUP                    24.99
      01 005 020 000 000 366   TRAV-SUPT                      93.15
      01 005 410 000 401 367   TRAV T1                       212.15
ADM   XP FN           15530                  749.47
      01 100 640 000 740 367   EL SP ED TRAV                 258.50
      01 200 415 000 359 430   GIFT - TAL                     30.00
      01 005 605 000 000 899   MIS INST EX                    67.00
      03 005 760 000 720 442   GAS - OIL                                      163.85
      01 005 810 193 000 899   MS EX EQ REPAIR                61.50
      01 005 960 000 000 870   ABTMT - FXD CHG                23.62
      01 300 341 000 814 430   MOD OFF SUP                    20.00
      01 300 331 000 809 430   HOME EC SUP                    75.00
      01 005 010 000 000 899   OTH SCH B EX                   50.00
ALD   APHIC SUPPL     15531                  447.13
      01 300 255 000 000 430   IND ART SUP                   447.13
ALL   BACON IN        15532                  868.32
      01 300 211 000 000 460   SEC TXT/WKBK                  868.32
AMB   MOTOR C         15533                  475.22
      03 005 810 000 720 370   RENT-PUP TRAN                          325.00
      03 005 760 000 720 420   VEHIC MAINT                            150.22
AME   N BINDER        15534                  294.27
      01 005 620 000 000 401   LIB SUP                       294.27
AME   N LINEN SUPP    15535                    5.04
      03 005 760 000 720 899   MS EX PT OP/MAI                         5.04
AMO   IL C            15536                  167.19
      01 200 258 000 000 430   INST MUS SUP                  167.19
APP   OMPUTER IN      15537                  150.38
      01 005 810 193 000 899   MS EX EQ REPAIR               150.38
AUC   TTER DRU        15538                   15.13
      01 200 490 000 749 430   SLBP SUPP                       4.74
      01 005 110 000 000 401   BUS OF SUPPL                    7.72
      02 005 770 000 701 401   LNCHRM SUP - EX                        2.67
AUG   G PUB HOUS      15539                    2.24
      01 300 258 000 000 430   VOC MUS SUP                     2.24
BAN   LIF             15540                 5047.64
      01 005 930 000 401 220   GRP HOSP T1                    75.32
      02 005 930 000 701 220   GRP HOSP                               71.36
      03 005 930 000 720 220   GRP HOSP                                       168.49
```

INDEPENDENT SCHOOL DISTRICT # 00
SAMPLEVILLE COLORADO
POSTING LEDGER (DISBURSEMENTS)

CODE	DESCRIPTION	VENDOR		AMOUNT	CHECK #
01 005 010 000 000 381	CON PR - PUB	ORT	LLE INDEPENDEN	321.13	15631
4 TOTAL***				321.13	
01 005 010 000 000 366	SCH BRD TRAV	CAR	HT ELAIN	28.90	15551
5 TOTAL***				28.90	
01 005 010 000 000 899	OTH SCH B EX	ADM	XP FN	50.00	15530
01 005 010 000 000 899	OTH SCH B EX	CAR	HT ELAIN	45.85	15551
01 005 010 000 000 899	OTH SCH B EX	PAY		307.00	----
6 TOTAL***				402.85	
01 005 010 000 000 311	CON LEG SER	PFL	R & KUN	7.50	15643
7 TOTAL***				7.50	
01 005 020 000 000 899	MIS EX SUPT OF	NAT	HOOL PUB RE	52.00	15620
01 005 020 000 000 899	MIS EX SUPT OF	NOR	N SCHL SU	6.92	15625
01 005 020 000 000 899	MIS EX SUPT OF	ORT	LLE INDEPENDEN	38.24	15631
01 005 020 000 000 899	MIS EX SUPT OF	PAM		1.33	15634
01 005 020 000 000 899	MIS EX SUPT OF	PET	ASH FUN	2.52	15642
01 005 020 000 000 899	MIS EX SUPT OF	ST	BK & STAT	203.49	15666
01 005 020 000 000 899	MIS EX SUPT OF	SUP	SCH SUPPLY C	69.77	15673
9 TOTAL***				374.27	
01 005 020 000 000 110	SAL SUPT	PAY		2599.38	----
10 TOTAL***				2599.38	
01 005 020 000 000 366	TRAV-SUPT	ADM	XP FN	93.15	15529
01 005 020 000 000 366	TRAV-SUPT	MOB	IL CRED COR	23.03	15616
11 TOTAL***				116.18	
01 300 050 000 000 366	TRAV/SEC ADM	TIE	ELF SERV IN	22.65	15678
12 TOTAL***				22.65	
01 300 050 000 000 110	SEC PRIN SAL	PAY		4300.20	----
14 TOTAL***				4300.20	
01 100 050 000 000 110	EL PRIN SAL	PAY		2341.66	----
16 TOTAL***				2341.66	
01 005 110 000 401 170	NEX SAL T1	PAY		235.74	----

```
                        INDEPENDENT SCHOOL DISTRICT # 00
                             SAMPLEVILLE COLORADO
                             LIST OF RECEIPTS
                              JANUARY 1982                        PAGE 1
```

DATE	VEN #		VENDOR	LINE #	DESCRIPTION	REC #	AMOUNT
01	343	BEN	KI ELNO	0071	SALE OF FOOD	856	179.96
01	343	BEN	KI ELNO	0072	FD SLS ADULT	856	13.84
02	343	BEN	KI ELNO	0071	SALE OF FOOD	857	96.58
02	343	BEN	KI ELNO	0072	FD SLS ADULT	857	10.62
03	343	BEN	KI ELNO	0071	SALE OF FOOD	858	261.16
03	343	BEN	KI ELNO	0072	FD SLS ADULT	858	71.50
03	024	ZAH		0071	SALE OF FOOD	859	48.60
03	024	ZAH		0072	FD SLS ADULT	859	16.25
03	343	BEN	KI ELNO	0071	SALE OF FOOD	860	162.85
03	343	BEN	KI ELNO	0072	FD SLS ADULT	860	13.75
06	343	BEN	KI ELNO	0071	SALE OF FOOD	861	603.74
06	343	BEN	KI ELNO	0072	FD SLS ADULT	861	65.01
06	024	ZAH		0071	SALE OF FOOD	862	9.60
07	005	PUB		0022	GRLS ATH AD SEC GRLS VB	863	48.75
07	005	PUB		0097	COM ED TUIT COMPUTER	864	81.00
07	005	PUB		0097	COM ED TUIT FOODS	864	42.00
07	005	PUB		0097	COM ED TUIT CALLIG	864	64.00
07	005	PUB		0097	COM ED TUIT MACRAME	864	82.00
07	005	PUB		0097	COM ED TUIT MICROWAVE	864	36.00
07	005	PUB		0097	COM ED TUIT ROSEMALING	864	18.00
07	005	PUB		0097	COM ED TUIT FIREARMS	864	2.00
07	005	PUB		0097	COM ED TUIT AEROBICS	864	408.00
07	006	STU		0082	ABTHT & OTH REV APPLETON FB	865	21.50
07	024	ZAH		0071	SALE OF FOOD	866	95.20
07	343	BEN	KI ELNO	0071	SALE OF FOOD	867	221.73
07	343	BEN	KI ELNO	0072	FD SLS ADULT	867	8.87
08	343	DEN	KI ELNO	0071	CALE OF FOOD	868	45.45
08	343	BEN	KI ELNO	0072	FD SLS ADULT	868	28.50
09	343	BEN	KI ELNO	0071	SALE OF FOOD	869	90.53
09	343	BEN	KI ELNO	0072	FD SLS ADULT	869	9.47
10	343	BEN	KI ELNO	0071	SALE OF FOOD	870	93.10
10	343	BEN	KI ELNO	0072	FD SLS ADULT	870	32.35
10	024	ZAH		0071	SALE OF FOOD	871	65.40
10	024	ZAH		0072	FD SLS ADULT	871	1.25
10	005	PUB		0021	BOYS ATH AD SEC FB CANBY	872	857.90
10	005	PUB		0097	COM ED TUIT AEROBICS	873	56.00
10	005	PUB		0097	COM ED TUIT ROSEMALING	873	131.00
10	005	PUB		0097	COM ED TUIT FOODS	873	4.50
10	005	PUB		0053	SALE OF MAT SM SALES	874	48.85
10	005	PUB		0G36	DUE TO OTH GVT UN SALES TAX	874	1.95
15	004	TRI	NTY ST BAN	0024	INTST INC CD #15711	875	4965.45
15	004	TRI	NTY ST BAN	00G4	INVESTMENTS CD #15711	875	70000.00
15	004	TRI	NTY ST BAN	0024	INTST INC CD #16001	875	7096.13
15	004	TRI	NTY ST BAN	00G4	INVESTMENTS CD #1601	875	253000.00
15	011	STA	F MIN	0040	SP ED AID 01S360M 1981	876	25737.07
15	343	BEN	KI ELNO	0071	SALE OF FOOD	877	353.14
15	343	BEN	KI ELNO	0072	FD SLS ADULT	877	17.01
15	024	ZAH		0071	SALE OF FOOD	878	49.00
15	024	ZAH		0072	FD SLS ADULT	878	2.50
15	343	BEN	KI ELNO	0071	SALE OF FOOD	879	100.87

```
                        INDEPENDENT SCHOOL DISTRICT # 00
                             SAMPLEVILLE COLORADO
                           POSTING LEDGER  (RECEIPTS)

CODE                    DESCRIPTION                 VENDOR          AMOUNT      RECEIPT #  DATE
--------------------------------------------------------------------------------------------------
01 300 294 000 000 060  BOYS ATH AD SEC FB CANBY    PUB             857.90        872      10
01 300 294 000 000 060  BOYS ATH AD SEC FB          TRA  UBLIC SCHOO   3.75       915      27

 21  TOTAL###                                                       861.65


01 300 296 000 000 060  GRLS ATH AD SEC GRLS VB     PUB              48.75        863      07
01 300 296 000 000 060  GRLS ATH AD SEC TRACY FB    PUB             380.55        894      20
01 300 296 000 000 060  GRLS ATH AD SEC GRLS VB DAWSON PUB           69.00        902      22
01 300 296 000 000 060  GRLS ATH AD SEC GRLS VB APPLE  PUB           87.00        918      27
01 300 296 000 000 060  GRLS ATH AD SEC GRLS VB MILAN  PUB          110.76        924      29

 22  TOTAL###                                                       696.06


01 005 000 000 000 092  INTST INC CD #15711         TRI  NTY ST BAN 4965.45       875      15
01 005 000 000 000 092  INTST INC CD #16001         TRI  NTY ST BAN 7096.13       875      15

 24  TOTAL###                                                      12061.58


01 005 000 000 000 093  RNT FM SCH FAC AUD RENT     FUL  SPEL BUSMAN  10.00       910      27

 25  TOTAL###                                                        10.00


01 005 000 000 000 099  MS REV FM LOC S JR GREAT BKS  STU           307.50        882      16
01 005 000 000 000 099  MS REV FM LOC S FLAG BOOTS    STU            15.00        884      16
01 005 000 000 000 099  MS REV FM LOC S REFUND        PIT  BOWE      46.24        885      16
01 005 000 000 000 099  MS REV FM LOC S REFUND        NAT  L WILDLIFE FE 9.95     886      16
01 005 000 000 000 099  MS REV FM LOC S HEALTH INS    FOR  EMPLOYEE  132.81       890      16
01 005 000 000 000 099  MS REV FM LOC S DWYER DAMAGE  AME  MILY IN    20.00       891      16
01 005 000 000 000 099  MS REV FM LOC S REFUND        ST   DISPATC    12.83       892      16
01 005 000 000 000 099  MS REV FM LOC S INST TR       SE   CS        152.31       901      22
01 005 000 000 000 099  MS REV FM LOC S PSAT          STU           123.75        904      22
01 005 000 000 000 099  MS REV FM LOC S JR GREAT BKS  PUB             7.50        911      27
01 005 000 000 000 099  MS REV FM LOC S LIB BK        PUB             5.20        914      27
01 005 000 000 000 099  MS REV FM LOC S JR GREAT BKS  PUB             7.50        922      29
01 005 000 000 000 099  MS REV FM LOC S COOP CR       AGR  E COO       9.70        923      29

 29  TOTAL###                                                       850.29


01 005 000 000 330 300  CDE MECC TR                 STA  F MIN       130.77        888      16
01 005 000 000 330 300  CDE ST FAIR REIMB           STA  F MIN      1618.58        927      30

 38  TOTAL###                                                      1749.35


01 005 420 000 000 360  SP ED AID 01S360M 1981      STA  F MIN     25737.07        876      15

 40  TOTAL###                                                     25737.07


01 005 000 000 382 382  CETA COMP PR                PRA  5 C.A.C    3000.00        896      20

 41  TOTAL###                                                      3000.00
```

INDEPENDENT SCHOOL DISTRICT # 00
SAMPLEVILLE COLORADO
DETAILED GENERAL LEDGER

PAGE 1

LINE #	ACCOUNT		DESCRIPTION	BEGINNING			PRESENT
TYPE	JOURNAL	REF #	VENDOR / DESCRIPTION	BALANCE	DEBIT	CREDIT	BALANCE
001	01-101.00		CASH				
			BEGINNING	-393531.70	625278.72	398856.70	-167109.68
R	CR10	863	PUBLIC		48.75		
R	CR10	872	PUBLIC		857.90		
R	CR10	874	PUBLIC		48.85		
R	CR10	874	PUBLIC		1.95		
R	CR10	875	TRI-COUNTY ST BANK		7096.13		
R	CR10	875	TRI-COUNTY ST BANK		70000.00		
R	CR10	875	TRI-COUNTY ST BANK		4965.45		
R	CR10	875	TRI-COUNTY ST BANK		253000.00		
R	CR10	876	STATE OF MINN		25737.07		
R	CR10	882	STUDENTS		307.50		
R	CR10	884	STUDENTS		15.00		
R	CR10	885	PITNEY BOWES		46.24		
R	CR10	886	NATIONAL WILDLIFE FED		9.95		
R	CR10	888	STATE OF MINN		130.77		
R	CR10	890	FORMER EMPLOYEES		132.81		
R	CR10	891	AMER FAMILY INS		20.00		
R	CR10	892	ST PAUL DISPATCH		12.83		
R	CR10	893	STUDENTS		3.59		
R	CR10	893	STUDENTS		89.72		
R	CR10	894	PUBLIC		380.55		
R	CR10	896	PRARIE 5 C.A.C.		3000.00		
R	CR10	896	PRARIE 5 C.A.C.		1500.00		
R	CR10	901	SE MN ECSU		152.31		
R	CR10	902	PUBLIC		69.00		
R	CR10	904	STUDENTS		123.75		
R	CR10	909	STUDENTS		19.71		
R	CR10	909	STUDENTS		0.79		
R	CR10	910	FULL GOSPEL BUSMANS		10.00		
R	CR10	911	PUBLIC		7.50		
R	CR10	914	PUBLIC		5.20		
R	CR10	915	TRACY PUBLIC SCHOOL		3.75		
R	CR10	918	PUBLIC		87.00		
R	CR10	922	PUBLIC		7.50		
R	CR10	923	AGRALITE COOP		9.70		
R	CR10	924	PUBLIC		110.76		
R	CR10	927	STATE OF MINN		1618.58		
J	GJ10	----	101380 TRANS GEN -> FS			76840.37	
D	CD10	----	PAYROLL			4300.20	
D	CD10	----	PAYROLL			1121.66	
D	CD10	----	PAYROLL			3428.80	
D	CD10	----	PAYROLL			1077.83	
D	CD10	----	PAYROLL			115.00	
D	CD10	----	PAYROLL			52.50	
D	CD10	----	PAYROLL			307.00	
D	CD10	----	PAYROLL			2599.38	
D	CD10	----	PAYROLL			165.00	
D	CD10	----	PAYROLL			5704.63	
D	CD10	----	PAYROLL			258.00	

INDEPENDENT SCHOOL DISTRICT # 00
SAMPLEVILLE COLORADO
DETAILED GENERAL LEDGER

PAGE 2

LINE #	ACCOUNT		DESCRIPTION	BEGINNING			PRESENT
TYPE	JOURNAL	REF #	VENDOR / DESCRIPTION	BALANCE	DEBIT	CREDIT	BALANCE
D	CD10	----	PAYROLL			1004.83	
D	CD10	----	PAYROLL			2887.33	
D	CD10	----	PAYROLL			1786.06	
D	CD10	----	PAYROLL			32671.27	
D	CD10	----	PAYROLL			8.50	
D	CD10	----	PAYROLL			1282.33	
D	CD10	----	PAYROLL			30.00	
D	CD10	----	PAYROLL			8.50	
D	CD10	----	PAYROLL			835.60	
D	CD10	----	PAYROLL			108.75	
D	CD10	----	PAYROLL			8407.41	
D	CD10	----	PAYROLL			2341.66	
D	CD10	----	PAYROLL			425.00	
D	CD10	----	PAYROLL			76.50	
D	CD10	----	PAYROLL			1359.99	
D	CD10	----	PAYROLL			1874.25	
D	CD10	----	PAYROLL			1530.33	
D	CD10	----	PAYROLL			235.74	
D	CD10	----	PAYROLL			22784.44	
D	CD10	----	PAYROLL			1295.80	
D	CD10	----	PAYROLL			7143.60	
D	CD10	----	PAYROLL			251.94	
D	CD10	----	PAYROLL			3299.70	
D	CD10	----	PAYROLL			1204.40	
D	CD10	----	PAYROLL			1100.65	
D	CD10	15529	ADMIN EXP FND			502.00	
D	CD10	15529	ADMIN EXP FND			42.00	
D	CD10	15529	ADMIN EXP FND			447.17	
D	CD10	15529	ADMIN EXP FND			1532.16	
D	CD10	15529	ADMIN EXP FND			262.00	
D	CD10	15529	ADMIN EXP FND			258.62	
D	CD10	15529	ADMIN EXP FND			5.00	
D	CD10	15529	ADMIN EXP FND			24.99	
D	CD10	15529	ADMIN EXP FND			5.00	
D	CD10	15529	ADMIN EXP FND			212.15	
D	CD10	15529	ADMIN EXP FND			40.00	
D	CD10	15529	ADMIN EXP FND			93.15	
D	CD10	15529	ADMIN EXP FND			42.00	
D	CD10	15530	ADMIN EXP FND			30.00	
D	CD10	15530	ADMIN EXP FND			258.50	
D	CD10	15530	ADMIN EXP FND			67.00	
D	CD10	15530	ADMIN EXP FND			50.00	
D	CD10	15530	ADMIN EXP FND			23.62	
D	CD10	15530	ADMIN EXP FND			61.50	
D	CD10	15530	ADMIN EXP FND			75.00	
D	CD10	15530	ADMIN EXP FND			20.00	
D	CD10	15531	ALDY GRAPHIC SUPPLY			447.13	
D	CD10	15532	ALLYN & BACON INC			868.32	
D	CD10	15534	AMERICAN BINDERY			294.27	
D	CD10	15536	AMOCO OIL CO			167.19	

```
                    INDEPENDENT SCHOOL DISTRICT # 00
                         SAMPLEVILLE COLORADO
                             BILL LIST
                            JANUARY 1982                    PAGE 1


    VEN #         VENDOR          LINE #    DESCRIPTION        AMOUNT
    --------------------------------------------------------------------
    041   ADM   XP FN            228    OTH CIV AC EX          73.75
    041   ADM   XP FN            051    BOYS ATH SAL            5.00
    041   ADM   XP FN            060    GIRLS TRK               5.00
    041   ADM   XP FN            142    CUSTODIAL SUP         258.62
    041   ADM   XP FN            048    GEN ATHL              447.17
    041   ADM   XP FN            022    COE                  1532.16
    041   ADM   XP FN            055    BOYS CC                42.00
    041   ADM   XP FN            059    GIRLS CC               42.00
    041   ADM   XP FN            057    BOYS FTBLL            502.00
    041   ADM   XP FN            144    OTH SUP/PLNT OP        40.00
    041   ADM   XP FN            063    GIRLS VBALL           262.00
    041   ADM   XP FN            045    VOC MUS SUP            24.99
    041   ADM   XP FN            011    TRAV-SUPT              93.15
    041   ADM   XP FN            077    TRAV T1               212.15
    041   ADM   XP FN            115    EL SP ED TRAV         258.50
    041   ADM   XP FN            081    GIFT - TAL             30.00
    041   ADM   XP FN            106    MIS INST EX            67.00
    041   ADM   XP FN            213    GAS - OIL             163.85
    041   ADM   XP FN            143    MS EX EQ REPAIR        61.50
    041   ADM   XP FN            167    ABTMT - FXD CHG        23.62
    041   ADM   XP FN            069    MOD OFF SUP            20.00
    041   ADM   XP FN            071    HOME EC SUP            75.00
    041   ADM   XP FN            006    OTH SCH B EX           50.00
    357   ALD   APHIC SUPPL      042    IND ART SUP           447.13
    155   ALL   BACON IN         066    SEC TXT/WKBK          868.32
    042   AMB   MOTOR C          209    RENT-PUP TRAN         325.00
    042   AMB   MOTOR C          214    VEHIC MAINT           150.22
    204   AME   N BINDER         109    LIB SUP               294.27
    044   AME   N LINEN SUPP     210    MS EX PT OP/MAI         5.04
    046   AMO   IL C             043    INST MUS SUP          167.19
    048   APP   OMPUTER IN       143    MS EX EQ REPAIR       150.38
    169   AUC   TTER DRU         100    SLBP SUPP               4.74
    169   AUC   TTER DRU         020    BUS OF SUPPL            7.72
    169   AUC   TTER DRU         173    LNCHRM SUP - EX         2.67
    387   AUG   G PUB HOUS       045    VOC MUS SUP             2.24
    049   BAN   LIF              159    GRP HOSP T1            75.32
    049   BAN   LIF              187    GRP HOSP              71.36
    049   BAN   LIF              219    GRP HOSP             168.49
    049   BAN   LIF              246    EMP GR HOS            56.00
    049   BAN   LIF              158    GRP HOSP            4676.47
    050   BAR   ELECTRI          142    CUSTODIAL SUP          62.73
    050   BAR   ELECTRI          042    IND ART SUP            58.02
    050   BAR   ELECTRI          249    REMODELING           324.99
    348   BEN   NKLI             233    CONT ED SUP             2.45
    348   BEN   NKLI             042    IND ART SUP             1.45
    348   BEN   NKLI             093    TMH SUP                13.75
    348   BEN   NKLI             020    BUS OF SUPPL            4.92
    058   BEN   BOOK             071    HOME EC SUP           123.18
    403   BIL   HSE FD           171    LNCHRM FD COSTS        19.46
    396   BIL   LDIN             203    MISC EQUIP             15.60
```

```
                    INDEPENDENT SCHOOL DISTRICT # 00
                          SAMPLEVILLE COLORADO
                              CHECK LIST
                            JANUARY 1982                    PAGE 1

              VENDOR                                AMOUNT
        ----------------------------------------------------------------
        ADM   XP FN                                4289.46
        ALD   APHIC SUPPL                           447.13
        ALL   BACON IN                              868.32
        AMB   MOTOR C                               475.22
        AME   N BINDER                              294.27
        AME   N LINEN SUPP                            5.04
        AMO   IL C                                  167.19
        APP   OMPUTER IN                            150.38
        AUC   TTER DRU                               15.13
        AUG   G PUB HOUS                              2.24
        BAN   LIF                                  5047.64
        BAR   ELECTRI                               445.74
        BEN   NKLI                                   22.57
        BEN   BOOK                                  123.18
        BIL   HSE FD                                 19.46
        BIL   LDIN                                   15.60
        BUR   PUB C                                  25.79
        CAL   Y HOUSE IN                             50.95
        CAR   SCHER-CHICAG                           31.42
        CAR   MALL MT                                22.20
        CAR   GHT DRU                                43.40
        CAR   HT ELAIN                               74.75
        CAS   N SERVIC                             6639.13
        CIT   ORTONVILL                            2860.29
        CLO   EAF DAIR                             3100.43
        COM   ILL BUILDER                           140.40
        COM   ENSIVE BKTBALL                         17.15
        COX   PRINTER                                83.58
        CUL                                          80.00
        DAK   WLDNG SUPP                            108.95
        DAV   IANO & ORGAN C                        268.00
        DEB   LYNN DESIGN                           187.20
        DEB   POTATO & PRO                           80.30
        DEV   MENTAL LRNING M                        15.37
        EDE   SS PUB C                                6.00
        EDU   OP SERV UNI                           986.00
        ELE   C MAID BAKER                          660.29
        ELV   G VIRGINI                              45.24
        FAR   HOME LB                               562.57
        FED   ED TELEPHONE C                         18.65
        FIS   ECTRI                                  81.42
        FRI   PTN GD                                 48.84
        GAM   ROBINSO                               521.15
        GAM                                          93.19
        GC    RSON MACHINER                         265.45
        GEN   ELEC C                                 45.75
        GIN   C                                    1068.36
        GHW                                         188.11
        GOD   DIAN                                   41.80
        GOO   R TIRE CNT                            254.51
```

```
ADM   XP FN            VOUCHER JACKET     DATE ALLOWED: 01/15/81
ISD#62                 SAMPLEVILLE
SAMPLEVILLE CO 10101   PUB SCH            DATE PAID ............

                                         CHECK NO ............
```

```
04 500 505 000 000 899    OTH CIV AC EX       73.75
01 300 294 000 000 140    BOYS ATH SAL         5.00
01 300 296 219 000 899    GIRLS TRK            5.00
01 005 810 000 000 410    CUSTODIAL SUP      258.62
01 005 292 000 000 899    GEN ATHL           447.17
01 005 140 000 330 899    CQE               1532.16
01 300 294 212 000 899    BOYS CC             42.00
01 300 296 226 000 899    GIRLS CC            42.00
01 300 294 211 000 899    BOYS FTBLL         502.00
01 005 810 000 000 401    OTH SUP/PLNT OP     40.00
01 300 296 230 000 899    GIRLS VBALL        262.00
01 300 258 000 000 430    VOC MUS SUP         24.99
01 005 020 000 000 366    TRAV-SUPT           93.15
01 005 410 000 401 367    TRAV T1            212.15
```

```
                          TOTAL             3539.99
```

```
AUDITED BY............
    *
    *
```

Microcomputers In Education

176

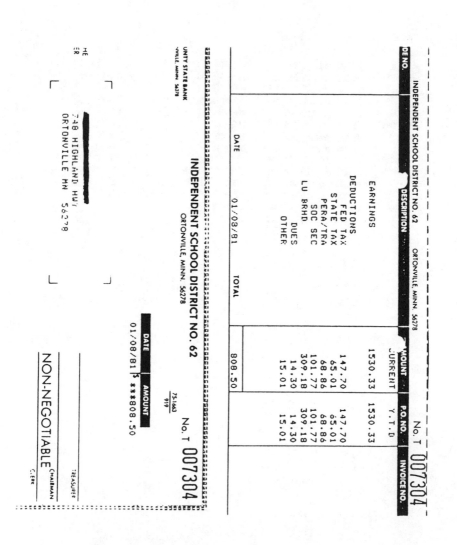

INVENTORIES

Inventories of all kinds, especially instructional materials and media, should be electronically stored to provide printouts as needed. Additions and deletions are easily made and the lists can be reorganized in a matter of seconds by item, vendor, purchase dates, cost, or purpose.

New administrative applications for the microcomputer continue to develop as increasing numbers of administrators begin to use them in the schools. Additional possibilities for microcomputer applications include energy analysis / conservation, library cataloging / circulation and future projections for use in planning. If the school is involved in a computer network, administrative data can be transferred through it to other administrators or a form of electronic conferencing can be set up, using networked microcomputers.

ADVANTAGES OF MICRO-ASSISTED ADMINISTRATION

- Equipment costs are low enough to be recovered in one year of operation. Hardware is discussed below.
- Users report that the equipment is easy to operate, but some programs are easier to use than others depending on how well they are written and the quality of their documentation.
- Microcomputer equipment used in the office can also be used for instruction. In most districts the micro is only needed one or two hours daily for office work.
- Software costs are low compared to the development costs for large computer systems.
- As more micro-administration programs become available their quality and ease of use is rapidly improving.
- Local districts of any size can process and control their own data instead of sending it out to large computer installations.
- Cost reductions are significant and staff time saved can be used for other purposes.
- Using microcomputers in school administration helps in the development of computer literacy throughout the school.

LIMITATIONS OF MICROS

- Preliminary expectations may exceed the system's capabilities. Micros are not magicians, they require that users be trained and that data entry be free of errors. Installation almost always entails some minor problems of one sort or another but once on line, reliability has been good.
- Memory size of the floppy disk units in use in 1980-81 are around 100 to 250 thousand bytes or characters. This limits the size of the data base that can be processed, i.e., small schools can make better use of micros. However, the hard disk systems now entering the market have millions of characters (megabytes) of storage and should alleviate this problem. Recent micros also have higher operating speeds in their central processing units which increase the speed at which tasks are performed.
- Data stored on floppy disks or any magnetic medium can be damaged by magnetic fields or extreme environmental conditions. If the hardware breaks down, it could erase or scramble data on a disk. For this reason, there must always be back-up copies of important data, preferrably stored in a safe environment. Back-up may be on disk or tape. Important archival data will soon be copied onto videodisks which are much more durable and unsusceptible to magnetism.

SYSTEM REQUIREMENTS

Administrative applications have large memory require-ments and involve special equipment. If the micro is to be used both for instruction and in the office, you are likely to need peripherals. Administrative offices large enough to use the microcomputer full-time can choose a system designed primarily for that purpose.

Assuming full-time use in the office, look first for a system having an 80 column display screen. Then, in word processing, what is scrolled up on the display is what it will look like printed out, making the task easier for the operator. Double disk drives with large capacities should be chosen or a floppy disk and a hard disk combination.

Multipurpose systems generally have a 40 column screen but most can have hardware installed to generate the 80 column screen at a cost of $200-$300. Instructional applications usually need only one disk drive so an extra drive needs to be obtained for office use, preferrably, a hard disk having megabytes of storage.

A printer will also be needed for most office applications. Letter quality output is obtained from full character impact printers in the $2,000-$3,000 price range. Dot matrix printers ranging in price from $500 to $1,500 have slightly less perfect character formation but operate two or three times as fast. Print quality of the dot matrix printers continues to improve and these models can create impressive graphics which could be very useful in reports. Ink jet printers that have fewer moving parts and can more easily produce color output are coming onto the market and may be the printing technology of the near future. Characters formed by ink jet printers are of letter quality and they can also create complex graphics. Printers that use special papers are not recommended for office use.

Workspace memory in the 8 bit microprocessor based systems common today is generally 16 to 64K bytes. Some have multiples of 64K and switch from bank to bank as needed. The 64K system is adequate for most present applications but trends indicate more memory space which can be directly addressed by the microprocessor will be needed. Several 16 bit microprocessor machines are now available which can directly address 8 megabytes. And 32 bit microprocessors are in the research and development stage. These second and third generations micros will eliminate the restrictions imposed by current hardware.

Networking will benefit administrative users by sharing common data bases and using electronic mail for memos. Microcomputers in one building can be linked into a local network for communicating and sharing a common hard disk for access to large data bases. Several manufacturers offer the needed hardware and software for these in-house networks. Between-school networking requires a modem device which connects the micro to the telephone lines. An acoustic coupler modem uses the standard handphone in a special cradle to make the connection. Direct connect modems bypass the telephone by having a standard phone jack connector to plug into any available socket. Direct connect modems are recommended because they result in fewer errors in data transfer.

FAREWELL TO THE BRIEFCASE

As the amount of information generated by our society escalates, the mountains of paper to be shuffled and reviewed begin to rival the Himalayas. Forms in triplicate and endless reports seem to reproduce in dark file cabinets and desk drawers. In the last three years, microcomputers have demonstrated an ability to reverse this trend. Information can be stored electronically at low cost and can be retrieved in very short periods of time. Scanning and retrieving relevant information will be a skill needed by future administrators.

Although most applications cited in the chapter include the generation of printed reports, the transfer of information over electronic networks will eliminate the need for much hardcopy. Information is a resource to be processed by the brain, not the hands, though the armies of filing clerks presently employed refute this idea. Administrators have much to learn about effective uses of available information in decision making. Trend analysis and future projections, made possible by such software as VisiCalc, hint at the possibilities for the future. As the microcomputer becomes the natural tool of the modern administrator, it will indeed replace the briefcase as a symbol of executive office.

Chapter VIII
MANAGEMENT INFORMATION SYSTEMS

Are educators turning into accountants and bookkeepers? The answer may be "yes" if what has happened in Head Start and special education programs is part of a general trend. Special educators, for example, must monitor and document 50 separate activities, required by federal regulations relating to one law, Public Law 94-142. For each student, documentation relating to the referral of students to services, nondiscriminatory assessment, the development of individualized education programs, and periodic re-evaluation must be recorded and kept accessible for review. With 200 students in a program, that means about 8,000 separate entries will be made somewhere in a bookkeeping and accounting system.

DATA MANAGEMENT TURMOIL

Head Start programs, suffering from declining funding but burgeoning enrollment have been characterized as being in a state of "data management turmoil" (Cogdill & Goldberg, 1981). These programs must gather data on student background, health services, dental services, student evaluations, handicap services, career development planning, food services, social services, attendance, and parent participation. To collect this data, check it for accuracy, store it somewhere, and then be able to locate it when needed is literally a nightmare. Without the help of computers it is nearly impossible to make any sense of this data or use it to help improve the quality of education. When you begin using a computer to control information for monitoring compliance with laws and regulations, cost control, deciding how to allocate your resources, or to make projections, you are involved in what is termed a management information system.

ADDICTION TO INFORMATION

When it comes to information it seems there are more suppliers than users. The dramatic growth of the "education industry" in the 1960's and 1970's resulted in the creation of many new expectations, programs, and "missions" that sharply increased the demand for information by state and federal agencies. Most of our recent growth in information acquisition and recording (human accounting) has been spurred by the demands of funding sources that have under-written the expansion of education and human services. It is also not altogether a matter of chance that these years saw the beginning of a transformation to an information society through the remarkable growth of the computer industry. The computer industry, and everyone whose fortune is linked to it, has a very strong economic interest in the production of information. It is the fundamental raw material of the computer industry. It is by encouraging the production of information that computers help manufacture the problems they solve.

In addition to the information that must be collected and stored for somebody else, educators themselves need information to:
- plan and target programs
- account for monies spent
- locate people and resources
- document student growth
- create instructional groupings
- plan budgets
- staff programs

ORGANIZATIONAL COMPLEXITY

What appears as an addiction to information is also sympto-matic of an increased organizational complexity in education that was noted earlier in other areas of our society such as business (Murdick and Ross, 1971). Looking back to the nineteenth century, there was the small country store where a single owner assumed all the duties and functions necessary to keep it running. The owner-operator

> "personally gathered all the information necessary to carry out his functions, either using it when gathered or storing the information in his memory for later retrieval...once a decision was made, the owner usually undertook the necessary action himself." (Radford, 1978, p. 4).

For the nineteenth century storekeeper there was no "data management turmoil." People working together shared information informally, as needs arose. Certainly record keeping was involved, but its scope was only a fraction of today's.

With the mass economies of the 20th century, and particularly during the post WWII period, came a high degree of specialization, hypermanagement with exponential growth in the number of persons involved in administrative functions, and a pattern of delegating authority and responsibility throughout the chain of command. All these trends involved substituting data and abstract information for first hand knowledge and observation. Diversification of roles and great organizational complexity, were accompanied in business, by information problems for management; both where to get it and how to use it.

ACCOUNTABILITY

All the recent organizational trends in business have occurred in education, too. One reason for this, in addition to recent population trends, is that education has historically endorsed the business model (Callahan, 1970). Management efficiency, inputs and outputs, products and resources are concepts that have been adopted by education from business. But there is one important difference that makes education far more complex than business. Unlike net profit in dollars, there is no simple figure at the end of the balance sheet.

Nonetheless, educators are expected, like businessmen, to demonstrate competent and effective management. These are fundamental to the concept of accountability. To demonstrate accountability, it isn't enough for educational leaders just to show that dollars were spent appropriately and in the authorized amount, nor that all necessary procedural mechanisms are in place. The public, through its legislative representatives, is interested in whether or not its "money's worth" is obtained. Do students become more capable? Does society benefit more than or at least equal to what programs cost?

A full accountability model suggests that longitudinal information will ultimately be required for all students, showing how each progresses through the school years on measures of academic achievement, social and occupational learning, physical growth, and emotional adjustment. For the school system without computerization, although much of this data is already collected, assembling and analyzing the data has been an impossible undertaking.

So accountability remains a problem, an unfortunate one in light of the declining political support for educational programs Guthrie, 1981). Especially vulnerable today are labor intensive and therefore costly programs for slow learners, bilingual pupils and children with mild handicapping conditions such as the learning disabled. To demonstrate that these costly programs yield benefit, extensive and convincing information must be assembled, analyzed and interpreted.

AN INFORMATION SYSTEMS APPROACH

With the advent of the microcomputer, some educators have begun experimenting with computer managed instruction and microcomputer based administration (see Chapters Five and Seven). Few, however, are aware that these two applications are part of a more general concept, "the management information system." A microcomputer based management information system would systematically assemble, code, store, format, and make available for retrieval at any time, information on staff, students, physical facilities, or financial questions. A management information system performs operations on one or more "data bases, - a synonym in information science jargon for a large store of information" (Sanderson, 1975).

An adequate microcomputer management information system entails two important features of a human system, such as the nineteenth century storekeeper's: 1) freedom to manipulate stored information in a variety of ways, and; 2) ability to selectively retrieve information stored in memory. With the complexity of modern school systems and the need for constant revision, updating, and sharing of information, our data bases have become so large and difficult to manipulate that automated procedures are required. Our schools, along with many other organizations, are just "too complex for a manager to hold all the relevant facts in his memory from which he can isolate the significant features to assist his decisions" (Sanderson, 1975).

In a management information system approach, emphasis is on decision making, not just facilitating clerical work. As discussed in Chapter Seven, there are many office applications for microcomputers that can ease the demands for clerical time devoted to routine record keeping and reporting. Attendance, class scheduling, optimization of bus routes, form generation, payroll and word processing are all legitimate and cost-saving applications of microcomputers. They are, however, paper processing as opposed to decision support functions. And computer systems that meet paper processing requirements often don't provide information of a type or format that can serve an educational administrator's decision and accountability needs.

Experience has shown that good management information systems have certain characteristics. According to Wilkinson (1974) they:

* provide relevant information to managers and other users

* operate efficiently and economically

* insure accurate and accessible information

* provide information with appropriate timeliness

* operate with an integrated and consistent framework

* provide adequate capacity for all legitimate needs

* exhibit simplicity of operation

* maintain sufficient flexibility, versatility, adaptability, and stability with respect to changing needs and conditions

* motivate managers and employees to act in ways that promote the organization's objectives. (p. 36-37)

CONFIGURATIONS

Centralized Computing

In the late 1960's and early 1970's, many states established centralized educational computing networks. The Minnesota Educational Computing Consortium is one example of such a network. Typically, centralized computing networks were organized around a star-structured data communications system with large, powerful computers at the center.

At the time centralized computing was established in state education agencies, the cost of CPU was many times higher than today's cost. Powerful microprocessors and high capacity disk storage units to accompany them were undeveloped. Given the extreme costs of computer hardware, centralized computing resulted in an economy of scale - computing costs being distributed among multiple users.

Today, the "economy of scale" advantage for centralized computing has just about disappeared because of market declines in microcomputer hardware costs. However, there are a number of features of centralized computer systems that should be noted and considered when designing a management information system to meet today's requirements. First, centralized computer operations are easier to control. Policies can be established that guarantee uniformity of equipment, compatibility of languages, and interchangeability of data and storage media.

Another advantage of centralized operations is that there continues to be a shortage of qualified data processing personnel; turnover is high in the data processing field. Glaser (1970) indicates that,

> "Centralization reduces the impact of this phenomenon by permitting fewer staffs of larger size, thus reducing dependence on individuals and enhancing the company's ability to recruit and retain a well-qualified staff."

Finally, centralized computing has often been endorsed by top level administrators because this organizational structure makes it easier for them to control individual school districts, when reporting systems are uniform. Unique, independent, data processing systems are regarded as an impediment to adequate control. It is through centralization that uniformity is enforced.

Decentralization

With the advent of powerful, inexpensive microcomputers, individual school districts are now able to acquire the computing capability of some of the earlier centralized networks, at least the portion available to them through telecommunications. The availability of computer hardware and software at reasonable cost makes it a near certainty that more and more school districts will begin to undertake limited purpose management information systems. Three economic considerations favor decentralization:

- The elimination of network membership fees
- The reduction of telecommunication costs that are involved in remote access to a centralized computer installation
- The elimination of expensive staff positions in computer bureaucracies.

In addition to the changing economics of computing, proponents of decentralization have articulated some other strong arguments favoring their position:

- Any effective application of computer power to the solution of complex problems presumes that analysts and programmers are familiar in details with local problems. There should be an identity between the problem solvers and those who want solutions.
- Telecommunication access to centralized computing results in too frequent and too lengthy delays because of the competition among multiple channels for access to CPU. Long distance telephone charges continue to rise. Long distance telephone charges continue to rise.

It appears that educators are beginning to experiment with management information systems at a time when the pendulum is swinging toward decentralized computing.

Distributed Systems

Decentralization, when carried to the extreme with each school district implementing its own information system, favors local management needs over state, regional, or federal information needs. Distributed systems are a hybrid. They retain the advantage of giving control over data entry and report production to local education agencies but provide mass storage and a communications network for assembling a data base for state and federal level strategic planning.

A distributed system consists of the following elements: (Canning, 1973)

- Distributed Processing
- Distributed Communications
- Distributed Data Bases
- System-wide Rules

Processing logic and storage are placed at the local level, where transactions occur. Microcomputers that can function both as intelligent terminals for existing network configurations and as host processors for stand-alone application would be the basic hardware unit. Richard Sprague, a computer pioneer, conceived of a distributed system for a large organization as consisting of a hierarchy of three or more types of processors, each matching the decision levels of an organization. Local computers would process data for local decision, state computers for state decisions, and federal computers for federal decisions.

Distributed communications allow interchange of data and programs both horizontally among local education agencies and vertically, between local and state-federal agencies. Uploading of data and downloading of programs are the two main types of transactions that would occur between state, federal and local agencies.

Distributed data bases are located where the data files are most frequently used. The data base, in its entirety, is distributed among the various participants in the system; any file within the system can be accessed from any place within the system if security rules have been followed.

A fundamental development problem in a distributed system is to establish the form of the entire data base and the procedures for its management. System-wide rules must be developed for security, data accessibility, the transfer of programs and data, along with universal data definitions.

MISPERCEPTIONS OF POWER

Many prospective users of information systems matured during a period of history when every generation of computer hardware was larger, faster, and more powerful. Partly due to this development trend, advertising hyperbole, and intellectual fashion, people acquired the belief that "the ultimate information system includes a vast data base that contains all important facts about the organization. It features an interactive output facility that allows management instantly to inquire about any combination of facts and, therefore, all aspects of the organization." (Clemson, 1978, p.13) Computing power, accessibility, and a large data base that breeds "facts" in variegated formats and cross-tabulations was the vision conveyed.

The trouble with this vision is that there is a consistent theme in management information system research: facts and more facts are not the critical need within the management decision structure. And there are many analysts who observe that all levels of management, in today's society, are inundated with disordered and undigested facts: "information overload." Observing managerial behavior suggests that the judgments about the implications of facts, rather than the availability of facts are the problem.

There are also real limits to the power of even the ultimate management information system. Clemson (1978) describes a school superintendent who wanted to systematically match student and teacher characteristics, using the variables sex, ethnicity, personality type, teaching methods, and learning styles. If we were to assume 300 different student types, 300 different teacher types, and an effectiveness rating to optimize placement, an information processing capability of 3×10^{92} bits would be required. According to Clemson, if all the matter in the earth were transformed into a computer and it had been processing data throughout the earth's history, about now its 10^{92} bit would have been reached.

> "In other words, the seemingly reasonable administrative question posed above requires a technologically perfect computer the size of the earth running eons of time just to handle its computations." (Clemson, 1978, p. 15).

Education experts harboring similarly unrealistic beliefs concerning the power of computer-based management information systems to support complex decision processes risk disappointment - a situation that could lead to complete rejection of the technology.

THE SYSTEM ISN'T THE DATA

Microcomputer technology is now available to support management information systems in the schools and there is an extensive literature on what has been learned by organizations involved with large systems. While educators have begun to endorse the technology, development efforts appear to ignore what has been learned about how systems development should proceed. Instead of determining how data will be used in supporting management control and planning, as a first step, the tendency is for the data base itself to become the focal point of the development effort.

A prototype of the primitive state of management information system design in public education is Michigan's recent involvement with a private contractor to design a statewide Special Education Information System at considerable expense. In Michigan, attention was focused on the data elements as the basic design unit of the system. After receiving inputs from various levels of prospective users, a master listing of variables was synthesized through a negotiation process. The focus of the development effort was the data base itself, not the decisions to be made from the data. No attempt was made to identify the features of the existing decision system, or how educators would use this data to provide better education for children.

The Michigan approach is characteristic of how computer experts approach management information systems. Emphasis is given to clerical and reporting requirements and establishing a data base that is very extensive, including information in hopes that something will be useful to someone, sometime. Unfortunately, it has been found that this approach, when used by major business organizations and universities results in an information system whose care and feeding is an increasingly burdensome financial undertaking without an offsetting gain in productivity (Clemson, 1978).

LIMITED PURPOSE MICROCOMPUTER INFORMATION PROLIFERATION OF REDUNDANT SYSTEMS

For the development of useful management information systems in schools, the heretofore more limited storage capacity of microcomputers may be an advantage. With limited storage capacity, it is likely that more attention will be given to precisely identifying problem areas for management and the data that is related to their solution.

An example of a carefully designed microcomputer management information system is the Intermountain Inter-Tribal School's MONITOR, developed by Richard Whitney and Alan Hofmeister of Utah State University (Whitney & Hofmeister, 1981). The system was designed to serve a limited purpose, that of allowing educators to economically document the fact that federal regulations had been complied with for each student. Mandated services and procedural safeguards were the focus of the system.

The microcomputer hardware selected were as follows:

- Horizon Northstar DOS 5.0,64K RAM
- Two double density 5¼ inch floppy disk drives
- A SOROC IQ video terminal
- Texas Instrument 810 RO bidirectional dot matrix printer

At the time of this writing, hardware costs for this configuration were $6,200. The Utah State University development team selected the Northstar because previous experience had convinced them of its reliability.

A requirement for building the microcomputer management information system was that users shouldn't need any computer operations or programming skills to use it. The system was "menu driven," meaning that user options were displayed on the screen and prompting was used to help the child study team enter new student records, create reports, or add / delete information. A highly desirable feature of the system was that users could obtain reports immediately, upon request, or similarly, update student records.

Four major types of activities relating to the provision of special education services were monitored, for each child, by the system:
- referral activities
- nondiscriminatory assessments
- individualized education program implementation
- annual reviews and re-evaluation

The Utah experience showed why it is so important to emphasize design, field testing, and revision of any major information system. As the system was originally designed, the data contained in it, its ease of operation, and its output were excellent. However, it was learned in the preliminary field test that users could and would "skip" required compliance activities, essentially violating the required sequence of activities. By skipping required activities, the compliance process was circumvented.

Other problems that were noted were: 1) data entry errors; 2) inconsistencies between school records and what was entered into the system; 3) a need to be able to delete cases and establish an "inactive" file; and 4) inability to format some data into reports. In a revision of the program and through inservice with staff, these problems were resolved. According to Whitney and Hofmeister (1981),

> "once the system has been in operation for a period of time, the special education coordinator can assess the 'Diagnostic Compliance Report' which provides an overall view of the school's compliance for each of the compliance activities monitored by the system. Using this document as a planning tool the coordinator can analyze which activities have 'positive slack' and which have 'negative slack.' "

PROLIFERATION OF REDUNDANT SYSTEMS

In addition to development efforts that are undertaken at universities such as Utah State, private vendors like Educational Turnkey Systems have begun to exploit the potential of microcomputers for relieving the school management burden induced by government regulations. Educational Turnkey System's product, like Utah State's, is a limited purpose management information system. It is addressed to the problem of Individualized Educational Program maintenance. Systems of this type update the federally required IEP for handicapped learners, help document the overall special education process and provide limited summary report capabilities based on selective sorts of the data base.

Although products such as this meet an important need for cost-reduction, the proliferation of different versions of limited purpose systems will make it very difficult to establish a uniform data base to support state and federal planning, assuming that such planning is desirable. What will undoubtedly occur is the creation of state and federal information systems that will require data transfer from local schools in a new format that is incompatible with existing systems. Therefore, we foresee an expensive conversion process beginning shortly after microcomputer management information systems become more widely adopted by local school districts. The reason: federal and state educational policies generally reflect social and technical changes that have already gained momentum at the local level.

THE ILLINOIS CLIENT INFORMATION SYSTEM

Building Specifications

The professional literature on management information systems uniformly advocates that careful preparations be made before acquiring and installing computer information systems. An important part of preparing your organization is the building of specifications for the information system.

First, a general planning phase allowing for the exploration of alternatives is recommended. In Illinois, the present authors were involved with the development of a prototype client information system for the developmentally disabled, a group composed of autistic, cerebral palsied, epileptic, and mentally retarded persons of all ages. Before actually implementing a system, the Governor's Planning Council on Developmental Disabilities undertook about one year of planning. As a consequence, when Southern Illinois University at Carbondale began the technical work to bring the system to operational status, it was a matter of following a detailed set of specifications that had been developed by prospective users: mental health facility staff, state administrators, and the systems design consultants, Bock Associates of St. Paul, Minnesota.

Part of the planning phase for the Illinois Client Information System was a feasibility analysis that examined variables such as the actions taken by prospective users and how client information related to these actions, the professional attitudes and orientations of persons who would be affected by computerization, and the structure of the mental health organization itself. An on-site design team worked with prospective users and those who would be responsible for supplying data, well in advance of the technical development effort.

A crucial planning task is to pinpoint the kinds of decisions that managers already are making and the types and formats of data that can support these decisions. The more attention that is given to decisions styles, information needs, and communication networks of prospective users, the more likely it is that an effective management information system will result.

A Multi-Purpose System

The Illinois Client Information System was a multi-purpose system designed to meet the needs of direct service providers, middle level management, and state planners. Although the system as originally designed entailed optical scanning of data and batch processing at Southern Illinois University, an effort is currently underway to convert to a distributed system using microcomputers.

As a distributed system, each facility would enter client information directly into a microcomputer according to a specified format. Data entry would be facilitated by screen prompts. Client data would be transmitted periodically to a large computer for entry into the statewide data base. Local facilities with printers would be able to use software supplied to them by the state to create individual case profiles.

The individual case profile is considered priority information for direct service providers. It serves as a case description and planning document, stored both electronically and in hardcopy. The individual case profile is a complete description of the client's legal, behavioral, medical, and

program status. Data from the Minnesota Developmental
Programming System Behavioral Scales (Bock, Weatherman, Joiner, and Kranz, 1979), also included in the Illinois
system, allows for the documentation of longitudinal trends in
client growth for accountability purposes. The information is
also used to group students, assign services, and identify skills
that should be taught (Silverstein, 1981). An example of a
computer generated case profile follows:

```
                          ILLINOIS
                  CLIENT INFORMATION SYSTEM


INDIVIDUAL CASE PROFILE              DATE OF ASSESSMENT:      04-17-80

NAME:_____             FACILITY/AGENCY CODE:      45C-10

INITIALS:           ID:      O       COMMUNITY WORKSHOP & TRN. CTR.
SEX:  M          BIRTH:  05-16-31    3215 N. UNIVERSITY
ETHNICITY:   WHITE
MARITAL STATUS:   SINGLE

HIS COUNTY OF (CURRENT RESIDENCE)       (ORIGIN)          (LAST PLACEMENT)

                TAZEWELL              MC LEAN             TAZEWELL

HIS PRIMARY DISABILITY IS MENTAL RETARDATION
HIS SECONDARY DISABILITY IS PHYSICAL/MEDICAL
HIS LAST I.Q. TEST SCORE =   51
HIS VISION IS IMPAIRED
HIS HEARING IS IMPAIRED/NOT DEAF
HE  WALKS UNAIDED WITH DIFFICULTY
HIS SEIZURES ARE CONTROLLED
HIS MEDICINE GIVEN BY SELF WITH SUPERVISION:   EMOTIONAL/BEHAVIORAL
HIS MEDICINE GIVEN BY SELF WITH SUPERVISION:   ANTI-CONVULSANT
HE  HAS NO BEHAVIORAL IMPEDIMENTS

HE  IS COMPLETELY INDEPENDENT IN TOILETING SKILLS
HE  IS COMPLETELY INDEPENDENT IN EATING SKILLS
HE  NEEDS ASSISTANCE, AND FURTHER TRAINING IN DRESSING/GROOMING SKILLS

HIS ON-SITE MEDICAL SUPPORT NEEDS:   NURSING
HIS ON-CALL MEDICAL SUPPORT NEEDS:   PHYSICIAN
HIS GENERAL PHYSICAL HEALTH:   GOOD

HIS TYPE OF CURRENT RESIDENCE: ICG SHELTERED CARE
DAY PROGRAM-RECEIVING:   WORK ACTIVITY
DAY PROGRAM-NEEDED:   WORK ACTIVITY
PRIMARY HEALTH & THERAPY NEED:   AUDIOLOGY SERVICES
SECOND HEALTH & THERAPY NEED:   OCCUPATIONAL THERAPY
PRIMARY COMMUNITY SUPPORT NEED:   LEISURE TIME/RECREATION
SECOND COMMUNITY SUPPORT NEED:   NONE NEEDED
VOCATIONAL STATUS-CURRENT:   DAYTIME/WORK ACTIVITY
VOCATIONAL STATUS-NEEDED:   DAYTIME/WORK ACTIVITY

HE  HAS  O YEARS IN REGULAR ED      HE  HAS  O YEARS IN SPECIAL ED

HIS ELIGIBILITY STATUS TITLE XIX:  UNKNOWN
HIS ELIGIBILITY STATUS TITLE XX:   RECEIVING
HIS ELIGIBILITY STATUS  SSI:   RECEIVING
HIS ELIGIBILITY STATUS  SSP:   UNKNOWN
HIS ELIGIBILITY STATUS PUBLIC AID:   RECEIVING
HIS ELIGIBILITY STATUS VOCATIONAL REHAB:   NOT ELIGIBLE
HIS ELIGIBILITY STATUS PURCHASE OF CARE:   NOT ELIGIBLE
HIS ELIGIBILITY STATUS DDSA:   NOT ELIGIBLE
HIS ELIGIBILITY STATUS DMH/DD GRANTS:   RECEIVING

HIS CURRENT "MEANINGFUL TIE" WILL REQUIRE:   REQUIREMENT NOT REPORTED
HIS FAMILY INVOLVEMENT:   FAMILY CONTACTS AT LEAST ANNUALLY
THIS CLIENT'S POINT COUNT IS   O         THE STAFF MEMBER CODE IS   1
```

```
                        MDPS  BEHAVIORAL  SCALE
                               FORM  A
                        RELATIVE PERFORMANCE INDEX**

NAME:_____        FACILITY/AGENCY CODE:   450-10

INITIALS:         ID:        0          SEX:  M       BIRTH:  05-16-31

DATE OF ASSESSMENT:   04-17-80
```

SCALE	PERCENTILES**	RAW TOTAL	ITEM SCORES

```
                                                         1111 111112
                   25%   50%   75% 100%          12345678 901234567890

:GROSS MOTOR      :****    |----|----|----|:-:  :C: 53 : ABABBBBA ACABBCCCDDDD:
:DEVELOPMENT      :                        :P:  :                            :

:FINE MOTOR       :*****   |----|----|----|:-:  :C: 38 : BBBCCABB BCDDDDDDDDDD:
:DEVELOPMENT      :                        :P:  :                            :

:EATING           :******  |----|----|----|:-:  :C: 43 : AAAABC BC CCBCDDDDDDDD:
                  :                        :P:  :                            :

:DRESSING         :*******  |----|----|----|:-: :C: 49 : AABB BBAB AABCCDDDDDDD:
                  :                        :P:  :                            :

:GROOMING         :******  |----|----|----|:-:  :C: 40 : AAAACDBCCDBCDDDDDDDD:
                  :                        :P:  :                            :

:TOILETING        :*********  |----|----|----|:-: :C: 64 : AAAAAAAA AAAABDBCCCDDB:
                  :                        :P:  :                            :

:RECEPTIVE        :******  |----|----|----|:-:  :C: 42 : DCCCCCDB ABAACCBCDDDD:
:LANGUAGE         :                        :P:  :                            :

:EXPRESSIVE       :**********  |----|----|:-:   :C: 54 : BBBAAAAA AABBBCDDDDDD:
:LANGUAGE         :                        :P:  :                            :

:SOCIAL           :***********  |----|----|:-:  :C: 64 : AAAAABAAC ACBALBABADD:
:INTERACTION      :                        :P:  :                            :

:READINESS &      :**********  |----|----|:-:   :C: 41 : AAAADCBCCDDDCCCCDDDD:
:READING          :                        :P:  :                            :

:WRITING          :**********  |----|----|:-:   :C: 42 : AABCCBDB ADDCACDDDDDD:
                  :                        :P:  :                            :

:NUMBERS          :**********  |----|----|:-:   :C: 31 : ACCCCCDCCDCDDDDDDDDD:
                  :                        :P:  :                            :

:TIME             :************  |----|----|:-: :C: 42 : AAAACBBBCCCDDDDDDDD:
                  :                        :P:  :                            :

:MONEY            :************  |----|----|:-: :C: 34 : AAACCDCDBCDDDDDDCDDDD:
                  :                        :P:  :                            :

:DOMESTIC         :********  |----|----|----|:-: :C: 27 : AACDDDDD DDDDDDDDDDDD:
:BEHAVIOR         :                        :P:  :                            :

:COMMUNITY        :*************  |----|----|:-: :C: 48 : AAAABBCCCDBBBUCDBDDD:
:ORIENTATION      :                        :P:  :                            :

:RECREATION &     :**********  |----|----|:-:   :C: 43 : ACAABA6BBCDCDDDDDDDD:
:LEISURE-TIME     :                        :P:  :                            :

:VOCATIONAL       :*************  |----|----|:-: :C: 57 : AACCBAABAABABBDCADDD:
                  :                        :P:  :                            :
```

```
**RELATIVE PERFORMANCE INDEX:   THESE PERCENTILES REFLECT WEIGHTED
COMPUTATIONS FOR COMPARING THIS PERSON'S PERFORMANCE ACROSS DOMAINS.
SHARP DEVIATIONS INDICATE SPECIFIC SKILL AREAS IN WHICH EXCEPTIONAL
PERFORMANCE(HIGH OR LOW) CAN BE NOTED WITH RESPECT TO PERFORMANCE IN
ALL OTHER DOMAINS.   EXCEPTIONALLY LOW PERFORMANCE IN A DOMAIN MAY
INDICATE A PROGRAM PRIORITY NEED.
NOTE:  RAW TOTAL CAN RANGE FROM 20 TO 80
```

MDPS

SUGGESTIONS FOR DEVELOPMENTAL PROGRAMMING LEVELS

NAME:_____   FACILITY/AGENCY CODE: 450-10

INITIALS: ID: 0   SEX: M   BIRTH: 05-16-31

DATE OF ASSESSMENT: 04-17-80

THE FOLLOWING LIST OF BEHAVIORS SUGGESTS THIS INDIVIDUAL'S CURRENT
CEILING LEVEL OF PERFORMANCE IN EACH OF THE 18 BEHAVIORAL DOMAINS.
GENERALLY, THE ITEMS THAT ARE LESS DIFFICULT THAN THOSE LISTED ARE
PERFORMED BY THE INDIVIDUAL AT A SATISFACTORY LEVEL. THE LIST OF
BEHAVIORS ARE NOT NECESSARILY THOSE FOR WHICH PROGRAMMING SHOULD BE
IMMEDIATELY PROVIDED; SUCH PROGRAM DECISIONS SHOULD BE MADE BY THE
INTERDISCIPLINARY TEAM. HOWEVER, ONCE A DOMAIN IS SELECTED AS A
PROGRAM PRIORITY, THE INITIAL LEVEL OF TRAINING MAY BE SUGGESTED
BY THE DIFFICULTY LEVEL OF THE BEHAVIORS BELOW.

	ITEM	
GROSS MOTOR	14:C	RUNS
DEVELOPMENT	15:C	SQUATS
FINE MOTOR	10:C	UNSCREWS A JAR OR BOTTLE LID
DEVELOPMENT	11:D	POURS LIQUID FROM PITCHER INTO OTHER CONTAINER-NO SPILLS
EATING	8:C	DRINKS FROM DRINKING FOUNTAIN USING HAND OR FOOT CONTROL
	9:C	USES A FORK TO PICK UP AND EAT FOOD
DRESSING	12:C	BUTTONS CLOTHING
	13:C	STARTS AND CLOSES A FRONT ZIPPER
GROOMING	5:C	PLACES A TOOTHBRUSH IN MOUTH AND BEGINS BRUSHING MOTION
	6:D	WIPES FACE WITH A WET WASHCLOTH
TOILETING	16:C	USES TOILET PAPER
	17:C	ASKS LOCATION OF BATHROOM IN A NEW SITUATION
RECEPTIVE	13:C	FOLLOWS TWO-STEP DIRECTIONS IN ORDER
LANGUAGE	14:C	POINTS TO LARGE OBJECT AND SMALL OBJECT UPON REQUEST
EXPRESSIVE	14:C	USES PRONOUNS IN COMPLETE SENTENCES
LANGUAGE	15:D	SPEAKS IN PHRASES TO BE UNDERSTOOD BY STRANGER
SOCIAL	19:D	INVITES OTHERS TO PARTICIPATE IN ACTIVITY
INTERACTION	20:D	RECEIVES AND MAKES LOCAL PHONE CALLS WITHOUT ASSISTANCE
READINESS &	5:D	IDENTIFIES DIFFERENT SOUNDS
READING	6:C	SORTS 3 OBJECTS BY SHAPE
WRITING	10:D	DRAWS CIRCLE WITH NO EXAMPLE TO LOOK AT
	11:D	DRAWS LINE CONNECTING 3 DOTS ON PAPER
NUMBERS	2:C	CREATES ORDER OUT OF A GROUP OF OBJECTS
	3:C	REPEATS 2 NUMBERS IN THE ORDER GIVEN
TIME	9:C	NAMES OR IDENTIFIES NUMBERS ON CLOCK
	10:C	NAMES OR IDENTIFIES SEASONS OF YEAR
MONEY	4:C	SORTS MIXED COINS INTO CORRECT GROUPINGS
	5:C	SELECTS PENNY, NICKEL, DIME & QUARTER FROM GROUP OF COINS
DOMESTIC	3:C	PROPERLY DISPOSES OF DIRTY CLOTHES
BEHAVIOR	4:D	MAKES BED (NOT INCLUDING CHANGING THE LINENS)
COMMUNITY	14:D	IDENTIFIES BUS STOP AND INDICATES ITS PURPOSE
ORIENTATION	15:C	ACTS APPROPRIATELY IN ALL NORMAL PUBLIC SITUATIONS
RECREATION &	10:C	PERFORMS ACTIVITIES NECESSARY TO VIEW TV/LISTEN TO RADIO
LEISURE-TIME	11:D	PARTICIPATES IN 3 OUTDOOR ACTIVITIES
VOCATIONAL	15:D	USES HAMMER, PLIERS & SCREWDRIVER APPROPRIATELY
	16:C	INCREASES SPEED OF WORK WHEN TOLD TO DO SO

At the next level, reports can be created that are useful to middle-level management; program directors and facility operators. After the information pertaining to individual clients has been entered into the data base, summary statistics, cross-tabulations, and selective sorts can be requested in response to particular management questions. Interestingly, few educational program directors today can accurately describe in detail the characteristics of the populations they serve. One of the authors was recently involved in a technical assistance project to a major suburban school district on the East coast. Despite the district's wealth, nobody knew for sure how many students were enrolled by program type. We have found, therefore, that simple tabulations and frequency counts are very useful as a starting point for program planning. The following is a sample management report for one facility (see page 200).

State planners generally will access a larger computer because of the magnitude of a statewide data base. In Illinois, for instance, a statewide client information system would produce a data base of 15 million bytes in one year. To perform longitudinal analysis would require even more capacity for storage.

There are many important analytic options that states need but that are unavailable for microcomputers. For instance, computer cartography and trend surface analysis has been very useful for displaying information to strategic planners (Joiner, 1979; Joiner, Silverstein & Bock, 1980). Powerful software such as SYMAP and ODESSEY are unavailable except in larger computer installations. Unavailable as yet for microcomputers are comprehensive software packages to perform "number crunching" analyses such as Statistical Analysis System (SAS).

However, the introduction of 16 and 32 bit microprocessors along with megabyte capacity disk drives for microcomputers will provide the capability to operate sophisticated statistical packages on desktop microcomputers. Complex statistical programs for microcomputers such as multiple linear regression, are marketed as individual software items. An illustration of the potential of management information

ILLINOIS CLIENT INFORMATION SYSTEM

NUMBER OF CLIENTS: 244

ASSESSMENT PERIOD: 05/15/80 - 07/08/81

FACILITY/AGENCY CODE: 001

AGE				SEX		
CATEGORY	N	%		CATEGORY	N	%
0- 2 YEARS	1	0.4		MALE	116	47.5
3- 5 YEARS	0	0.0		FEMALE	128	52.5
6-12 YEARS	0	0.0				
13-17 YEARS	0	0.0		MARITAL STATUS		
18-21 YEARS	3	1.2		CATEGORY	N	%
22-33 YEARS	76	31.1		NOT REPORTED	3	1.2
34-54 YEARS	127	52.0		SINGLE	241	98.8
55-64 YEARS	31	12.7		MARRIED	0	0.0
65 AND OVER	6	2.5				

ETHNICITY				LEGAL STATUS(ES)		
CATEGORY	N	%		CATEGORY	N	%
BLACK	4	1.6		UNREGULATED	0	0.0
WHITE	236	96.7		LTD. GUARD-TEMP	0	0.0
NATIVE AMERICAN	2	0.8		LTD. GUARD-PERM	0	0.0
SPANISH SURNAME	0	0.0		FULL GUARD-TEMP	0	0.0
ORIENTAL	0	0.0		FULL GUARD-PERM	0	0.0
OTHER	0	0.0		TEMPORARY	0	0.0
UNKNOWN	1	0.4		DIAGNOSTIC	0	0.0
NOT REPORTED	1	0.4		ADMINISTRATIVE	0	0.0
DMH/DD ID				EMERGENCY-MR	0	0.0
CATEGORY	N	%		JUDICIAL-MR	0	0.0
NOT REPORTED	1	0.4				
YES, REPORTED	243	99.6				

FACILITY/AGENCY CODE: 001

LEVEL OF INTELLECT

CATEGORY	N	%
NOT REPORTED	243	99.6
NOT RETARDED	1	0.4
BORDERLINE	0	0.0
MR-MILD	0	0.0
MR-MODERATE	0	0.0
MR-SEVERE	0	0.0
MR-PROFOUND	0	0.0
UNDETERMINED	0	0.0

MOBILITY

CATEGORY	N	%
NOT REPORTED	11	4.5
WALKS INDEP	131	53.7
WALKS/DEVICES	18	7.4
WALKS UNAIDED	9	3.7
WHEELCHAIR/SELF	16	6.6
WHEELCHAIR/HELP	37	15.2
NO MOBILITY	22	9.0

VISION

CATEGORY	N	%
NORMAL	196	80.3
IMPAIRED	25	10.2
LEGALLY BLIND	4	1.6
NO FUNCTIONAL	14	5.7
UNKNOWN	5	2.0
NOT REPORTED	0	0.0

HEARING

CATEGORY	N	%
NORMAL	207	84.8
IMPAIRED	27	11.1
DEAF	2	0.8
UNKNOWN	8	3.3
NOT REPORTED	0	0.0

CATEGORY	TOILETING		EATING		DRESS/GROOM	
	N	%	N	%	N	%
NOT REPORTED	3	1.2	1	0.4	2	0.8
COMPLETELY INDEPENDENT	92	37.7	98	40.2	41	16.8
NEEDS ASSISTANCE, NO TRAINING	18	7.4	14	5.7	22	9.0
NEEDS ASSISTANCE AND TRAINING	52	21.3	81	33.2	102	41.8
COMPLETELY DEPENDENT	79	32.4	50	20.5	77	31.6

FACILITY/AGENCY CODE: 001

SEIZURE HISTORY

CATEGORY	N	%
CONTROLLED	40	16.4
SEIZURES IN PAST 2 YEARS	25	10.2
CURRENTLY HAS SEIZURES	25	10.2
NONE	154	63.1
NOT REPORTED	0	0.0

MEDICAL SUPPORT

	ON-SITE		ON-CALL	
CATEGORY	N	%	N	%
NONE	2	0.8	1	0.4
NURSING	242	99.2	0	0.0
PHYSICAN	0	0.0	243	99.6

PHYSICAL HEALTH STATUS

CATEGORY	N	%
NOT REPORTED	3	1.2
GOOD	130	53.3
INTERMITTENT PROBLEMS	51	20.9
CHRONIC PROBLEMS	60	24.6

MEANINGFUL TIE

CATEGORY	N	%
NOT REPORTED	102	41.8
COUNSELING ONLY	121	49.6
POSSIBLE DUAL PLACEMENT	17	7.0
MANDATORY DUAL PLACEMENT	4	1.6

ELIGIBILITY STATUS

CATEGORY	RECEIVING		NOT RECEIVING BUT ELIGIBLE		NOT ELIGIBLE		UNKNOWN	
	N	%	N	%	N	%	N	%
TITLE XIX	0	0.0	0	0.0	0	0.0	244	100.0
TITLE XX	0	0.0	0	0.0	0	0.0	244	100.0
SSI	0	0.0	0	0.0	0	0.0	244	100.0
SSP	0	0.0	0	0.0	0	0.0	244	100.0
PUBLIC AID	0	0.0	0	0.0	0	0.0	244	100.0
VOC. REHAB	0	0.0	0	0.0	0	0.0	244	100.0
PURCHASE CARE	0	0.0	0	0.0	0	0.0	244	100.0
DDSA	0	0.0	0	0.0	0	0.0	244	100.0
DMH/DD GRANTS	0	0.0	0	0.0	0	0.0	244	100.0

FACILITY/AGENCY CODE: 001

MEDICATION ADMINISTRATION

CATEGORY	N	%
NOT REPORTED	6	2.5
NO MEDICATION	39	16.0
YES, MEDICATION	199	81.6

	BY SELF		BY SELF WITH SUPERVISION		BY OTHERS	
CATEGORY	N	%	N	%	N	%
EMOTIONAL/BEHAVIORAL	0	0.0	38	19.1	61	30.7
FOR DIABETES	0	0.0	1	0.5	1	0.5
ANTI-CONVULSANT	0	0.0	14	7.0	60	30.2
CARDIAC	0	0.0	5	2.5	2	1.0
OTHER	0	0.0	32	16.1	95	47.7

VOCATIONAL STATUS

	CURRENT		NEEDED	
CATEGORY	N	%	N	%
NONE/DUPLICATE OF CURRENT	4	1.6	209	85.7
COMPETITIVE EMPLOYMENT	0	0.0	0	0.0
JOB SKILL TRAINING	0	0.0	0	0.0
SHELTERED EMPLOYMENT	1	0.4	10	4.1
DAYTIME/WORK ACTIVITY	30	12.3	22	9.0
WORK ADJUSTMENT	0	0.0	0	0.0
VOCATIONAL EVALUATION	0	0.0	2	0.8
GENERAL EDUCATION DEVELOPMENT	206	84.4	1	0.4
UNOCCUPIED	3	1.2	0	0.0

FACILITY/AGENCY CODE: 001

DAY PROGRAMS

CATEGORY	CURRENTLY RECEIVING		NEEDED WITHIN 1 YEAR	
	N	%	N	%
NONE REPORTED/DUPLICATE OF CURRENT	244	100.0	244	100.0
ADULT-TRAINING PROGRAMS--SHELTERED WORKSHOP	0	0.0	0	0.0
CASEFINDING/INFORMATION AND REFERRAL PGM	0	0.0	0	0.0
DAY TRAINING FOR DD ADULTS	0	0.0	0	0.0
DAY TRAINING FOR DD CHILDREN, THRU AGE 21	0	0.0	0	0.0
DENTAL PROGRAM	0	0.0	0	0.0
GENETIC TESTING/COUNSELING PROGRAM	0	0.0	0	0.0
HOMEBOUND PROGRAM	0	0.0	0	0.0
LOW PREVALENCE OUTREACH--FOLLOW ALONG PGM	0	0.0	0	0.0
OUTPATIENT COMPREHENSIVE DIAGNOSTIC PROGRAM	0	0.0	0	0.0
OUTPATIENT PROGRAMS	0	0.0	0	0.0
PUBLIC SCHOOL	0	0.0	0	0.0
PROTECTIVE SERVICES PROGRAM	0	0.0	0	0.0
RESIDENTIAL CAMP PROGRAM	0	0.0	0	0.0
SPECIAL HABILITATION PROGRAM	0	0.0	0	0.0
SUMMER DAY CAMP PROGRAM	0	0.0	0	0.0
SUSTAINING CARE	0	0.0	0	0.0
WORK ACTIVITY	0	0.0	0	0.0

FACILITY/AGENCY CODE: 001

FUNCTIONAL AND DISABILITY STATUS

	PRIMARY		SECONDARY		TERTIARY	
CATEGORY	N	%	N	%	N	%
NONE	0	0.0	39	16.0	145	59.4
ALCOHOLISM	0	0.0	0	0.0	0	0.0
AUTISM	1	0.4	0	0.0	0	0.0
CEREBRAL PALSY	14	5.7	44	18.0	7	2.9
CHEMICAL DEPENDENCY	0	0.0	0	0.0	0	0.0
EPILEPSY	6	2.5	37	15.2	23	9.4
IMPAIRMENTS OF AGING	0	0.0	1	0.4	1	0.4
MENTAL RETARDATION	208	85.2	29	11.9	4	1.6
NEUROLOGICAL IMPAIRMENT	2	0.8	4	1.6	2	0.8
PSYCHIATRIC (DIAGNOSED)	4	1.6	9	3.7	5	2.0
SPECIAL LEARNING	0	0.0	2	0.8	1	0.4
UNDETERMINED	0	0.0	0	0.0	0	0.0
OTHER	0	0.0	0	0.0	0	0.0
PHYSICAL/MEDICAL & SUBPARTS	9	3.7	79	32.4	56	23.0
(1) GROWTH IMPAIRMENT	0		3		6	
(2) MUSCULO-SKELETAL	3		32		34	
(3) SPECIAL SENSE	4		15		13	
(4) RESPIRATORY	1		4		1	
(5) CARDIOVASCULAR	0		16		1	
(6) DIGESTIVE	0		6		6	
(7) GENITO-URINARY	0		5		3	
(8) HEMIC/LYMPHATIC	0		2		0	
(9) SKIN	1		15		5	
(10) ENDOCRINE	1		12		7	
(11) MULTIPLE BODY SYSTEMS	0		0		1	
(12) NEUROLOGICAL	2		6		11	
(13) NEOPLASTIC DISEASE	0		1		0	

HEALTH AND THERAPY NEEDS

CATEGORY	PRIMARY		SECONDARY	
	N	%	N	%
NONE NEEDED/DUPLICATE OF PRIMARY	243	99.6	244	100.0
ONGOING MEDICAL	0	0.0	0	0.0
PHYSICAL THERAPY	1	0.4	0	0.0
OCCUPATIONAL THERAPY	0	0.0	0	0.0
NURSING SUPERVISION	0	0.0	0	0.0
MENTAL HEALTH SERVICES	0	0.0	0	0.0
DENTAL SERVICES	0	0.0	0	0.0
SPEECH THERAPY	0	0.0	0	0.0
PHYSICAL REHABILITATION	0	0.0	0	0.0
AUDIOLOGY SERVICES	0	0.0	0	0.0

REGULAR EDUCATION			SPECIAL EDUCATION		
YEARS	N	%	YEARS	N	%
NONE	243	99.6	NONE	242	99.2
(1) ONE	0	0.0	(1) ONE	0	0.0
(2) TWO	0	0.0	(2) TWO	0	0.0
(3) THREE	0	0.0	(3) THREE	0	0.0
(4) FOUR	0	0.0	(4) FOUR	1	0.4
(5) FIVE	1	0.4	(5) FIVE	0	0.0
(6) SIX	0	0.0	(6) SIX	0	0.0
(7) SEVEN	0	0.0	(7) SEVEN	0	0.0
(8) EIGHT	0	0.0	(8) EIGHT	1	0.4
(9) NINE	0	0.0	(9) NINE	0	0.0
(10) TEN	0	0.0	(10) TEN	0	0.0
(11) ELEVEN	0	0.0	(11) ELEVEN	0	0.0
(12) TWELVE	0	0.0	(12) TWELVE	0	0.0
(13) OR MORE	0	0.0	(13) OR MORE	0	0.0

FACILITY/AGENCY CODE: 001

BEHAVIORAL IMPEDIMENTS (MOST)

CATEGORY	N	%
NO IMPEDIMENTS	145	59.4

COGNITIVE PROBLEMS

DELUSIONS OR HALLUCINATIONS	3	1.2
DISORIENTATION TO TIME OR PLACE	0	0.0
PERSEVERATION	1	0.4
ECHOLALIA	0	0.0

AFFECTIVE PROBLEMS

EXTREME MOOD CHANGES	9	3.7
APPROPRIATE AFFECT NOT DISPLAYED	1	0.4
LACK SOCIAL OR INTERPERSONAL RESPONSIVENESS	6	2.5
SUICIDE THREATS OR ATTEMPTS	1	0.4
DEPRESSION	5	2.0
EXTREME IRRITABILITY	10	4.1

BEHAVIOR PROBLEMS

PHYSICAL ASSAULT UPON OTHERS	6	2.5
PROPERTY DESTRUCTION	5	2.0
PROPERTY THEFTS	4	1.6
FIRE-SETTING OR ATTEMPTS AT	0	0.0
COERCIVE SEXUAL BEHAVIOR	1	0.4
GENITAL DISPLAY IN PUBLIC SETTING	1	0.4
DISROBING IN PUBLIC SETTING	2	0.8
SELF-INJURIOUS ACTIONS	5	2.0
HYPERACTIVITY	1	0.4
STEREOTYPIC/REPETITIVE MOVEMENTS	3	1.2
ACTIVELY RESISTS SUPERVISION	5	2.0
CRYING, TEMPER TANTRUMS	9	3.7
VERBALLY ABUSIVE TO OTHERS	1	0.4
WANDERING, ROAMING, OR RUNNING AWAY	9	3.7
HANDLES/PLAYS WITH BODILY WASTES	6	2.5
EATS NON-FOOD SUBSTANCES	3	1.2
SCAPEGOATING	0	0.0
SUBSTANCE ABUSE	0	0.0
TOILET STUFFING	0	0.0
OTHER BEHAVIOR	2	0.8

COMMUNITY SUPPORT SERVICES

	PRIMARY		SECONDARY	
CATEGORY	N	%	N	%
NONE NEEDED/DUPLICATE OF PRIMARY	242	99.2	244	100.0
LEISURE TIME/RECREATION	0	0.0	0	0.0
HOMEMAKER SERVICES	0	0.0	0	0.0
HOME HEALTH SERVICES	0	0.0	0	0.0
CHORE SERVICES	0	0.0	0	0.0
HOME DELIVEREE MEALS	0	0.0	0	0.0
LEGAL SERVICES	0	0.0	0	0.0
RESPITE CARE	0	0.0	0	0.0
ADVOCACY SERVICES	0	0.0	0	0.0
EVENING CONTINUING EDUCATION	0	0.0	0	0.0
FINANCIAL GUARDIAN	2	0.8	0	0.0
FINANCIAL COUNSELING	0	0.0	0	0.0
LIFE COUNSELING	0	0.0	0	0.0

systems for state level policy is the Illinois Mental Health Department's exploration of differential funding for the developmentally disabled on a case by case basis. Presently, funding is sensitive to only gross client differences and needs; adjustments for such things as gains in behavioral competence are impossible. With shrinking state dollars it would be desirable to allocate financial support according to the client's status on a large array of measures. But to do so requires the existence of a large data base on clients and cost variables; in essence, an information system.

Silverstein (1981) has developed procedures to perform multivariate groupings of Illinois' developmentally disabled on a sub-set of items contained in the Illinois Client Information System. Bock Associates of St. Paul has developed specifications for establishing differential funding algorithms. Together, these procedures, in conjunction with a management information system, can save the State of Illinois millions of dollars per year, while insuring that each developmentally disabled client receives optimal services.

Estimating Costs

The exact dollar figures for implementing a management information system depends on the magnitude of the data base, staffing, computer hardware, inservice training, programming, and the overall complexity of the specifications. At the lower end of the scale, the authors implemented an information system for budget management in a university department on an Apple II microcomputer, for less than $500. Cogdill and Goldberg (1981) reported a per pupil cost of $13.50 for a Head Start information system on the IBM 8100. The Illinois Client Information System cost about $5 per client for programming, data processing, technical assistance, and report generation. What these cost figures overlook, however, are the "soft" start-up, planning, and staff development costs that are fundamental requirements of a successful application.

Sanderson (1975) has provided time and cost estimates of

the several stages of MIS research and development. Of particular interest are the preliminary analysis of feasibility, feasibility study, and the systems analysis and design. Together, these activities represent an estimated 25 percent of the cost and 40 percent of the time in establishing a management information system.

Unfortunately, these three stages too often are either overlooked entirely or only informally pursued.

	Cost	Time
Preliminary analysis of feasibility	2%	5%
Feasibility study	5%	10%
Systems analysis and design	18%	25%
Programming	45%	40%
Installation	30%	20%

THE CRUCIAL NATURE OF ACCURATE DATA

A disastrous oversight in the design of information systems is insufficient attention to developing procedures that guarantee the accuracy of basic data. Computer generated reports, data tapes, and print-outs tend to convey, because of their orderliness, an impression of authority and accuracy. In reality, however, the data upon which an entire system is based is often assembled and coded by poorly trained and supervised professional and even paraprofessional employees.

The need for accuracy in the basic data contained in an information system is paramount. And to achieve this accuracy, pre-service and inservice training of staff is often necessary. Both skills development and attitudinal changes are often required, the latter because employees far removed from the decision context may have little or no appreciation of the significance of the data they collect or code.

According to Putnam (1977),

"it is foolhardy to assume that the automation of the present system and/ or use of existing data will be good enough to do

the job...While there is tremendous redundancy in manual
systems, frequently the errors may be isolated or averaged;
however, in the computer system, each item of data is used
and reused." (p. 108)

Therefore, an advised practice is to assign data auditors at the
beginning of the design phase.

Also relating to the need for accurate data, a further
tightening of controls is possible through a format EDIT, built
into data entry programs. These provisions will result in the
rejection of transactions if fields have missing data or invalid
characters. There are also a number of logical checks that
can be built into programs to detect data entry errors.

OBSTACLES

Organizational Impact

Two decades ago, Mann and Williams (1960) described the
distress and organizational problems that arose when a
manual information system was converted to a computerized
system in an organization. Those observations remain valid
today. The three main problems that Mann and Williams
noted were: alterations in previous managerial responsibilities, changes in existing patterns of personnel control, and
uncertainty concerning the future management roles and
responsibilities of those most affected by the system.

Demb (1979), in a study of conversion by a university to a
centralized MIS, reviewed information system literature and
identified five most frequently discussed concepts relating to
the installation of management information systems in
organizations:

- The installation of any automated system that supplies
  information to managers must be considered a major
  organizational change.

- Fear and anxiety among personnel affected by the change
  is inevitable.

- Organizational norms will determine whether the overall reaction to a MIS is positive and supportive or negative and hindering.

- The impact of MIS will vary according to the decision styles of users, their management functions, and the type of tasks impacted.

- Smaller organizations are more likely to be able to effectively assimilate MIS technology by making appropriate and timely modifications in managerial responsibilities.

Avoidance Behaviors and Passive Sabotage

One type of information system that has been frequently tried is in career education. To assist students in making wise career choices, computer-based information systems such as SIGI, DISCOVER, CHOICES, and GIS have been made available to secondary students, counselors, and career education staff. In a recent study of the impact of these systems, Ryan and Drummond (1981) noted "serious problems remain unresolved before computer information systems receive a positive endorsement by staff in human service agencies" (p. 81). Despite the fact that these information systems function well technically and contain timely and relevant information, "professionals in human service agencies have a fear of computer systems and their reputed power that seemed to cause a variety of avoidance behaviors."

Lack Of Technical Knowledge

Lack of technical knowledge is often a source of resistance to the introduction of computer technologies in an organization. For higher level administrators, a lack of technical knowledge can alter their relationships with subordinates. At the present time, few, if any, colleges of education offer courses for education administrators that prepare them to effectively use computer technologies, appraise them of the nomenclature, and provide them with a conceptual base that would allow them to evaluate and control the performance of technically trained subordinates. Most can't even read computer printouts.

Lacking adequate training in the basics of computer applications, administrators must rely upon outside experts or younger staff members who have acquired knowledge and skills independently. Given this situation, it is easy for administrators to become opponents of computer applications in school management. They may endorse enthusiastically the use of computers in classroom instruction, but not support their use as a management tool.

Disruptions of the prevailing patterns of subordinate relationships in organizations that adopt computerized systems occur with such regularity that the phenomenon has been discussed at length in the literature under the rubric: "inversion of formerly normal superior-subordinate relationships," (Reynolds, 1969). It has been observed that subordinates with access to and control over management information systems may, in a sense, "program" less skillful or technically aware top level administrators who become dependent upon them.

Information Overdemand

A major obstacle to the implementation of an efficient, comprehensive management information system in fields like special education is the reporting requirements and procedures that are already in place. All too frequently, state and federal offices, for strategic planning or management control, require the collection and transmission of data whose purpose either isn't well understood or is considered trivial by line staff.

While information overload may be a significant impediment to effective management (Joiner, 1979), information overdemand is likely to contribute to a climate of resistance to computerized information systems. It is, therefore, crucial that a careful plan be drawn up, even prior to implementing limited purpose systems, that addresses the consolidation of reporting requirements, levels within the organization, and guaranteeing the production only of information of significant worth to strategic planners, managers, and direct service staff.

Demb's (1979) research in university management information systems has resulted in several crucial recommendations concerning development activities that should be undertaken prior to the installation of a system:

* Design a process which involves all affected parties in the setting of priorities and diagnosis of needs.

* Develop a plan of action which has realistic timetables and level-of-effort estimates for each activity.

* Make top management support highly visible and explicit.

* Establish institutional rewards which encourage the development and utilization of the new system; establish mechanisms which encourage its use in the conduct of daily business.

* Develop a clear understanding of the relationships between users and the information system, particularly their level of dependence on it.

Chapter IX

COMPUTER CONFRONTATION

This chapter is about how microcomputers became the object of intense conflict between local educators and a state education agency's computer establishment. It describes how, despite shrinking dollars to support schools and the proven cost-effectiveness of microcomputers in doing the job, a state supported computer bureaucracy was able to compel local schools to participate in a statewide financial information system at the excess cost of hundreds of teacher salaries. It reveals that local educators will endorse a proven cost-effective technology, but that state organizations are quite willing to ignore costs and local needs when organizational interests and control are threatened.

RELUCTANT VOYAGERS

"A Congressional report quotes an industrialist who happens also to be a school board president as saying, 'the aircraft industry would go out of business in two years if it changed as slow as education.' Always the public whipping boy, education as been accused by 'experts' of harboring a 30-year lag between innovation and widespread adoption of the innovation." (Hoos, 1975).

Professional educators have often been portrayed as unimaginative functionaries whose dedication is to the status quo and turn-of-the-century methods. Contributing to this portrayal is the fact that many "authorities" in our society are convinced that the adoption of new technologies by education is both desirable and progressive. It is "the way" to efficiency. According to Hoos (1975): "education to an extent greater, perhaps than any other societal institution, has been vulnerable to invasion, if not takeover, by 'technology', in its myriad manifestations."

As members of an industrial society, our daily lives abound with technologies, air travel, television, autos, and telecommunications. From this may arise the tendency to equate the use of any technology by schools with enlightened practice. Technologies are tangible, but mysterious and compelling to laypeople. Even high level professionals gravitate toward them, without even knowing why. Harvard professor David McClelland admitted:

> Educational technology should be helpful in getting the facts across to the participants, in creating an atmosphere which is conducive to learning and increasing confidence, and in making the information presented more vivid and understandable. We have found it essential to make use of educational technology from the very beginning, although it is only recently that we have begun seriously with a self-conscious attempt to understand how and why they work" (McClelland, 1969).

Faith abounds. Unfortunately, great faith in technologies has often been misplaced. Some reluctance to become involved in technologies surely stems from earlier monumental failures of technology based instruction. The IBM Computer Assisted Instruction 1500 Program, after years of development and eight million dollars, was terminated -- a failure. Project IMPACT, the ultimate CAI as described by Radio Corporation of America, was also terminated prior to implementation, after millions of dollars were spent. (Steg & Schenk, 1977).

Nonetheless, as any administrator will attest, technologies have made their way into the schools. Almost all schools are now, to some degree, involved with data processing, sometimes provided through a central district office and sometimes contracted to computer service agencies. The availability and power of microcomputers, however, adds an interesting new dimension to education's presumably reluctant voyage into the land of technology. Arising now are confrontations between existing, established technologies and microcomputing. This conflict is enacted with appeals for greater cost-effectiveness on one side and a desire to protect major financial and organizational vested interests on the other.

As the following case discloses, efficiency rationalizations are rarely, except in extreme circumstances if ever, powerful enough to produce acceptance of new technologies when old ones supported by large and powerful organizations are at stake. More importantly, it illustrates that the presence of elaborate technologies is, in and of itself, an inexorable conservative force in education.

Emerging human needs, aspirations and new ways of doing things set the stage for the introduction of technologies. For like any other machine, even computers have no intrinsic purpose or world-view. There is no technological imperative, but only the changes in human activities that provide the momentum for the takeover of a field by technology.

Recently, we have experienced major changes in the way of doing things in education. One of these changes is the widespread endorsement of rational, centralized planning requiring vast, accurate, and accessible data. Data based management, management by objective, and operational analysis have become widely accepted models for talking about and analyzing data and events. Uniform administrative practices and especially uniform reporting are key features of this approach.

Consistent with and flowing from their acceptance of the information-based, centralized planning model, states are beginning to adopt uniform financial accounting and reporting standards for "independent" school districts. Uniform financial accounting and reporting systems govern the structure that reports of financial data must take, the data that must be collected, the manner in which school funds are accounted, and permit the establishment of computerized "statewide" data bases pertaining to school finances.

Obviously, school districts got, spent, and kept track of money long before somebody thought of uniform financial accounting and reporting systems. And it is safe to say that financial accounting and reporting hasn't been cited in professional literature as one of the crucial issues of modern education. The fact is most schools are quite able to manage their own financial affairs and do so accurately and responsibly -- especially smaller school districts.

But what works for local districts may not always suit the state education directorate. So it was for one midwestern state in the area of finance. The state department of education and the legislature wanted uniform accounting and reports from all school districts, under the auspices of improved planning.

It is worth keeping in mind that our present capacity for generating uniform data far exceeds our capability for understanding its implications and for using it in planning. Joiner (1979) observes that:

> The computer-induced quantitative revolution has led to a
> glut of quantitative data, with a resulting information
> overload...Undoubtedly, much data is readily available
> today for use by planners. But can they understand it?

Despite dismal prospects, evidenced by past performance, training and background for doing anything remarkable or even valuable with masses of data, state officials forged ahead. The existing statewide computer network, a member of the state department of education family of enterprises, was the organizational vehicle for implementing the uniform accounting and reporting system.

THE BIG SYSTEM

The centralized computer system of this mid-western state was slated to provide services of two types to school districts: 1) student instruction, and 2) management information services. Management information services included student support services, payroll personnel services, and finance subsystems. Centralized management information data analysis services were performed on large computers,

Burroughs 6700 / 6800 at regional "service offices" across the state. At the time of this writing, however, student support services was not operational due to delays and problems in implementing the financial and payroll subsystems.

Member districts entered their financial data into regional computers through a telephone line using a local terminal, or by transporting data on paper or keypunched cards to the regional center. Summary reports, vouchers, and checks were returned to the district by mail or common carrier. Many districts did not use the statewide computer services since they were optional and required payment of a set fee per student. However, a state statute was enacted requiring all districts to provide fiscal reports to the state in compliance with Uniform Financial Accounting and Reporting Standards (UFARS) by July 1, 1980.

THE MICRO ALTERNATIVE

The compelling idea behind the UFARS was that the data would be of a consistent type and format, allowing the aggregation of a statewide fiscal data base. Assuming that the existence of such a financial data base would support better and more rational financial planning, perhaps even cutting costs, it would also seem reasonable to assume that the most cost-effective computer configuration to support it would be widely endorsed. As might be expected, then, educators began wondering whether microcomputers, distributed in individual school districts, might be able to process and report data to the state at a lower cost than that of a statewide system based upon a price per student formula.

About the same time, a state agency responsible for encouraging cost-effective education funded a local school district's microcomputer-based effort to meet Uniform Financial Accounting and Reporting requirements. During its three years of operation, the project developed, among other things, a complete financial package for schools that could run on the Apple II microcomputer. The financial package included general ledger, revenues, disbursements, payroll, vendor list, check printing, and a variety of report formats.

STUDYING RELATIVE COSTS

In order to evaluate microcomputer programs and procedures for meeting Uniform Financial Accounting and
Reporting requirements, independent evaluators conducted a
study to estimate the relative costs of four options, involving
microcomputers and timesharing computers, for meeting
state requirements. The study was supported by educators at
both the state and local levels. An option of special interest
was the "Stand-Alone Microcomputer" model.

The state was organized into several computer service
regions and the study was addressed to the costs of
implementing the four alternative models within one of those
regions. Financial reports, operating plans, and interviews
with administrators and clerical staff were the data from
which cost-effectiveness estimates were drawn.

The region selected for study contained 87 independent
school districts and was predominantly rural. At the time of
the study, only 16,099 of the 66,000 students in the region were
as yet being served by the statewide financial information
system. These facts show that the region was at a point in its
development where no irreversible commitment had been
made to any one system. At the local school district level,
there were, as yet, no strong financial or organizational
interests in any existing model.

FOUR MODELS FOR DISTRICT FINANCIAL
MANAGEMENT

Two of the four models studied involved membership in the
statewide system and two involved independent operation
using microcomputers. The statewide system models required
transmission of district revenue and expenditure data to a
regional computer, either on paper or keypunched cards,
processing at the regional headquarters, and the mailing of
reports, vouchers, and checks back to the district.

Both microcomputer models involved independent data
processing and the printing of vouchers and summary reports
in the district's own offices. Microcomputer models involved

no keypunching or transportation charges. All cost estimates included a 5 year depreciation of equipment. A description of each model follows:

Centralized Computing With Paper-Pencil Reporting

A district with an enrollment of 1,000 students subscribes to the region's financial information service, transporting data recorded with paper and pencil, monthly, by private carrier to regional headquarters. Estimated five year costs for the model were:

1. Transporting data to regional office by private carrier
   ($30 per month x 60 months)...................................... $ 1,800

2. Keypunching at regional office
   ($.06 per transaction x 300 transactions x 60 months).............. $ 1,080

3. District fees for "membership" in financial information system
   ($100 membership per year x 5 years) +
   ($2.00 per student x 1000 students x 5 years)...................... $10,500

4. Staff costs at $6.50 per hour
   (Five days of data preparation and report handling) + (One day editing hardcopy of vouchers and report) = (Six days per month x 60 months).. $18,720

Total five year cost = $32,100 = 1.95 full time teaching positions or .39 positions per year at statewide average salary. (At the time of publication it has been learned that key punching rates doubled, membership fees were raised to $500, and per pupil costs for the full financial system more than doubled to $5.70)

The $32,100 estimate is for a district with an enrollment of 1,000 students. Extrapolating to the 87 district region yielded an estimated regional cost of $2,792,700. Converting this to a full-time teacher metric yielded a total estimated regionwide cost of 169.82 full-time teaching positions over a five year period, or 33.96 full-time positions per year.

Characteristics of "Paper and Pencil" Model.
1. No editing of reports or vouchers on site until results were returned from the regional office.
2. The delay between transportation of the data to the regional office and the receipt of vouchers and reports

was two weeks. Reporting errors were corrected in the next batch, one month later. Voucher errors were corrected by handwritten checks. To insure monthly reports for board meetings at the district level, data had to be submitted at least two weeks in advance. This excluded transactions occurring within two weeks of the board meeting from summary reports to district policy-makers.

3. Bookkeeping and administrative staff reported dissatisfaction with the system's performance to date. Due to slow response, errors and the complexity of summary reports, the district bookkeeper maintained a duplicate set of books. Local school boards were required to adjust their meeting dates because the regional center couldn't handle the peak demand during "traditional" meeting times.

Centralized Computing With Local Keypunching And CRT Editing

A district with an enrollment of 1,000 students accesses statewide services by transporting "in-house" keypunched data to the regional office, which is then edited using a video display terminal in the district office. Estimated five year costs for the model were:

1. Hardware
   (CRT - synchronous processor = $2,219) + (telephone coupler at $782 - Maintenance at $421.68 per year)...........................$ 5,109

2. Keypunching
   (Machine at $2075) + (Maintenance at $100 per year) + (Supplies at $30 per year)...$ 2,725

3. Transportation of keypunched data............................... $ 1,800

4. District fees for membership in financial information system
   ($100 membership per year x five years) + ($2.00 per student X 1000 students x five years)............................ $10,500

5. Staff costs at $6.50 per hour
   (Two and one half days of data preparation) + (Two days of keypunching per month) + (One day editing per month) = 5.5 days per month x 60 months... $17,160

Total five year costs = $37,294 = 2.27 full-time teaching positions or .45 positions per year at statewide average salary.

The above $37,294 estimate is for a district with an enrollment of 1,000 students. Projecting this cost to an 87 district region yielded a total estimated regional cost of $3,244,578 to the region's districts. Conversion to the full-time teacher metric resulted in a total estimated regionwide cost of 197.3 full-time teaching positions over a five year period of 39.46 teaching positions per year at average statewide salaries.

Characteristics of "Keypunched Cards plus CRT" Model.
Editing of data on site was accomplished through a video terminal "on line" to the region's computer. Errors in keypunching or processing were reduced, but the response of the region's computer was slow, involving up to two minutes per keyboard entry. In other words, the district's terminal operator waited two minutes for the computer to respond to each entry made on the terminal's keyboard. Bookkeeping staff reported that this delay caused considerable frustration. Data editing required one full day per month.

Delay between submission of keypunched cards to the regional center and the return of vouchers and reports to the district involved four to six day's time. An additional six days were required if keypunching service had to be purchased through the region.

Bookkeeping and administrative staff reported strong dissatisfaction with the system's performance. Due to slow response, errors and the complexity of summary reports, the district bookkeeper maintained a duplicate set of books.

Micro Plus (Apple II, Decwriter, And Central Processing)

Using a combination of an Apple II microcomputer and the timeshare system accessed by a printing terminal, locally generated reports made available:
1. check register
2. vouchers and voucher jackets
3. clerk's register of disbursements

The system operated as follows:

1. A list of vendors and addresses was stored on disk.
2. As bills arrive they were coded according to vendor number, line item, and amount.
3. The above information was transmitted by telephone line to the central computer for processing.
4. Reports and vouchers were printed on a Decwriter printing terminal.

Costs were:

1. Hardware (terminal)
   (Decwriter printing terminal = $1200) + (Maintenance: $285 per
   year x five years)..$2,625

2. Hardware (microcomputer)
   (Apple II microcomputer with 48K memory, dual disk drives,
   telephone coupler, monitor, printer = $3300) + (Maintenance:
   $195 x 5 years)..$4,275

3. Staff costs at $6.50 per hour
   (Three days per month x 60 months)...............................$9,380

Total five year cost = $16,260 = .99 full time teaching positions or .20 positions per year at statewide average salary.

Projecting micro plus costs to an 87 district region yielded a total cost to the region of $1,414,620. Conversion to the "full-time teacher" metric yielded an estimated five year regionwide cost of 86.02 full-time teaching positions or 17.2 positions per year at the average statewide pay scale.

Characteristics of Micro Plus Model. Editing was done on site before data was transmitted. Reports were printed when data was entered or any time thereafter. Local staff was up-to-date on the status of all accounts. No duplication of effort: bookkeeping reported a 40 to 50 percent reduction in staff time required for fiscal management. In addition, reports were formatted to district specifications for interpretability.

"Stand-Alone" Microcomputer System

All three previously described models used centralized processing at regional offices with reports sent back to the districts by mail or through the telephone linkage for printing at the local district level. Under the "stand-alone" microcomputer model, fiscal programming for the Apple II, with UFARS coding of the data, processed raw fiscal data on site and sent summary reports to a central computer for aggregation with other districts. This "distributed processing" method met local needs for rapid turnaround for report generation and reduced processing time on the large centralized computer.

Estimated five year costs for the model were:

1. Hardware
   (Apple II microcomputer with 48k memory, dual disk drive, modem, monitor, and printer = $3300) + (Maintenance: $195 x five years).. $4,275

2. Local staff at $6.50 per hour
   (Three days x 60 months)... $9,360

Total five year cost = $13,635 = .83 teaching positions or .17 positions per year at the state average salary.

Multiplying the cost to a district with a 1,000 student enrollment by 87 districts yielded a subtotal cost for compliance with uniform financial system requirements of $1,186,245. In addition, certain additional costs would accrue to the region itself:

3. Regional consultant... $115,000
   To insure proper system operation, a regional microcomputer consultant would be needed
   ($20,000 x 5 years) + travel ($3,000 x 5 years).

4. District staff training... $ 5,000
   Reportedly, training local staff to operate the microcomputer model is easy because of the simplicity and self-direction built into the program. One of the investigators, with no bookkeeping experience, interacted with the program easily. It is estimated that a one-day workshop for a bookkeeper

from each district would provide the skills necessary for independent system operation. An estimated nine workshops would be needed at intra-region locations. Total five year costs = $1,306,245 = 79.43 full-time teaching positions over the five year period or 15.88 positions per year.

Characteristics of the "Stand-Alone" Microcomputer Model.

1. Continuous on-site editing capabilities.
2. Access to necessary information is only dependent on the speed of the printer. Printing of all vouchers and reports took less than 45 minutes at the local school district.
3. There was no duplication of effort. Reports were formatted specifically for district use and compliance with UFARS was built into the system.
4. Unlike large timesharing systems, if a microcomputer failed, another machine could be substituted and work continued.

SUMMARY OF FINDINGS

Figure 5 displays the relative costs of the four fiscal management and reporting models. "Stand-Alone" Model is the least expensive, least time consuming and yields the highest degree of local control over access to information and formatting of reports.

Figure 6 displays the projected five year total regional costs of the two models employing financial information system membership, and the "stand-alone" microcomputer model.

Estimates for each model include, where applicable, region expenditures prorated at 43 percent for financial information services, hardware, staff time, consulting and training, transportation of data and keypunching. It should be noted that the stand alone model avoids a $4,500,000 regional office expenditure and saves the equivalent of 293.75 full-time teaching positions or $4,830,000 when compared to "system membership without terminal or keypunch."

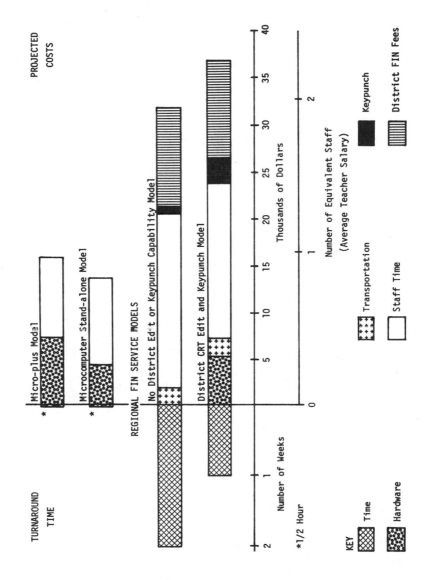

Figure 5

When compared to "system membership with CRT terminal and keypunch," the "stand-alone" microcomputer saves the equivalent of 321.24 full-time teacher positions or $5,282,713 over a five year period. This assumes the state chooses to have the data from the distributed processing network of local districts sent directly to the state computer without prior aggregation at regional offices.

Even if regional aggregation was to be used, the cost of operating the regional offices for MIS services would be greatly reduced. More powerful microcomputer systems now entering the market will be able to process much larger data bases in more complex ways which should further reduce the need for central processing, hastening the formation of distributed processing networks.

SUBSEQUENT EVENTS

School administrators at the local level began seeking help in adopting the stand-alone microcomputer model to meet state reporting requirements as soon as they heard of its success. Instead of providing that help, the statewide computing agency mounted a legislative and professional assault to discredit and prohibit the adoption of the new technology for meeting state reporting requirements. At stake was a multi-million dollar educational establishment, an empire of expanding job opportunities for non-instructional staff, and lucrative hardware contracts for mainframe computer vendors.

The spearhead of the attack was legislation requiring all school districts in the state to purchase membership in the statewide MIS, or "legislated cost-ineffectiveness." After a protracted struggle and at least one "major" (expensive) study, it was more or less concluded that microcomputers might possibly work, but only for small schools. The end result was the adoption of two models. Larger school districts were required by legislative act to purchase memberships in the statewide system; small schools were able to exercise the microcomputer option...at least for now.

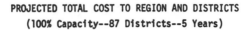

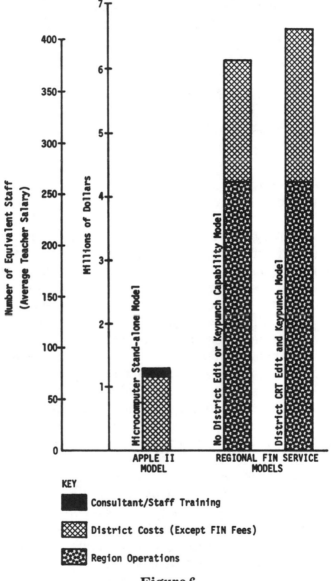

Figure 6

EPILOGUE

In spring, 1981 the legislature of that midwestern state was in extended session, debating and pondering the need for budget cuts due to inflation, overtaxation, a shrinking tax base, and the depopulation of the schools. Articles appeared in local newspapers almost daily, describing the cuts in educational programs. Included in the cuts were over 600 special education teaching positions.

MEANINGS

There are many lessons to be learned from this case, conclusions to be drawn, and points of interest. Among them are:

1. The adoption of a reporting requirement, in this case a a financial information system, paved the way for an expensive technical conversion. Hundreds of teacher salary equivalents were displaced by a lust for orderly and uniform data, regardless of the "cost-efficiency" of the technology ultimately adopted.
2. Teacher displacement by technology is a reality, not a paranoid's boogey-man. In this case, displacement is a far better term than replacement. While professional polemic addresses the virtues and failings of instructional technologies and what they portend for the welfare of the teaching profession, a technology far removed from the classroom itself threatens to gobble up the resources that might underwrite hundreds of teachers.
3. The expenditure of public monies on glamorous and elaborate "systems" and hardware, touted by technocrats, received far greater political support, despite its cost-ineffectiveness, than the felt needs, desires, and best interests of local educators and students. The statewide computing agency, an established, unified organization was able to muster the support to achieve widespread adoption of what might appear to be an ill-timed and misguided policy. Local education was weakened by its organizational diversity.

4. Technologies propagate organizations to control them. Once in place, these organizations resist the introduction of any competitive technology that cannot be subsumed within the control mechanisms or directed by the organization.

5. Microcomputers are aligned with diversity and independence among schools, because it is at the local level that their care and feeding occurs.

6. Local educators will endorse and support technologies in the schools when it is absolutely clear that they are cost-effective. Fifteen years of rhetoric about the resistance of educators to technology has overlooked the fact that cost-effective technologies are rare.

7. Cost-effectiveness is a catechism administered selectively. In this case, it had little bearing on the decision process of the education directorate. In fact, no cost studies were ever conducted and made public by state officials.

APPENDIX A

MICROCOMPUTER VENDORS

Aladdin Computer Corp.
3420 Kenyon Street
San Diego, CA 92110

ALTAIR
MITS
2450 Alamo SE
Albuquerque, NM

Altos Computer Systems
2360 Bering Drive
San Jose, California 95131

Apple Computer Inc.
10260 Bandley Dr.
Cupertino, CA 95014

ATARI, Inc.
Customer Service
1340 Bordeaux Avenue
Sunnyvale, CA 94086

Bell & Howell Audio-Visual Products Division
7100 McCormick Road
Chicago, IL 60645

Commodore Business ..Machines Inc.
3300 Scott Boulevard
Santa Clara, CA 94611

Commodore Pet
901 California Avenue
Santa Clara, CA 94611

Compucolor Corporation
Intecolor Drive Technology Park
Atlanta-Norcross, GA 30092
404-449-5996

Computer Data Systems
5460 Fairmont Drive
Wilmington, DE 19808
302-738-0933

Cromemco Inc.
280 Bernardo Ave.
Mountain View, CA 94040

Digital Equipment Corp.
Education Computer Systems
Maynard, MN 01754

Digital Systems
6017 Margorido Drive
Oakland, GA 94618
415-428-0950

Dyna Byte
1005 Elwell Court
Palo Alto, CA 94303
415-965-1010

Exidy Inc.
969 W. Maude Avenue
Sunnyvale, CA 94086

Exo Electronics Company
P.O. Box 3571
Culver City, CA 90230
213-390-6527

Heath Data Systems
Hilltop Road
St. Joseph, MI 44085

Hewlett-Packard Company
1507 Page Mill Road
Palo Alto, CA 94304

Honeywell
200 Smith Street
MS 487
Waltham, MA 02154

IMSAI
14860 Wicks Blvd.
San Leandro, CA 94577
415-483-2093

Industrial Micro Systems
628 N. Eckhoff Street
Orange, CA 92668
714-978-6281

Intelligent Systems Corp.
5965 Peachtree Corners
   East
Norcross, GA 30071
404-494-5961

Intertec Data Systems
2300 Broad River Road
Columbia, SD 29210
803-798-9100

Micro Dasys
P.O. Box 36061 Dept. B-12
Los Angeles, CA 90036
213-935-4555

**Midwest Scientific
   Instruments**
220 W. Cedar
Olathe, KS 66061
913-764-3273

**Monroe Systems for
   Business**
The American Road
Morris Plains, NJ 07950
Attn: Monroe Education
   Center

NEC America, Inc.
1401 Estes Avenue
Elk Grove Village, IL 60007

Netronics R&D LTD
Dept. cc9
333 Litchfield Road
New Milford, CT 06776

North Star Computers, Inc.
14440 Catalina Street
San Leandro, CA 94577

Nova Inc.
8404 Aero Drive
San Diego, CA 92123
714-277-8700

Ohio Scientific
1333 South Chillicothe Road
Aurora, OH 44202
216-831-5600

Osborne Computer Corp.
16500 Corporate Avenue
Hayward, CA 94545

Polymorphics
460 Ward Drive
Santa Barbara, CA 93111

Prodigy Systems Inc.
497 Lincoln Highway
Iselin, NJ 08830
201-283-2000

Radio Shack
1300 One Tandy Center
Fort Worth, Texas 76102

RCA VIP Marketing
New Holland Avenue
Lancaster, PA 17604
717-291-5848

Sinclair Research Ltd.
475 Main Street
Box 3027
Wallingford, CT 06492

Smoke Signal Broadcasting
31336 Via Colinas
West Blue Village, CA 91361
213-889-9340

Soroc Technology Inc.
169 Freedom Avenue
Anaheim, CA 92801
800-854-0147

**Southwest Technical
   Products Corporation**
219 W. Rhapsody
San Antonio, TX 78216
512-394-0241

Systems Engineering Ent.
1749 Rockville Pike
Rockville, MD 20852
301-468-1822

Tanyo Corporation
4301 Poche Court West
New Orleans, LA 70129

Technico Inc.
9130 Red Branch Road
Columbia, MD 21045
301-596-4100

TEI, Inc.
5075 S. Loop East,
Houston, TX 77033
713-738-2300

Tektronix Inc.
P.O. Box 500
Beaverton, OR 97077
800-547-1512

Terak Corp.
14405 North Scottsdale Road
Scottsdale, AR 85254
602-491-1580

Texas Instruments Inc.
Consumer Relations
P.O. Box 53
Lubbock, TX 79408

Vector Graphic Inc.
31364 Via Colinas
Westlake Village, CA 91362

Vista Computer Company
1317 E. Edinger Avenue
Santa Ana, CA 92705
714-953-0523

XYCON III
Computer Systems
   Unlimited
P.O. Box 870
Milpitas, CA 95035
408-262-6271

APPENDIX B

PRINTERS AND VIDEO DISPLAYS

Alphacom, Inc.
2323 South Bascom
Campbell, CA 95008

Anadex, Inc.
9825 Desota Avenue
Chatsworth, CA 91311

Arrom
5932 San Fernando Road
Glendale, CA 91202

Axiom Corporation
1014 Griswold Avenue
San Fernando, CA 91340

Centronics Data Computer Corp.
Hudson, NH 03051

Computers Peripherals
1225 Conecticut Avenue
Bridgeport, CT 06607

Computer Printers International, Inc.
340 E. Middlefield Road
Mountain View, CA 94043

Cybennex Limited
3221 Council Rins Road
Mississauga, Ontario
Canada

Datamedia Corp.
7300 N. Crescent Blvd.
Pennsauken, NJ 08110

Dataroyal, Inc.
Main Dunstable Road
Nashua, NH 03061

Datasouth Computer Corp.
4740 Dwight Evans Road
Charlotte, NC 28210

Diablo Systems
Xerox
Box 2639
Columbus, OH 43216

Digital Eq. Corp.
Education Computer
 Systems
Maynard, MN 01754

DIP, Inc.
745 Atlantic Avenue
Boston, MA 02111

E & L Instruments
61 First Street
Derby, CT 06418

Electrohome Electronics
809 Wellington Street North
Kitchener, Ontario N2G4J6
Canada

Epson America, Inc.
23844 Hawthorne Blvd.
Torrance, CA 90505

Excel Company
618 Grand Avenue
Oakland, CA 94610

Heath Company
Department 350-820
Benton Harbor, MI 49022

Input Output Unlimited
5922 Kester Avenue
Van Nuys, CA 91411

Integral Data Systems, Inc.
Milford, NH 03055

**Intertec Data Systems
  Corp.**
2300 Broad River Road
Columbia, SC 29210

Local Data Inc.
2701 Toledo Street
Suite 706
Torrance, CA 90503

Malibu Electronics Corp.
2301 Townsgate Road
Westlake Village, CA 91361

Marcom Inc.
124 10th Street
Ramona, CA 92065

Micro Peripherals
2099 West South
Salt Lake City, UT 84119

**National Computer
  Communications**
171 Worchester Road
Weliesley Hills, MA 02181

NEC America, Inc.
1401 Estes Avenue
Elk Grove Village, IL 60007

Okidata
111 Gaither Drive
Mount Laurel, NJ 08054

Otto Electronics
P.O. Box 3066
Princeton, NJ 08540

Soroc Technology Inc.
165 Freedom Avenue
Anaheim, CA 92801

Superbrain, Inc.
P.O. Box 403
Los Angeles, CA 90073

Syntest Corp.
169 Millhan Street
Marlboro, MA

Technical Products Corp.
219 West Rhapsody
San Antonio, TX 78216

Teletype Corp.
5555 Touhey Avenue
Skokie, IL

Telray
P.O. Box 24064
Minneapolis, MN 55424

Texas Instrument
P.O. Box 63
Lubbock, TX 79408

Trevcom
484 Oakmead Parkway
Sunnyvale, CA 94086

U.S. Robotics Inc.
1035 W. Lake Street
Chicago, IL 60607

APPENDIX C

MISCELLANEOUS PERIPHERALS

BIOFEEDBACK EQUIPMENT

Total Digital Engineering
210 D.W. Hwy.
S. Nashua. NH 03060
608-883-0991

COMPUTER ASSISTED VIDEO INSTRUCTION

CAVRI
26 Trumbull Street
New Haven, CT 06511
203-562-4979

TecLan
1010 Hurley Way
Sacramento, CA 95825
916-922-7729

Whitney Educational
  Services
1499 Bayshore Office Center
Suite 232
1499 Bayshore Highway
Burlington, CA 94010
415-692-7133

IN-HOUSE NETWORKING SYSTEMS

Corvus Systems
2029 O'Toole Avenue
San Jose, CA 95131
408-946-7700

Nestar Systems
2582 East Bayshore Road
Palo Alto, CA 94303
415-493-2223

GRAPHIC SYSTEMS

Datamax, Inc.
350 North Eric Drive
Palatine, IL 60067
312-991-7410

Micro Technology
  Unlimited
2806 Hillsborough Street
Box 12106
Raleigh, NC 27605
919-833-1458

MASS MEMORY STORAGE (TAPE, DISK, ETC.)

Apparat, Inc.
4401 So. Tamarac Parkway
Denver, CO 80237
303-741-1778

**Braemer Computer
Devices, Inc.**
11950 12th Avenue South
Burnsville, MN 55337

Cameo Electronics, Inc.
1626 Clementine
Anaheim, CA 92802
714-535-1682

CGRS Microtech, Inc.
P.O. Box 102
Langhorne, PA 19047

Corvus Systems
2029 O'Toole Avenue
San Jose, CA 95131
408-946-7700

Digital Research
P.O. Box 579
Pacific Grove, CA 93950

Exatron, Inc.
181 Commercial Street
Sunnyvale, CA 94086
408-737-7111

General Micro-Systems
12369 W. Alabama Pl.
Lakewood, LA 80228

ICOM
20630 Nordhoff Street
Chatsworth, CA 91311
213-998-1800

Lobo Drives, International
354 South Fairview Avenue
Goleta, CA 93117
805-683-1576

Matchless Systems
18444 South Broadway
Gardena, VA 90248
213-327-1010

MECCA
7026 O.W.S. Road
Yucca Valley, CA 92284
714-365-7686

Micro Squared
Suite 5B
7131 Owensmouth Avenue
Canoga Park, CA 91303

**Microcomputer
Technology, Inc.**
3304 W. MacArthur
Santa Ann, CA 92704
714-979-9923

Micro-Sci
17742 Irvine Blvd.
Suite 205
Tustin, CA 92680
714-731-9461

**Midwest Computer
Peripherals**
1467 South Michigan
Chicago, IL 60605
312-987-1024

Morrow Designs
5221 Central Avenue
Richmond, CA 94804
415-524-2101

**Percom   Data   Company,
Inc.**
211 North Kirby
Garland, TX 95042
214-272-3421

Tar Bell Electronic
950 Dolven Pl.
Suite B
Carson, CA 90746
213-538-4251

Vista Computer Company
1317 E. Edinger Avenue
Santa Ana, CA 92705
714-953-0523

MODEMS

ESI Lynx
123 Locust Street
Lancaster, PA 17602

**Hayes Microcomputer
  Products, Inc.**
5835 Peachtree Corners
  East
Norcross, GA 30092
404-449-8791

Microperipheral Corp.
2643 151st Place N.E.
Redmond, WA 98052
206-881-7544

Novation, Inc.
18664 Oxnard Street
Tarzana, CA 91356
213-996-5060

Omnitee Data
2405 South 20th Street
Phoenix, AZ 85034

Prentic Corp.
266 Casplan Drive
Sunnyvale, CA 94086
408-734-9519

U.S. Robotics, Inc.
203 N. Wabash
Suite 1718
Chicago, IL 60601
312-346-5650

Universal Data Systems
5000 Bradford Drive
Huntsville, AL 35805
205-837-8100

MUSIC SYNTHESIS

ALF Products, Inc.
1448 Estes
Denver, CO 80228

Micro Music, Inc.
309 Beaufort
Normal, IL 61761

Mountain Computer, Inc.
300 El Pueblo
Scotts Valley, CA 95066
408-438-6650

**Newtech Computer
  Systems, Inc.**
230 Clinton Street
Brooklyn, NY 11201

Passport Designs
Box 478
La Honda, CA 94020

OPTICAL SCANNERS / CARD READERS

Chatsworth Data Corp.
20710 Lassen Street
Chatsworth, CA 91311

SCAN-TRON Corp.
3398 E. 70th Street
Long Beach, CA 90805
213-633-4051

PLOTTERS

Hewlett-Packard Company
1507 Page Mill Road
Palo Alto, CA 94304
415-857-3752

Houston Instruments
One Houston Square
Austin, TX 78753
512-837-2820

Mauro Engineering
Rt. 1, P.O. Box 133
Mt. Shasta, CA 96067
916-926-4406

Nicolet Zeta Corp.
2300 Stanweel Drive
Concord, CA 94520

Summagraphics Corp.
35 Brentwood Avenue
Fairfield, CT 06430
203-384-1344

Versa Computing, Inc.
887 Conestoga Circle
Newbury Park, CA 91320
805-498-1956

POWER SURGE PROTECTORS

Electronic Specialists Inc.
171 South Main Street
Natick, MA 01760

RKS Enterprises Inc.
643 South 6th Street
San Jose, CA 95112

REMOTE CONTROL EQUIPMENT

Connecticut
    Microcomputer Inc.
34 Del Mar Drive
Brookfield, CT 06804
203-775-4595

E-Z Associates
5589 Starcrest Drive
San Jose, CA 95123
408-578-8096

Intelligent Control Systems
    Inc.
Box 14571
Minneapolis, MN 55414
612-699-4342

SPECIALIZED EQUIPMENT FOR THE HANDICAPPED

John Giem
1904 Westfield Drive
Fort Collins, CO 80526
303-223-0844

Grover & Associates
Creekside Center,
  Suite D116
7 Mount Lassen Drive
San Rafael, CA 94903
415-479-5906

Gregg Vanderheiden
Trace Research & Dev.
  Center
University of Wisconsin
314 Waisman Center
Madison, WI 53706
608-262-6966

Prentke Romich Co.
R.D. 2, Box 191
Shreve, OH 44676
216-767-2906

SPEECH RECOGNITION / SYNTHESIS

Computalker Consultants
1730 21st St., Suite A
Santa Monica, CA 90404
213-392-5230

Heuristics, Inc.
1285 Hammerwood Avenue
Sunnyvale, CA 95066
408-734-8532

Mountain Computer, Inc.
300 El Pueblo
Scotts Valley, CA 95066
408-438-6650

Vodex
500 Stephenson Hwy.
Troy, MI 48084
313-588-0341

VIDEO DIGITIZERS

The Micro Works
Box 1110
Del Mar, CA 92014
714-942-2400

Vector Graphic Inc.
31364 Via Colinas
Westlake Village, CA 91362

APPENDIX D

SOFTWARE

Aardvark Software
P.O. Box 26505
Milwaukee, WI 53213
1-800-558-8570

Activity Resources Co., Inc.
P.O. Box 4875
Hayward, CA 94540

Adventure International
P.O. Box 3435
Longwood, FL 32750

AJA Software
P.O. Box 2528
Orange, CA 94702
415-548-2805

Alternate Source
1806 Ada Street
Lansing, MI 48910

Apple Computer Inc.
10260 Bandley Drive
Cupertino, CA 95014

Basics & Beyond
P.O. Box 10
Amawalk, NY 10501

Borg-Warner Educ'l Systs
600 W. University Drive
Arlington Hgts., IL 60004

Computalker Consultants
1730 21st Street, AE
Santa Monica, CA 90404
213-392-5230

**Computer Components-
  Orange Co.**
6791 Westminster Avenue
Westminster, CA 92683
714-891-2584

Computer Factory
485 Lexington Avenue
New York, NY 10017
212-687-5001

CONDUIT
P.O. Box 388
Iowa City, IA 52244

Cow Bay Computing
Box 515
Manhasset, NY 11030

**Creative Computing
  Software**
39 E. Hanover Avenue
Morris Plains, NJ 07950
201-540-0445

Dynacomp
P.O. Box 162
Webster, NY 14580

Educational Activities Inc.
P.O. Box 392
Freeport, NY 11520

Educational Courseware
3 Nappa Lane
Westport, CT 06880

Educational Programs
P.O. Box 2345
W. Lafayette, IN 47906

Educ'l Software & Design
3338 No. 4th Street
W. Lafayette, IN 47906

Edu-Ware Services Inc.
22035 Burbank Blvd.
Woodland Hills, CA 91367

ENTELEK
P.O. Box 1303
Portsmouth, NH 03801

Folio Books
P.O. Box 4100 H
Los Angeles, CA 90041
800-423-4864

George Earl
1302 S. Gen. McMullen
San Antonio, TX 78237

**Graham-Dorian Software
   Systems Inc.**
211 North Broadway
Wichita, KS 67202
316-265-8633

Hartley Software
3268 Coach Lane   2A
Kentwood, MI 49508

**H. Geller Computer
   Systems**
Dept. M, P.O. Box 350
New York, NY 10040

Hugh Ward
1615 Falmouth Avenue
Deltona, FL 32725

Interpretive Education
2306 Winters Drive
Kalamazoo, MI 49002

Jo Ann Comito
State Univ. of N.Y.
Tech. & Society Dept.
Stony Brook, NY 11790

Lifeboat Associates
2248 Broadway
New York, NY 10024
212-580-0082

Ligori Data Services
P.O. Box 2482
Anaheim, CA 92804

MECC Publications
2520 Broadway Drive
St. Paul, MN 55113

Mentor Software Inc.
515 Park Street
Anoda, MN 55303

Merlan Scientific
P.O. Box 25
Depew, NY 14043

**Microcomp. Software
   Systems**
4716 Lakewood Drive
Metairie, LA 70002

MICRO-ED, Inc.
P.O. Box 24156
Minneapolis, MN 55424

Micro Learningware
P.O. Box 2134
Mankato, MN 56001
507-387-1649

Micro-Music, Inc.
309 W. Baeufort
Normal, IL 61761

Microphys
2048 Ford Street
Brooklyn, NY 11229

Microsoft
10800 NE Eighth
Suite 819
Bellevue, WA 98004
206-455-8080

Microspan Software
2213A Lanier Drive
Austin, TX 78758

Oregon Software
2340 SW Canyon Road
Portland, OR 97210
503-226-7760

Osborne & Associates
P.O. Box 2036
Berkeley, CA 94702
415-548-2805

Personal Software, Inc.
592 Weddell Drive
Sunnyvale, CA 94086
408-745-7841

Petsoft - Radclyffe House
66-68 Hagley Road
Birmingham B16 8PF
England

Powersoft Inc.
P.O. Box 157
Pitman, NJ 08071
609-589-5500

Program Design Inc.
11 Idar Court
Greenwich, CT 06830

**Programma International
Inc.**
3400 Wilshire Blvd.
Los Angeles, CA 90010
213-384-0579

**Programs for Learning,
Inc.**
P.O. Box 954
New Milford, CT 06776

Progressive Software
P.O. Box 3
South Chelmsford, MA
01824
617-256-3649

Pygmy Programming
P.O. Box 3078
Scottsdale, AZ 85257

Queue
5 Chapel Hill Drive
Fairfield, CT 06432

**Radio Shack - Software
Dept.**
One Tandy Center
Fort Worth, TX 76102

Rainbow Computing Inc.
10723 White Oak Avenue
Department CC
Granada Hills, CA 91344
213-360-2171

**Random House School
Division**
Dept. 985, Suite 201
2970 Brandywine Road
Atlanta, GA 30341

Scharf Software Services
P.O. Box 18445
Irvine, CA 92713

Sheridan College, F. Winter
1430 Trafalgar Road
Oakville, Ontario
L6H 2L1 Canada

Small Software Systems
P.O. Box 366
Newbory Park, GA 91320

Softape
10432 Burbank Blvd.
North Hollywood, CA 91601

Softouch
P.O. Box 511
Leominster, MA 01453

Softside Subscriptions
P.O. Box 68
Milford, NH 03055

**Softswap (public domain
    software)**
Educational Resources
    Library
San Mateo Co. Office of
    Education
333 Main Street
Redwood City, CA 94063

Software House
P.O. Box 966
Mishawaka, IN 46544
219-255-3408

Supersoft
P.O. Box 1628
Champaign, IL 61820
217-359-2112

The Computerists Inc.
P.O. Box 3
South Chalmsford, MA
    01824
617-256-3649

T.H.E.S.I.S.
P.O. Box 147
Garden City, MI 48135

The Software Works
8369 Vickers
San Diego, CA
214-569-1721

The Teaching Assistant
22 Seward Drive
Huntington Station, NY
    11746

Tycom Associates
69 Velma Avenue
Pittsfield, MA 01201

United Software of America
750 Third Avenue
New York, NY 10017

APPENDIX E

SOFTWARE REVIEWS

Apple Education Foundation
20605 Lazaneo Drive
Cupertino, CA 95014

Apple for the Teacher
c / o Ted Perry
9525 Lucerne
Ventura, CA

CONDUIT
P.O. Box 388
Iowa City, IA 52244

Materials Review & Evaluation Center
Computer Courseware Project
Division of Educational Media
State Department of Public Instruction
Raleigh, NC 27611

MicroSIFT
Northwest Regional Educational Laboratory
500 Lindsay Building
710 2nd Ave., S.W.
Portland, OR 91204
(505) 248-6974

Project LOCAL
200 Nahatan Street
Westwood, MA 02090

Purser's Magazine
Box 466
El Dorado, CA 95623

Queue
5 Chapel Hill Drive
Fairfield, CT 06432

School Microware
A Directory of Educational Software
Dresden Associates
P.O. Box 246
Dresden, ME 04342

Technical Education Research Centers
8 Eliot Street
Cambridge, MA 02138

APPENDIX F

NEWSLETTERS

ACH Newsletter
(Association for Computers and the Humanities)
Queens College
Flushing, NY 11367

(quarterly: computer applications in literature, music, arts, and social sciences)

Computer Using Educators
127 O'Connor Street
Menlo Park, CA 94025

(bi-monthly: contains conferences, software sources, new products)

Counterpoint
Dissemin Action
3705 South George Drive
Suite C-4 South
Falls Church, VA 22041

(Bi-annual: newspaper size review of special education computer applications)

Education USA NEWSLINE
National Schools Public Relations Association
1801 North Moore Street
Arlington, VA 22209

(on-line newsletter on education through the SOURCE network)

The Harvard Newsletter on Computer Graphics
Laboratory for Computer Graphics
Harvard University
48 Quincy Street
Cambridge, MA 02138

(news and trends in computer graphics applications in government, business, and education)

Mean Brief
(Microcomputer Education Application Network)
256 North Washington Street
Falls Church, VA 22041

MICRO-SCOPE
JEM Research
Discovery Park
University of Victoria
Box 1700
Victoria, British Columbia
V8W 2Y2 CANADA

APPENDIX G

MAGAZINES AND JOURNALS

AEDS Journal. Reports of original research, searches of literature, and conceptual / theoretical discussions of computer applications in education. An official publication of the Association for Educational Data Systems, 1201 Sixteenth Street, N.W., Washington, DC 20036

AEDS Monitor. Short articles, book and software reviews, announcements, and current information relating to computers in education and the profession. An official publication of the Association for Educational Data Systems, 1201 Sixteenth Street, N.W., Washington, DC 20036

BYTE. A magazine for more advanced computer enthusiasts. 70 Main Street, Peterborough, NH 03458

CLASSROOM COMPUTER NEWS. A bi-monthly magazine focusing on educational applications, new products and governmental programs. Box 266, Cambridge, MA 02138

THE COMPUTING TEACHER. A magazine for teachers who are interested in classroom applications and curriculum. c / o Howard Baily, Eastern Oregon State College, La Grande OR 97850

CREATIVE COMPUTING. A widely distributed magazine for broad audiences, available on newstands. Applications, software, hardware, and advertising. A wide range of interests. P.O. Box 789-M, Morristown, NJ 07960

EDUCATIONAL TECHNOLOGY. A wide range of articles about all forms of technology in education, including microcomputers. 140 Sylvan Avenue, Englewood Cliffs, NJ 07632

INTERFACE AGE. Trade magazine with a wide range of topics. Box 1234, Cerritos, CA 90701.

KILOBAUD. Both beginners and experts can find articles of interest in this magazine on small computers. 1001001 Inc., Peterborough, NH 03458

MACUL JOURNAL. Michigan Association for Computer Users in Learning's journal. Over 100 descriptions of Apple, Pet, and TRS-80 programs were provided in the Spring, 1980, issue. Larry Smith, Wayne County ISD, 33500 Van Born Road, Wayne, MI 48184

MEDIA & METHODS. Educational journal focusing on instructional delivery and is beginning to feature microcomputer applications. 1511 Walnut Street, Philadelphia, PA 19102

MICROCOMPUTING 80. General interest articles over a broad range of microcomputer topics. Box 997, Farmingdale, NY 11737

NIBBLE. Dedicated to Apple computer applications and products and featuring several program listings in each issue. Box 325, Lincoln, MA 01773

ON COMPUTING. Product reviews, hardware, and especially, information about how to get started. 70 Main Street, Peterborough, NH 03458

PERSONAL COMPUTING. Generally consumer-oriented, for business and home applications of microcomputers. 1050 Commonwealth Avenue, Boston, MA 02215

PURSER'S MAGAZINE. Published four times per year. This contains reviews of software for the Apple, Atari, TRS-80 computers. Robert Purser, P.O. Box 466, El Dorado, CA 95623

RECREATIONAL COMPUTING. A source of ideas about how computers can be used for fun and learning. People's Computing Company, 1263 El Camino Real, Box 3, Menlo Park, CA 94025

T.H.E. JOURNAL. (Technological Horizons in Education). A journal for educators (free to principals) that describes technological approaches to solving current educational problems. 7 Spruce Street, Acton, MA 01720

THE COMPUTING TEACHER. Elementary and secondary educators who use computers in teaching, whether beginners or advanced users, are the target audience. Using and teaching about computers represent the major themes. Department of Computer and Information Science, University of Oregon, Eugene, OR 97403

APPENDIX H

DIRECTORIES AND CATALOGS

Appleseed
Software Publications
6 South Street
Milford, NH 03055
(software for Apple, Pet, TRS-80 and Atari, free)

Educational Software Directory
Sterling Swift Publishing Co.
P.O. Box 188
Manchaca, TX 78652
(commercial and non-commercial software for elementary through college applications, $11.95)

HUMRRO
300 N. Washington Street
Alexandria, VA 22314
(a directory of nationwide computer projects in education)

Huntington Computer Catalogue
Box 787
Corcoran, CA 93212
(free)

Instant Software
Peterborrough, NH 03458
(educational games and simulations, business and scientific utilities, frequently up-dated and revised)

K-12 Micro Media
Box 17
Valley Cottage, NY 10989
(free)

School Microware Directory
Dresden Associates
P.O. Box 246
Dresden, ME 04342
(a directory of educational software for Apple, Atari, Pet, and TRS-80, $25 / year for four editions)

Skarbeks Software Directory
11990 Dorsett Road
St. Louis, MO 63043
($11.95, lists over 1,000 programs)

The Software Directory
Software Central
P.O. Box 30424
Lincoln, NE 68503
(educational, games, home, professional and scientific software)

TRS-80 Software Directory
Radio Shack
1600 One Tandy Center
Fort Worth, TX 76102
($10.95)

Ye Compleate Computer Catalogue
6 South Street
Milford, NH 03055
(software, hardware, books, and supplies)

APPENDIX I

ORGANIZATIONS

ACM   Task Group - Administrators and School Boards
Rem Aranda, Office of Policy, Planning and
Management, 249 High Street, Hartford, CT 06103

ACM   Task Group - Microcomputers
Dan Isaacson, Department of Computer Sciences,
University of Oregon, Eugene, OR 97403

ADCIS   Association for the Development of Computer-
Based Instruction
Western Washington State College, Bellingham,
WA 98225

AECT   Association for Educational Communications and
Technology
1126 16th Street N.W., Washington, D.C. 20036

AEDS   Association for Educational Data Systems
1201 16th Street, N.W., Washington, DC 20036

Apple for the Teacher
Operates a national CAI library for the Apple
microcomputers
Ted Perry, 5848 Riddio Street, Citrus Hts., CA
95610

Association for Computing Machinery
1133 Avenue of the Americas, New York, NY 10036

BCS   The Boston Computer Society
17 Chestnut Street, Boston, MA 02108

CONDUIT   Jim Johnson and Hal Peters, P.O. Box 338, Iowa
City, IA 52240
CONDUIT is a source of information on
instructional materials and instructional applica-
tions for computers. Their newsletter,
"Pipeline," is published three times each year.

CUE   Computer Using Educators
Don McKell, Independence High School, 1776
Education Park Drive, San Jose, CA 95133

EDUCOM   Serves colleges and universities across the U.S.
Box 364, Princeton, NJ 08540

EDUSIG   Digital Equipment Company Users Group
One Iron Way, Marlboro, MA 01752

ICCE   International Council of Computer Educators
Eastern Oregon State College, La Grande, OR 97850

MACUL   Michigan Association for Computer Users in Learning
33500 Van Born Road, Wayne, MI 48184

MEAN   Micro Education Applications Network
Suite 800, 1030 15th Street, N.W., Washington, DC

MECC   Minnesota Educational Computing Consortium
2520 Broadway Drive, Lauderdale, MN 55113

NRCC   National Research Council Canada
Associate Committee on Instructional Technology, Ottawa, Canada

NWREL   The Northwest Regional Educational Laboratory
A clearinghouse of microcomputer-related programs and materials for education.
Judith Edwards, Director, Computer Technology Program NWREL, 710 S.W. Second Avenue, Portland, OR 97204

Society of Data Educators
983 Fairmeadow Road, Memphis, TN 38117

SMALL   Society for Microcomputer Applications in Language and Literature
Wendell Hall
University Station
Box 7134
Provo, UT 84602

APPENDIX J

RESOURCE CENTERS

Apple Computer Clearinghouse for the Handicapped
Prentke Romich Company
R.D. 2, Box 191
Shreve, OH 44676

Computers in Education as a Resource
Exhibition Road
London, S.W. 7
United Kingdom
(resource project at the Imperial College)

Computer Resource Center
8 Eliot Street
Cambridge, MA 02138
(microcomputer hardware, software, curricular, and technical information)

CONDUIT
Box 388
Iowa City, IA 52244
(source of materials and R & D center)

Dataspan
University of Michigan
109 E. Madison Street
Ann Arbor, MI 48104
(information on computer applications in science education)

Educator's Hot Line
Vital Information Inc.
913-384-3860
(answers questions about educational microcomputing)

EPIE Institute
Box 620
Stony Brook, MY 11790
(educational consumer advocacy group, software evaluation)

Math / Computer Education Project
Lawrence Hall of Science
University of California
Berkeley, CA 94720
(workshops for teachers and students)

Microcomputer Center (Softswap)
Micro Center
San Mateo County, Office of Education
Educational Resource Library
333 Main Street
Redwood City, CA 94063
(public domain software available for exchange; microcomputer hardware from major manufacturers on display, commercial software available for evaluation)

Microcomputer Resource Center
Room 655G
Thorndike Hall
Teacher's College / Columbia University
525 West 120th Street
New York, NY 10027
(books, periodicals, software and microcomputers)

MICROSIFT
Microcomputer Software and Information for Teachers
Northwest Regional Educational Laboratory
710 S.W. Second Avenue
Portland, OR 97204
(software evaluation)

APPENDIX K

ANSWERS: MICROCOMPUTER LITERACY ASSESSMENT

1. false
2. true
3. false
4. false
5. false
6. true
7. true
8. true
9. false
10. c
11. b
12. b
13. d
14. d
15. b
16. d
17. a
18. a
19. c
20. c

APPENDIX L

RECOMMENDED READINGS ON COMPUTER LITERACY

An Alternative Curriculum for Computer Literacy Development.
Denenberg, Stewart A.
AEDS Journal, pp. 156-173, Winter 1980.
   An alternative curriculum for computer literacy development (ACCOLADE) is a system that allows people to use computers and to achieve a degree of computer literacy. Preliminary results of a pilot study on the PLATO IV Computer System indicate moderate success.

EJ179598
Computer Awareness Laboratory
Powell, James D.; Speece, Herbert E.
Journal of Educational Technology Systems, v. 6, n. 1, pp. 45-50, 1977-78.
   Describes a project involving a traveling van, equipped with several small computers, which visits high schools giving demonstrations, allowing students to access the computers, and providing teachers with backup material. An evaluation of the first year's activities is presented and plans for the future are given.

ED142200
Computer Literacy
Rosen, Elizabeth; Hicks, Bruce
Illinois University, Urbana, Department of Secondary Education
June 1977 10p.; Illinois Series on Educational Applications of Computers
Report No.: ISEAC-22
EDRS Price MF - $.83 HC - $1.67 Plus Postage.
   A brief review is made of informational books dealing with simple concepts and terminology related to computers. Recommendations are made as to those which are better for children and high school students. A bibliography lists all books considered.

Computer Literacy Courses
Hansen, Thomas P.: et al
AEDS Monitor, v. 18, n. 4-6, pp. 29-30, November 1979.
    An overview of computer literacy courses from 50 school
districts. They are categorized by courses / units and by
content.

EJ139385
Computer Literacy in the High School
Thomas, Rex A.
AEDS Journal, v. 9, n. 3, pp. 71-77, Spring 1976.
    Describes an instrument created to measure the general
level of computer literacy of high school students and to obtain
baseline data on student awareness of computer concepts.

ED117116
The LACE (La Crosse Computers in Education)
Castek, John; And Others
Wisconsin University, La Crosse
10 December 1975, 8p.
EDRS Price MF - $.76 HC - $1.58 Plus Postage
    The University of Wisconsin-La Crosse Computer Center's
LACE Project is designed to familiarize teachers and students
with the use of computers. The project offers a wide range of
instructional computing services through timesharing
computer terminals located across the state of Wisconsin. The
success of the program is measured in part by its growth from
10 terminals in 1972 to 47 today. Users enjoy all the benefits of
the central site computer at their terminal, including the
ability to write their own programs or to use prewritten
programs in nearly every subject area. The university's
secondary education department has been instrumental in
insuring the success of the programs and thus improving the
quality of teacher education. The department has taught
experienced and prospective teachers the effective use of
computers in the classroom. Some of this has been done by
specially designed courses, and, in addition, a notable effort
has been made to expose all education students to the
computer's potential in methods classes. As a result of these
efforts, the LACE Project has been productive in improving
the quality of teacher education at the university, as well as
the quality of instruction in Wisconsin Schools.

The Mind Revolution
Miller, Merle; Ueker, Ed
Interface Age, pp. 52-53, January 1980.
    An argument for a high level of computer literacy in our
society.

"The Minnesota Computer Literacy Tests: A Technical
    Report on the MECC Computer Literacy Field Study,"
    MECC, October 1979,
"Computer Literacy Study - An Update," MECC Memo, June
    2, 1978,
"Minnesota Computer Literacy and Awareness Assessment"
    (eighth-grade form) and scoring key,
"The Computer Mystique," MECC, August 1979
    All of the above are available from:
    Minnesota Educational Computing Consortium (MECC)
    2520 Broadway Drive
    St. Paul, MN 55113
    This project, funded by the National Science Foundation,
began with a survey of teachers concerning the nature and
scope of computer instruction in Minnesota schools. A
computer literacy assessment instrument was developed and
administered to statewide samples of eighth and eleventh
graders. A laboratory study will be used to determine the
impact of actual computer use on student attitudes toward
computers.

EJ187471
The Next Great Crisis in American Education: Computer
    Literacy
Molnar, Andrew R.
Journal of Technological Horizons in Education, v. 5, n. 4, pp.
    35-8, July-August 1978.
    Discusses the importance of the computer in today's
complex society. Argues strongly in favor of integrating the
computer into education by introducing computer-related
curricula at all levels of education, and thus developing a
computer literate society.

EJ173607
Training Preservice Teachers to Teach with Computers
Dennis, J. Richard
AEDS Journal, v. 11, n. 2, pp. 25-30, Winter 1978.

Describes an instructional model for training preservice teachers to teach with computers. The preservice level is seen as the appropriate time for such training because intense, long-duration experiences are required to develop functional competence with the instructional medium.

APPENDIX M

GLOSSARY OF COMPUTER TERMS

The computer revolution has brought many new terms into the language. Without knowledge of the meaning of some of these terms, the lay person will find it difficult, if not impossible, to discuss computer applications, either among themselves or with computer specialists. Most of the terms pertaining to the technical aspects of computer operations or programming have been deleted from the glossary. What has been retained are the terms that are more fundamental to computer literacy. These terms represent only the "tip of the iceberg," but knowing their meaning is a major step toward understanding the functions and characteristics of computers.

Access time - The amount of time that is required for a microcomputer to locate a piece of information such as a name, stored in memory. Information stored on tape requires more access time than information stored on disk because the information is searched sequentially.

Acoustic coupler - A piece of equipment that enables the remote transmission of information in the form of audio tones between two microcomputers through telephone lines. An "originate / answer" coupler permits information to flow in either direction. Typically, the telephone handset is inserted into a special cradle.

Algorithm - A series of fixed steps, performed repeatedly, to solve a problem. Students are taught algorithms for finding the least common denominator of a fraction or the square root of a number. Algorithms are an important part of computer programs.

Alphanumeric - Computers are programmed to decode alphanumeric symbols; the letters of the alphabet, the digits 0-9, and several special characters such as ",". Alphanumeric symbols are represented on the keys of a computer terminal.

Array - An arrangement of information in a fixed pattern so that it can be stored and recalled efficiently. A multiplication table is an array of data; so is a distance-between-cities table on a roadmap.

ASCII Code - American Standard Code for Information Interchange. Alphanumeric symbols are represented in ASCII as a unique pattern of ones and zeros in groups of eight "bits." For instance, the number seven (7) is 00110111.

Authoring Languages - Higher level languages that in one instruction, may execute many operations in BASIC or some other language. Designed only to produce lessons for computer delivery and are thus easier to learn and use than general purpose languages.

Assembler - A program that translates assembly language into the computers native language (binary).

Assembly Language - A low level language similar to the computers native language (binary), but more convenient to use.

Backplane Board - A surface which is designed to interconnect smaller boards using the same bus. Often called a motherboard.

BASIC - Beginners All Purpose Symbolic Instruction Code, a "high-level" computer programming language commonly used with microcomputers. It is very "English sounding" and its rules can be learned very quickly. It was developed in the early 1960's by John Kemeny and Thomas Kurtz.

Batch Processing - A method of data processing where data is logically grouped prior to input. Processing occurs during a single "run."

Baud rate - Refers to the transmission of data, the number of bits of information that can be sent or received by computer or terminal in one second. A teletypewriter operates at a baud rate of 110 bits per second. Microcomputer acoutical couplers usually operate at a baud rate of 300 and higher speeds will be accomplished with improved equipment.

Binary - A number system with base 2 represented by the digits 1 and 0. Information is translated into binary for computers, where 1's and 0's are represented as different voltages. The number 12 in binary is represented as 1100.

Bit - Each binary digit (0 or 1) is a bit, the fundamental unit of information that a computer processes. BInary digiT = BIT.

Board - A rectangle of composition material on which computer components (chips, diodes, etc.) are attached.

Bootstrap Procedure - A sequence of events that causes a system to be "brought up," i.e., made operational.

Bug - An error, usually in programming, that causes the computer to produce an incorrect output.

Bus - An electrical connector between components of a computer system.

Byte - Usually a group of eight (8) adjacent binary bits that the computer reads as a unit. Newer microprocessors use 16 or 32 bit bytes which allows them to access much more memory.

CAI - Computer Assisted Instruction.

Central Processing Unit (CPU) - The central processing unit is composed of control and arithmetic-logic units. It organizes, rearranges, and performs arithmetic operations on the data and instructions that are entered via the program.

Character - A symbol that carries significant meaning such as "7", or represents a process, e.g. * indicates multiplication. Characters are translated to binary for processing.

Chip - An integrated circuit contained on a tiny silicon surface. A microprocessor is composed of 10's of thousands of microscopic circuits. Some chips are manufactured by exposing a sensitized surface to light and then coating the exposed pattern of circuitry with metal. As chips are developed containing more circuits, fewer chips will be needed in the computer, which lowers costs.

CMI - Computer Managed Instruction.

Cobol - A computer language oriented to business applications.

Core memory - A permanent memory used in early computers, composed of ferrite, a magnetic material. Microcomputers have volatile or non-permanent memories in the form of semiconductor chips.

Command - An instruction given to a computer through a terminal or other peripheral.

Compiler - Computers respond to patterns of 1's and 0's. Therefore, all characters or words used in "high level" languages such as BASIC must be translated into patterns of 1's and 0's. A compiler makes the translation once and stores the data in binary code. When needed by the computer, the binary form is input directly, with no need for repeated translations.

Courseware - Computer programs that deliver instruction.

CRT - Cathode Ray Tube, the "screen" of a TV set, the video-display output device that is attached to most microcomputers.

Cursor - A symbol, usually an arrow or flashing square, that can be moved around on a CRT display to identify and refer to a location.

Data - The alphanumeric information that is entered into a computer for processing.

Debug - To locate and remove errors from a computer program. It is a time-consuming, but fundamental part, of computer programming.

Disk - An information storage device for computers that looks like a phonograph record but is usually floppy (flexible). A disk-drive is the mechanism into which the disk is inserted and that accesses the information stored there. Searching for data on a disk is fast because the search pattern is not sequential (starting at the beginning and going through to the end). The surface of a disk must be kept very clean, they cannot be removed from their protective jackets and handled.

Documentation - A written description of a computer program, including its purpose, instructions for operation, suggestions to the user, and samples of output. Documentation tells you how to use a program and what to expect as output.

DOS - Disk Operating System.

Downloading - Receiving a computer program or data from a computer at another site.

EPROM - Electrically Programmable Read Only Memory. A permanent memory that contains operating system programs. Although it can be altered by special procedures, it is unlikely that this "built in" memory would need to be changed from its state as provided by the manufacturer. A peripheral is available for microcomputers which allows a given program to be loaded into blank EPROM chips. Once in the chip, the program can be sold in this format as opposed to being sold on floppy disks.

Erase - Clearing data or programs from the computer's memory.

Execute - To perform a manipulation of data according to specification contained in the program. To perform the computing task.

File - A set of series of information, all in the same format (form). A computer file may contain such things as the names and addresses of vendors supplying goods and services to the school district. A file is composed of "records" representing the information on each vendor that is to be stored and / or analyzed.

Firmware - Programs (instructions) that are stored in ROM chips.

Flicker - CRT displays require rapid electronic stimulation to retain an image. A CRT display is made up of hundreds of pixels that are independently controlled. The eye does not constantly perceive the flicker that results from the very rapid stimulation and restimulation of points on the screen. However, the flicker can lead to eye-fatigue under prolonged exposure at close distances. Plasma displays do not flicker. This technology is not wide-spread because of production costs. Many PLATO installations use plasma displays.

Floating Point Arithmetic - Simply stated it is computer arithmetic that allows decimal representation of numbers.

Floppy disk - See DISK.

Flow chart - A system with established rules for pictorially describing, with diagrams, the sequence of steps and their interrelationships, that occur when a computer program runs. Flowcharts are usually drawn on paper before programming is begun.

FORTRAN - A computer language oriented to scientific applications.

Garbage In Garbage Out (GIGO) - The principle that the results of computer operation can not be better than the quality of the data that is entered. Unreliable data will produce unreliable results, even if they appear authoritative.

Hard copy - Results printed on paper as opposed to displayed on a screen.

Hardware - Computer equipment, including peripheral attachments.

Input - The programs and data entered into a computer for processing.

Integrated Circuit (IC) - Contained on the surface of a chip, hundreds of microtransistors and circuits that are interconnected in complex patterns (See Chip).

Intelligent terminal - See Smart Terminal.

Interface - The connection or device that links a computer to its peripherals.

Interpreter - A program similar to, but slower than, a compiler, that executes commands immediately and does not keep the intermediate representation as does the compiler.

I / O - Input-Output. Input programs and data; output results.

Job - Everything that is submitted to computing operations; programs and data.

Joystick - A mechanical device that inputs Cartesian coordinates to the computer. Operates much like the aviators "steering wheel" in many aircraft.

K - Refers to units of computer memory; 1024 equals 1K "bits" of memory capacity; kilo; roughly one thousand.

Keyboard - The interface between the operator and the computer terminal; a typewriter-like array of alpha-numeric symbols and special function keys.

Label - A name or acronym assigned to a variable or program statement.

Language - All of the symbols and rules that together compose a method of informing a computer how to input data, read it, manipulate it, and output results.

Library routines - Tested and documented programs that are available to users of a networked computer system; many library routines are available in high demand areas such as statistical analysis.

Line feed - A line-at-a-time movement of paper through a printer.

Line noise - Interference on telecommunications lines that can disrupt computer data being transmitted.

Line printer - A peripheral hardware that prints a whole line of type simultaneously; a rapid form of printing computer output.

Load - Entering data and programs into the computer memory.

Loop - A series of computer instructions that are repeatedly performed until a specified condition is met.

Machine language - The "low level" binary code into which all "high level" languages such as BASIC are ultimately translated, by a separate program, in order for the computer to respond.

Magnetic tape memory - A peripheral device that stores and recalls binary coded information from a magnetic recording tape.

Memory - Computer components that store data, including magnetic disk memory, magnetic tape memory, video disk, and others.

Menu - A list of choices displayed in a computer program to guide the user.

Microcomputer - A digital computer with most of the capabilities of larger computers; the nerve center of the microcomputer is the microprocessor composed of large scale integrated circuits on silicone chips. An FCC designation of class B computer has been used.

Microprocessor - The control, arithmetic logic unit (ALU), and part of the memory of a microcomputer. Carries out the processing of the data.

Minicomputer - A mid-range computer (in size and cost); larger than a microcomputer.

Mnemonic - An abbreviation that is suggestive of the underlying word or words, e.g. COMSAT / communications satellite, pronounced, "nu-monic."

Modem - Modulator / Demodulator, a device that is used to permit transmission of information over a telephone line, by a computer.

MOS - Metal-Oxide-Semiconductor.

Multiplex - In network systems, incoming signals from independent telephone sources are combined onto a single channel by a multiplexor.

Nanosecond - One thousandth of one millionth of a second (microsecond), i.e., one billionth of a second.

Network - A computer system made up of a central computer, telecommunications, and a number of "users" with input / output devices; can be made up of several or many microcomputers.

Nibble - Half a byte; four bits; 0111.

Noise - Random signals, with no meaning, that can interfere with computer operations and produce errors. Too high a volume setting when reading data from magnetic tape into a microcomputer can produce noise. Concentrations of fluorescent lights in proximity to the microcomputer can produce noise.

Off-line - Activities that occur outside the computer system but that relate to it. For example, in CAI, students do much reading off line.

Peripheral - Not part of the computer itself but involved in its operation; terminals, printers, card readers, voice synthesizers, etc.

Port - A connection on the computer where peripheral devices, such printers, can be plugged in.

Printer - A device that produces hard copy output from a computer; "selectric" typewriter; dot matrix printer, or line printer are examples. Printing speed varies from 10 to 140 characters per second on printers that are typically attached to microcomputers. Character width is often controllable. Upper and lower case letters may or may not be printed, depending on the equipment.

Processor - A set of integrated circuits that executes instructions.

Program - The instructions, written in a computer language, that control the computer's operation.

RAM - Random Access Memory; a method of storing and recovering data that is independent of sequential order; a memory unit whose contents can be readily altered. Also referred to as workspace memory inside microcomputers.

ROM - Read Only Memory; the contents of ROM are fixed by the manufacturers; the user cannot store information there or alter the contents.

Real-time - Information processing that occurs in response to situations when and as they arise in reality. Computer assisted instruction occurs in real time.

Register - A section of memory where a binary digit (bit) is stored.

Remote - A remote terminal is located at a distance, often considerable, from the computer.

Routine - Part of a program that is used in performing a computer task.

RS-232 (EIA) - A standard interfacing configuration by which computers can communicate with peripheral devices.

Run - The operation of the computer, controlled by the program, to perform a job from start to finish.

Seek-time - The amount of time required to locate a record within a file.

Smart terminal - A terminal that can temporarily store some data and perform some limited independent processing activities while connected to a host computer. Microcomputers can serve as smart terminals.

Software - The program that controls a computer procedure and the written documents describing what it does and how to use it.

Sort - The reordering of a data file according to some specification; e.g., a file of students can be sorted according to their ages.

Source program - A computer program written in a high level language such as BASIC or FORTRAN.

Statement - One line in a computer program.

Store - To enter data into a memory device.

Storage capacity - The amount of information that a memory is capable of retaining; temporary or permanent.

Storage device - Peripheral equipment that serves a memory function for the computer.

Subroutine - Part of a computer program that is used repeatedly in performing a job.

System - All the hardware and software that together perform computing operations; systems vary according to scale and complexity.

Teleprinter - Generic term for equipment that is used to produce printed documents by computer.

Terminal - A device that is used to input and output information to a computer; typically contains a keyboard and a CRT display. It cannot function unless connected to a host computer, which can be a microcomputer.

Third generation - Computers based on integrated circuits, as opposed to tubes (first generation) or transistors (second generation). This terminology can also be applied to microcomputers. Those common today are first generation, those coming out of research labs are the second generation.

Turn-Key - A computer program that starts automatically when the computer is turned on and gives prompts to help guide the user.

TUTOR - An authoring language for creating CAI lessons.

Uploading - Sending a computer program or data from a computer over telecommunications lines to another computer.

User's group - An association of people with an interest in a particular computer. The group serves as a medium for exchanging information.

Variable - Something that can take on different values, e.g. age, price, weight, etc.

Video display - Data displayed on a TV-type monitor, characters and graphics. Future displays will not use cathode ray tubes, e.g., plasma displays, LEDs, CCDs, and fluorescent displays.

Volatile storage - Temporary memory that depends on the continuing presence of an electrical current. If the electricity goes off, information in volatile storage is lost.

Write - To put data into storage or move it from storage to a peripheral device.

APPENDIX N

REFERENCES

ADVENTURES OF THE MIND, A SERIES ON PERSONAL COMPUTING. Falls Church, Va.: ITV Co-op, 1980 (A Television Series).

Alderman, D. L. EVALUATION OF THE TICCIT COMPUTER-ASSISTED INSTRUCTIONAL SYSTEMS IN THE COMMUNITY COLLEGE: FINAL REPORT. Princeton: Educational Testing Service, 1978.

Alspaugh, J. COMPUTER ASSISTED BUS ROUTE CONSTRUCTION WITH A MICROCOMPUTER. Paper presented at Association for Educational Data Systems National Conference, Minneapolis, May 1981.

Alterman, I. Computer graphics maps help execs quickly understand volumnous data. MARKETING NEWS, Harvard Laboratory for Computer Graphics and Spatial Analysis, July, 1979.

Alvir, H. P. WHAT INSTRUCTIONAL RESOURCES CAN'T DO AND SHOULDN'T TRY TO DO. Albany, N.Y.: Claire Gelinas, 1977, ED 150 945.

Anastasio, E. & Morgan, J. FACTORS INHIBITING THE USE OF COMPUTERS IN INSTRUCTION. Princeton: EDUCOM, Inc., 1972.

Armsey, J. & Dahl, N. AN INQUIRY INTO THE USE OF INSTRUCTIONAL TECHNOLOGY. New York: Ford Foundation, 1973.

Atkins, J. A. and Lockhart, L. Flexible vs. instructor paced college quizzing: a behavioral analysis of preference and performance. In L. E. Fraley and E. Z. Vargas (Eds.), BEHAVIOR RESEARCH AND TECHNOLOGY IN HIGHER EDUCATION. Gainsville, Florida: Society for Behavioral Technology & Engineering. Psychology Department, University of Florida, 1976.

Avner, R. A. Cost-effective applications of computer-based education. EDUCATIONAL TECHNOLOGY, April 1978, 24-26.

Bagley, Carole A. Comprehensive Offender Program Effort. Final Progress Report. A paper prepared for the Minnesota State Department of Corrections, 1977, ED 152 226.

Barrette, P. R. THE MICROCOMPUTER AND THE SCHOOL LIBRARY MEDIA SPECIALIST. Littleton, Co.: Libraries Unlimited, 1980.

Barrette, P. R. Microcomputers in the school media program. CATHOLIC LIBRARY WORLD, 53(1), in press.

Berthold, H. & Sachs, R. Education and the minimally brain damaged child by computer and by teachers. PROGRAMMED LEARNING AND EDUCATIONAL TECHNOLOGY, 1974, 11(3), 121-124.

Bigelow, R. THE MARKETING AND DISTRIBUTION OF SOFTWARE: SOME LEGAL ISSUES. Paper presented at the Second International User's Conference on Computer Mapping Hardware, Software and Data Bases, Cambridge, Mass., July 1979.

Bock, W., Weatherman, R., Joiner, L., & Kranz, G. THE ASSESSMENT OF BEHAVIORAL COMPETENCE OF DEVELOPMENTALLY DISABLED INDIVIDUALS: THE MDPS. Minneapolis: University of Minnesota, 1979.

Bork, A. Machines for computer assisted learning. EDUCATIONAL TECHNOLOGY, 1978, 17, 17-20.

Bork, A. Stand alone computer systems--Our educational future. JOURNAL OF EDUCATIONAL TECHNOLOGY SYSTEMS, 7(3), p. 201-207, 1978-79.

Bork, A. & Franklin, S. D. The role of personal computer systems in education. AEDS JOURNAL, Fall 1979, 13(1), 17-30.

Borry, L. Meet the music teacher's new assistant - A microcomputer. AEDS MONITOR, November 1979, p. 21.

Boyce, J. C. MICROPROCESSOR AND MICROCOMPUTER BASICS. Englewood Cliffs, N.J.: Prentice-Hall, Inc., 1979.

Braun, L. How do I choose a personal computer? AEDS JOURNAL, Fall 1979, 13(1), 81-87.

Briggs, L. & Wagner, W. HANDBOOK OF PROCEDURES FOR THE DESIGN OF INSTRUCTION. Englewood Cliffs, N.J.: Educational Technology Press, 1981.

Brown, B. & O'Neil, H. Computer terminal selection: Some instructional and psychological implications. Washington, D.C.: Office of Naval Research, 1971, ED 054 651.

Butman, R. CAI-there is a way to make it pay (But not in conventional schooling). EDUCATIONAL TECHNOLOGY, December 1973, 5-9.

Callahan, R. EDUCATION AND THE CULT OF EFFICIENCY. Chicago: University of Chicago Press, 1970.

Canning, R. G. In your future: Distributed system. EDP ANALYZER. 1973, 11(8), 1-13.

Carroll, J. D. Service, knowledge, and choice: The future as post-industrial administration. PUBLIC ADMINISTRATION REVIEW, November-December, 1975, 35, 580.

Carter, J. R. Thematic mapping on low-resolution color CRT terminals. Paper presented at the Second International User's Conference on Computer Mapping Hardware, Software and Data Bases, Cambridge, Mass., July 1979.

Cartwright, G. P., & Hall, K. A review of computer uses in special education. L. Mann & D. Sabatino (Eds.), THE SECOND REVIEW OF SPECIAL EDUCATION. Philadelphia: JSE Press, 1974.

Cartwright, P., & Dervensky, J. L. An attitudinal study of computer assisted testing as a learning method. PSYCHOLOGY IN THE SCHOOLS, 1976, 13(3), 317-321.

Cleary, A., Mayes, T. & Packham, D. EDUCATIONAL TECHNOLOGY: IMPLICATIONS FOR EARLY AND SPECIAL EDUCATION. New York: John Wiley & Sons, 1976.

Cleary, A. & Packham, D. A touch-detecting teaching machine with auditory reinforcement. JOURNAL OF APPLIED BEHAVIOR ANALYSIS, 1968, 1, 344-345.

Clemson, B. Beyond management information system. EDUCATIONAL ADMINISTRATION QUARTERLY. 1978, 14(3), 13-38.

Cogdill, L. & Goldberg, A. An information system for managing headstart. PROCEEDINGS OF AEDS CONFERENCE, May 1981, 56-58.

Coldeway, D. C. and Scheller, W. J. Training proctors for the personalized system of instruction. In R. Rulskin and S. Bono (eds.), PERSONALIZED INSTRUCTION IN HIGHER EDUCATION. Washington, D.C.: Center for Personalized Instruction, Georgetown University, 1974, 111-118.

Control Data Corporation. CONTROL DATA PLATO CMI AUTHOR'S GUIDE. Minneapolis: Author, 1978.

Crandall, N., & Mantano, M. An analysis of CAI in a program designed to ameliorate the effects of racial isolation in the Los Nietos School District. Testimony presented to the House Committee on Domestic Applications of Science and Technology, October 6, 1977.

D'Angleo, J. The microprocessor as a pencil. AEDS MONITOR, November 1979, 2214-17.

Demb, A. COMPUTER SYSTEMS FOR HUMAN SYSTEMS. Oxford: Pergamon Press, 1979.

Dennis, J. R. Training preservice teachers to teach with computers. AEDS JOURNAL, 1978, 11(2), 25-30.

Deringer, D. & Molnar, A. TECHNOLOGY IN SCIENCE EDUCATION: THE NEXT TEN YEARS. Washington D.C.: Science Education Directorate of the National Science Foundation, 1979.

Doerr, C. MICROCOMPUTERS AND THE 3 R's: A GUIDE FOR TEACHERS. Rochell Park, N.J.: Hayden Book Co., Inc., 1979.

Dunn, T., Lushene, R. F., & O'Neill, H. F. The complete automation of the Minnesota Multiphasic Personality Inventory and a study of its response latency (Technical Memo No. 28). Tallahassee: Florida State University, Computer-Assisted Instructional Center, 1971.

Education Turnkey Systems, Inc. PROGRAMMING FOR INDIVIDUALIZED INSTRUCTION. Monograph, Author, 1981.

Edwards, J., Norton, S., Taylor, S., Van Dusseldorp, R., & Weiss, M. Is CAI effective? AEDS JOURNAL, Summer 1974, 7(4), 123-127.

English, F. & Sharpes, D. STRATEGIES FOR DIFFEREN-TIAL STAFFING. Berkeley, Cal.: McCutchan Pub. Corp., 1972.

Experimental Development Unit, NCAVAE Technical Report: Bell & Howell Language Master Model 701, VISUAL EDUCATION, April 1970, 13-14.

Foecke, J. An educational computing consortium: A sociological perspective. AEDS JOURNAL, Winter, 1979, 12(2), 84-94.

Gearheart, B. LEARNING DISABILITIES. St. Louis: C. V. Mosby, 1973.

Glaser, G. The centralization vs. decentralization issue: arguments, alternatives, and guidelines. DATA BASE. 1970, 2(3), 1-7.

Goodenough, F. R., & Harris, D. GOODENOUGH-HARRIS DRAWING TEST. New York: Harcourt, Brace, and World, 1963.

Guthrie, J. W. Emerging politics of educational policy. EDUCATIONAL EVALUATION AND POLICY ANALY-SIS, May-June 1981, 3(3), 75-82.

Hadalski, J. A management perspective on computer graphics in local government. Paper presented at the Second International User's Conference on Computer Mapping Hardware, Software and Data Bases, Cambridge, Mass., July, 1979.

Hamm, R. Effects of CAI in a microcounseling model for training facilitative use of verbal communication skills. (Doctoral dissertation, East Texas State University, 1975). DISSERTATION ABSTRACTS INTERNATIONAL, 1975, 36, 7209-A. (University Microfilms No. 76-11, 948)

Hanson, T., Klassen, D., Anderson, R., & Johnson, D. Computer literacy courses. AEDS MONITOR, November 1979, 2229-30.

Hausmann, K. Tips on writing instructional software for microcomputers. AEDS MONITOR, November 1979, 22, 46.

Hicks, B. & Hyde, D. Teaching about CAI. JOURNAL OF TEACHER EDUCATION, Summer 1973, 24, 120.

Hively, W. A multiple-choice visual discrimination apparatus. JOURNAL OF EXPERIMENTAL ANALYSIS OF BEHAVIOR, 1964, 7, 279-298.

Hoos, I. R. The cost of efficiency: Implications of educational technology. JOURNAL OF HIGHER EDUCATION. 46(2), 1975, 141-159.

Hyer, A. L. & McClure, R. M. New patterns of teacher tasks and other implications: The effect of innovations on staffing patterns and teacher roles in the United States. A paper prepared for the Organization for Economic Cooperation and Development, 1973, ED 086 684.

Jacobsen, E. Putting computers into education. Paper presented at the American Educational Research Association meeting, 1973, ED 087 477.

Johnson, J. Microcomputers: Promise or reality? PIPELINE, Spring 1979, 4(2), 2.

Joiner, L. EVALUATION OF THE MINNESOTA LEARNING DISABILITIES CONSORTIUM: PROJECT MLDC. St. Paul: Minnesota State Department of Education, 1979.

Joiner, L. When a map is worth one-thousand ANOVAS: Applications of statistical cartography in special education research and planning. THE JOURNAL OF SPECIAL EDUCATION, 1979, 13(4), 421-432.

Joiner, L. M. A TECHNICAL ANALYSIS OF THE VARIATION IN SCREENING INSTRUMENTS AND PROGRAMS IN NEW YORK STATE. New York: Center for Advanced Study in Education, City University of New York, 1978.

Joiner, L. & Silverstein, B. MICRO IN-HOUSE COMPUTERS: INTERIM EVALUATION REPORT. St. Paul: Minnesota Council on Quality Education, 1979.

Joiner, L., Silverstein, B., & Bock, W. A spatial analysis of interstate traffic in mental retardation. THE HARVARD MAPPING COLLECTION VOL. XI, Urban, Regional and State Government Applications of Computer Mapping. Cambridge: Harvard University, 1980.

Joiner, L. M., Miller, S. R. & Silverstein, B. J. Potential and limits of computers in schools. EDUCATIONAL LEADERSHIP, March 1980, 37(6), 498-501.

Jung, P. New learning aids offer help for the handicapped. APPLE, N.D., 1(1), 20-21.

Kehrberg, K. Microcomputer software development: New strategies for a new technology. AEDS JOURNAL, Fall 1979, 13(1), 103-110.

Keyser, E. The integration of microcomputers into the classroom or now that I've got it, what do I do with it? AEDS JOURNAL, Fall 1979, 13(1), 113-117.

Kniefel, K. & Just, S. Impact of microcomputers on educational computer networks. AEDS JOURNAL, Fall 1979, 13(1), 41-52.

Kock, H. Inductive experiences using the Apple II microcomputer. AEDS MONITOR, November 1979, 10-13.

Leventhal, L. INTRODUCTION TO MICROCOMPUTERS: SOFTWARE, HARDWARE, PROGRAMMING. Englewood Cliffs, N.J.: Prentice-Hall, 1978.

Libes, S., Byte News, BYTE, July, 1979, 4(7), 100.

Licklider, J. Impact of information technology on education in science and technology. TECHNOLOGY IN SCIENCE EDUCATION. Washington, D.C.: Science Education Directorate of the National Science Foundation, 1979.

Loomis, H., & Sucher J. Finding substitutes in a hurry. SCHOOL MANAGEMENT, October 1972, 24-25.

Lynch, M. A computor error: Trying to use one in your own home. THE WALL STREET JOURNAL, May 14, 1979.

Mann, F. C., & Williams, L. K. Observations in the dynamics of a change to electronic data processing equipment. ADMINISTRATIVE SCIENCE QUARTERLY, 1960, 5(2), 217-256.

Magidson, E. Issue overview: Trends in computer assisted instruction. EDUCATIONAL TECHNOLOGY, 1978, 18(4), 5-8.

Matthews, J. Problems in selecting a microcomputer for educational applications. AEDS JOURNAL, Fall 1979, 13(1), 69-79.

McClelland, D. C. The role of educational technology in developing achievement motivation. EDUCATIONAL TECHNOLOGY, October 1969, 7-16.

McIsaac, D. N. Impact of personal computing on education. AEDS JOURNAL, Fall 1979, 13(1), 7-15.

McKinley, R. & Reckase, M. Computer applications to ability testing. AEDS JOURNAL, Spring 1980, 13(3), 193-203.

Miller, L. D., Waver, F. H., and Semb, G. A. A procedure for maintaining student progress in a personalized university course. JOURNAL OF APPLIED BEHAVIOR ANALYSIS, 1974, 7, 87-91.

Milner, S. Learner controlled computing: A description and rationale. Paper presented at the American Educational Research Association's annual meeting, Chicago, Illinois, April, 1974.

Molitor, G. The information society: The path to post-industrial growth. THE FUTURIST, April 1981, 23-30.

Montague, J. A preliminary methodological verbal computer content analysis study of preschool black children. JOURNAL OF EDUCATIONAL RESEARCH, 1976, 69(6), 236-240.

Moore, O. K. Autotelic responsive environments and exceptional children in O. J. Harvey, EXPERIENCE, STRUCTURE AND ADAPTABILITY, New York: Springer, 1966.

Moursund, D. Microcomputers will not solve the computers-in-education problem. AEDS JOURNAL, Fall 1979, 13(1), 31-39.

Murdick, R. G. & Ross, J. E. INFORMATION SYSTEMS FOR MODERN MANAGEMENT. New York: Prentice-Hall, 1971.

National Advisory Committee on the Handicapped. Implementing the IEP concept. AMERICAN EDUCATION. August-September 1977, 6-8.

Nisen, W. G. (ed.). THE HARVARD NEWSLETTER ON COMPUTER GRAPHICS. July 1979, p. 8.

O'Gara, G. Where are the children? The new data game at HEW. THE WASHINGTON MONTHLY, June 1979, pp. 35-38.

Overheu, D. Computer aided assessment and development of basic skills. EXCEPTIONAL CHILD, March 1977, 24(1), 18-35.

Papert, S. & Solomon, C. Twenty things to do with a computer. EDUCATIONAL TECHNOLOGY, 1972, 12(4), 9-18.

Price, C. C. Microcomputers in the classroom. MATHEMATICS TEACHER, May 1978, 425-427.

Putnam, A. O. MANAGEMENT INFORMATION SYSTEMS: PLANNING, DEVELOPING, MANAGING. Boston: Herman Publishing, Inc., 1977.

Radford, D. J. INFORMATION SYSTEMS FOR STRATEGIC DECISIONS. Reston, Virginia: Reston Publishing Company, 1978.

Reith, H. & Semmel, M. The use of microcomputer technology to prepare and enable teachers to meet the educational needs of handicapped children. TEACHER EDUCATION AND SPECIAL EDUCATION, Winter 1978, 2(2), 56-59.

Reynolds, W. H. The executive synecdoche. MSU BUSINESS TOPICS, 1969, 17,(4), 21-29.

Ricketts, D. & Seay, J. Assessing inexpensive microcomputers for classroom use: A produce oriented course to promote instructional computing literacy. AEDS JOURNAL, Fall 1979, 13(1), 89-99.

Roblyer, M. Instructional design vs. authoring of courseware: Some crucial differences. PROCEEDINGS OF AEDS CONFERENCE, May 1981, 243-247.

Ryan, C. W., & Drummond, R. J. Differential impacts of a computer information system on selected human service agencies. AEDS JOURNAL, 1981, 14,(2), 73-83.

Sabatino, D. A. Are appropriate educational programs operationally achievable under the mandated promise of P.L. 94-142. JOURNAL OF SPECIAL EDUCATION, 1981, 15, 9-23.

Salisbury, G. The "talking page" machine. VISUAL EDUCATION, May 1971, 12-13.

Sampson, J. P., & Stripling, R. O. Strategies for counselors intervention with a computer-assisted career guidance system. VOCATIONAL GUIDANCE QUARTERLY, 1979, 27, 230-238.

Sanderson, P. C. MANAGEMENT INFORMATION SYS-TEMS AND THE COMPUTER. London: Pan Books Ltd., 1975.

Schwartz, L. & Oseroff, A. THE CLINICAL TEACHER FOR SPECIAL EDUCATION. Tallahassee, Florida: Educational Research Institute, 1975.

Silverstein, B. Toward a grouping typology: A profile analysis of the behavioral competence of the mentally retarded. (Doctoral dissertation, Southern Illinois University at Carbondale, 1981).

Sippl, C. J. MICROCOMPUTER HANDBOOK. New York: Petrocelli / Charter, 1977.

Smelser, E. K. Microcomputers: Fad or function. AEDS MONITOR, November 1979, 27.

Smith, L. Microcomputers in education. AEDS MONITOR, November 1979, 18-20.

Spero, S. W. A micro-processor based system as a classroom teaching tool. T.H.E. JOURNAL, February 1979, 31-33.

Steg, D. R. & Schenk, R. Intervention through technology: The talking typewriter revisited. EDUCATIONAL TECH-NOLOGY, October 1977, 45-47.

Stevens, D. J. How educators perceive computers in the classroom. AEDS JOURNAL, Spring 1980, 13(3), 221-232.

Suppes, D. The use of computers in education. SCIENTIFIC AMERICAN, September 1966, 215, 207-220.

Suppes, P., & Morningstar, M. COMPUTER ASSISTED INSTRUCTION AT STANFORD. 1966-68: DATA, MODELS, AND EVALUATION OF THE ARITHMETIC PROGRAM. New York: Academic Press, 1972.

Sydow, B. Using the computer terminal to motivate typing students. BUSINESS EDUCATION FORUM, April 1975, 25-26.

Tekawa, K. The machine that talks for the non-verbal. INTERFACE AGE, January 1980, 70-72.

Thelen, H. Profit for the private sector. PHI DELTA KAPPAN, 1977, 58(6), 458.

Thomas, D. B. The effectiveness of computer assisted instruction in secondary schools. AEDS JOURNAL, 1979, 12(3), 113-116.

Thomas, D & McClain, D. Selecting microcomputers for the classroom. AEDS JOURNAL, Fall 1979, 13(1), 55-68.

Tolor, A. AN EVALUATION OF A NEW APPROACH IN DEALING WITH HIGH SCHOOL UNDERACHIEVE-MENT. Final Report, Fairfield University, Connecticut, 1969, 27.

Travers, R. AN INTRODUCTION TO EDUCATIONAL RESEARCH. New York: MacMillan Publishing Co., 1978.

Uncovering health dangers in VDT's. BUSINESS WEEK. July 28, 1980, 68.

Unger, A. J. Getting more for less-polygon graphics using a microcomputer. Paper presented at the Second International User's Conference on Computer Mapping Hardware, Software and Data Bases, Cambridge, Mass., July 1979.

Vensel, G., & Joiner, L. Microcomputer R & D in the elementary school. AEDS MONITOR, Winter 1981, 19(7,8,9), 26-28.

Vensel, G., & Joiner, L. Micros for group instruction. AEDS MONITOR, Winter 1981, 19(7,8,9), 9.

vonFeldt, J. R. A national survey of the use of computer assisted instruction in schools for the deaf. JOURNAL OF EDUCATION TECHNOLOGY SYSTEMS, 1978-79, 7, 29-40.

Wachtel, E. A five year time line for the integration of computers into the Shaker Heights City Schools. PROCEEDINGS OF THE AEDS CONFERENCE, May 1981, 270-274.

Weatherman, R. Special education student and compliance system. Paper presented at the National Convention of the Council for Exceptional Children. Dallas, Texas, August 1979.

Wells, R. Planning and the American computer machine. Paper presented at the Harvard Graphics Week Conference, Cambridge, Mass., July 1979.

Wheat, L. Computer in my classroom? I vote no. CALCULATORS AND COMPUTERS, January & February 1979, 3(1), 32-34.

Whitney, R. & Hofmeister, A. MONITOR: A Computer Based Management Information System for Special Education. Proceedings of AEDS Conference, May 1981, 279-286.

Wilkinson, J. W. Guidelines for designing systems. JOURNAL OF SYSTEMS MANAGEMENT. 1974, 25(12), 36-40.

Withrow, M. Computer animation and language instruction. AMERICAN ANNALS OF THE DEAF, 1978, 123, 723-25.

Wood, R. K. and Soulier, J. S. The Utah State University Videodisc Innovation Projects: Implications for Educational Data Systems. THE AEDS MONITOR, 19(10,11,12), 18-23, 1981.

Zinn, K. The impact of microcomputers on college teaching. PIPELINE, Spring 1979, 4(2), 3-8.

Zinn, K. L. Considerations in buying a personal computer: what, which, when, how much? CREATIVE COMPUTING, 1978, 4(5), 102.

AUTHOR INDEX

SUBJECT INDEX

DATE DUE